IN THE MARGINS OF THE YERUSHALMI

Number 55

IN THE MARGINS OF THE YERUSHALMI
Glosses on the English Translation

Edited by
Jacob Neusner

IN THE MARGINS OF THE YERUSHALMI
Glosses on the English Translation

Edited by
Jacob Neusner

Scholars Press
Chico, California

IN THE MARGINS OF THE YERUSHALMI
Glosses on the English Translation

Edited by
Jacob Neusner

In memory of
Saul Lieberman
and
Solomon Zeitlin

Library of Congress Cataloging in Publication Data
Main entry under title:

In the margins of the Yerushalmi.

(Brown Judaic studies ; no. 55)
Includes index.
1. Talmud Yerushalmi. English. 1982. I. Neusner, Jacob, 1932- . II. Series.
BM498.5.E5 1982a 296.1'2405 83-20113
ISBN 0-89130-663-3

Printed in the United States of America

CONTENTS

PREFACE

When I translated twenty-nine of the thirty-nine tractates of the Talmud of the Land of Israel into English and supervised the translation of the other ten by my former students and a colleague (all: The Talmud of the Land of Israel: A Preliminary Translation and Explanation (Chicago: The University of Chicago Press, 1982-1988), I-XXXV), I aimed to attain a modest goal. I hoped to be able to render an accurate account of as much as 80% of the whole, hoping that in time to come, others would improve upon my work. I recognized, in particular, that the three principal requirements for a suitable translation had yet to come to hand. I had no critical text. I had no up-to-date dictionary of Palestinian Aramaic. I had no commentary on modern lines for the text. Yet, it seemed to me, even what I did have permitted a first systematic effort at rendering the whole into English.

Having specified the problems confronting anyone who wishes to approach the Yerushalmi for scholarly purposes, let me now point to a model for a truly reliable text-edition. It is Mordecai Margulies, Midrash Wayyikra Rabbah. A critical edition based on manuscripts and Genizah fragments with variants and notes (Jerusalem, 1953-1960) 1-5. Just now I made a translation of Margulies' text, following his commentary. With the work of sifting among textual variants and selecting the best possible reading complete, with a systematic account of the meanings of all difficult passages and words, and with a complete reference system, all of us have an entirely fresh view of Leviticus Rabbah. We may proceed to the next stages of study -- definition of the problems of description, analysis, and interpretation -- secure that, now at last, we know what the text says. So we may ask what, in itself and in its context, it means. That is what Margulies has made possible in his work of surpassing industry and intelligence. For the Yerushalmi there is no equivalent. For other rabbinic texts there are few equals, none of the concision and taste displayed by that great man.

When I came to the Yerushalmi, I recognized that we are far from that ideal situation to which Margulies has brought us for Leviticus Rabbah. I determined simply to do my best, in the conviction that the provision of a preliminary account of the whole would do two things. First, it would isolate for further study those passages that require it. Second, it also would give a decent picture of those many more passages that are accessible in accord with our present text, dictionary, and exegetical tools. Marking the many passages on which further work was needed, therefore, I also distinguished those that seemed to me reliably rendered into intelligible English. Underlining the numerous words on which lexicographical work had not reached a conclusion, I assessed how much, or how little, difference for the meaning of discourse as a whole such progress would bring. Above all, relying heavily on Moses Margulies' great commentary, Pene Moshe, I gave ample testimony to the need for further exegetical work, line by line. At the same time, I did, and do, claim for myself success in rendering the sense and structure and character of the whole. Indeed, my goal, as I said, was to give a fair account of about 80% of the document, but in the end, I reckoned I had done so for no less than 90%.

That is to say, for most, though not all, of the Yerushalmi, the contents and the language of discourse, the main points and the detailed way in which they are made -- these stand firm. True, others will correct details, whether involving translations of odd words or whole phrases. These corrections are always welcome, whether phrased in friendly or other ways. Indeed, everyone who thinks he or she knows the original text will not only have better ideas than the translator on how to translate that text, but also strong feelings on how much better qualified than the translator would the critic have proved for the work. That may well be so. The critic invariably improves. But the original translator did the work. No translation but one that mattered very much to no one has ever failed to attract suggestions on improvement. That is all to the good.

Recognizing that fact at the outset, I turned to critical readers, in two stages, to review and correct my translations of each of the tractates as they were completed. The first stage of critical reading was done by my graduate students. Their work was to see to it that my translation omitted nothing and conformed, as much as possible, to the Leiden MS, the first printed edition, and the available printed edition, or at least to indicate when it did not.

The second set of critical readers consisted of colleagues who undertook to review, slowly and word for word, every line of my translation. This process of critical review involved two quite distinct sorts of comment. First, the critical reviewer would see points on which I had simply made mistakes, omitted words, misconstrued or mistranslated lines, and the like. These I asked the reviewer to correct forthwith; a mistake is a mistake. Second, the critical reviewer would form a thesis different from mine, recognizing that what I gave was defensible, if not beyond cavil. Here I asked the reviewer to give in his own name what he thought better than what I had provided. I did not wish to take credit for other peoples' work. Finally, I invited the critical reviewer to add his own comments, using such other resources as he wished beyond those to which I had referred. The result was an important corpus of scholarly work. Not only did the critical reviewers save me from needless error. They also vastly enriched the process of translation and improved on the possibilities for interpreting a given passage available to the reader of the English language.

My original intention was to print the ample comments of the critical reviewers as appendices in the several volumes of translations. However, some of the contributions clearly took on the status of major essays in their own right. Accordingly, it seemed only fair to publish the work of the critical reviewers in an independent volume, for reference and study by others interested in the meaning of the tractates on which I had worked. That is why I undertook to edit and publish this book.

How shall I thank these scholars! They took time from their own work to help me with mine. They labored through not the text alone, but my version of the text -- itself, of necessity, a commentary. They restudied the text and its commentaries as well as a sizable ancillary literature. They then systematically scrutinized my work and also contributed the results of their own research and reflections upon the same problems on which I had worked.

Before us in this book is the result of a labor not only of scholarship and criticism but also of commitment to a common task -- a labor of extraordinary generosity. Recognizing that, whatever my limitations of learning and intelligence, I was surely going to do the work, these critical reviewers determined to help me make the translation as accurate and reliable as possible. With improved tools, text, dictionary, and commentary, later generations will surely do better than has ours. But because of those who gave so generously of their time and learning, the preliminary translation and explanation at hand have emerged far better than they might otherwise have been. For that many will be grateful.

Nor am I any less grateful to those who write reviews and propose improvements in the translation of words or phrases. I am entirely confident that no critic will be able to demonstrate the essential inaccuracy of the picture of discourse as a whole provided in my translation. Concentration on correcting details confirms the basic accuracy and reliability of my account of the sense as a whole. However phrased, whether in a generous or ungenerous way, these criticisms are welcome and will be taken into account in future versions of the English translation.

Each contribution to this book consists of comments upon, and improvements of, the English translation of the Talmud of the Land of Israel. The reference system follows that devised by me. The Arabic numerals refer to the chapter and paragraph of the Mishnah passage under discussion, thus 1:1 refers to the first paragraph of the first chapter of a tractate. These references further follow the division of the Yerushalmi's tractates by Mishnah-chapter and paragraph in the standard printed text. I further subdivided each passage of the Talmud by "unit of discourse," by which I mean a completed discussion of a given subject or problem, and by subdivision of said unit or completed thought. The Roman numeral refers to the former, the capital letter to the latter, thus 1:1.I.A. refers to the first unit of discourse and the first completed thought of the first paragraph of the first chapter of the Mishnah -- hence also of the Yerushalmi -- of a given tractate. While at first glance the system appears to be "technical," in fact it facilitates ready reference to both the original text and the translation.

This book is dedicated, with the permission of all contributors, to the memory of the two paramount Talmud scholars of our day, Saul Lieberman and Solomon Zeitlin. The two have much in common. Both attained formidable mastery of the sources at hand. Particularly in their younger years, both produced work of a revolutionary character, in method and in results. Both far transcended their origins.

Zeitlin's use of rabbinic writings for historical purposes was far more critical, imaginative, and genuinely secular than any of his predecessors' readings of those same materials. Looking backward from Zeitlin, we discern none who compared either in productivity or in critical acumen.

Lieberman's exegesis of rabbinic writings flowed from what must be an unparalleled mastery of relevant cognate, as well as alien, sources. His greatest achievements, however, rest not only on erudition but also upon critical imagination, particularly his

Talmud of Caesarea (1931) and his Tosefet Rishonim (completed by 1939). True, much of his later work flowed from no more sophisticated "method" than juxtaposing things no one before had seen to be associated -- that is, free association out of a remarkable knowledge of many things. But the earlier works in his long career, like Zeitlin's, show entirely new possibilities, a wholly other conception of learning in the rabbinical writings from any held before his time.

Both Lieberman and Zeitlin won loyal circles of disciples and admirers, as indeed each had every right to expect. Both of them were capable of acts of enormous generosity and even grace among those near at hand. Both of them changed for all time the way in which work might be done on the documents on which they labored.

To be sure, like all truly great persons, Zeitlin and Lieberman exhibited remarkable flaws in learning. Zeitlin in his middle and later years proved unable to learn anything from anyone else. He ceased to wish even to engage in civil discourse about matters on which reasonable people normally may agree to differ. He made himself a pariah.

Like Zeitlin, Lieberman, for his part, never produced a student able to carry on his work in his way. He taught this and that to many people. But he did not seem able to explain how he reached his conclusions or in what way someone else might either replicate or even validate them. The result is that his later writings, rich as they are in erudition and containing moments of remarkably suggestive insight, generate no succession, no continuation. Tosefta Kishutah is a reference work, magisterially closing many doors, but opening none.

Lieberman and Zeitlin had in common, also, a certain ungenerous capacity to reject, out of hand and often for trivial reasons, the work of their successors. Both of them failed to realize that the truly important aspect of learning lies in its continuity, in the ongoing process of which each scholar is a part. Both of them seemed therefore to want to mark the end of a tradition rather than the beginning of one. In their ways, they were, alas, right. That is why each of them taught to their students not method but mere facts, not how to do what the master was doing -- and to improve on it -- but only the result of the master's incomparable and unattainable learning (in Lieberman's case) and critical acumen (in Zeitlin's).

So their academic narcissism did make it difficult for them, particularly in later life, to show much sympathy for people who would take up the same texts, but in different ways, people equipped with different qualifications and aiming at answering a different set of questions from their own. Zeitlin, to be sure, had the honesty to print what he thought. But he would never fairly print others' replies. His was mere destruction. Lieberman expressed his opinions everywhere but in print -- until after he died, when any response would be (and was) impossible. Still, the picture, even for those of us who have had to bear the murderous contempt, expressed both in public and in lashon hara, of Solomon Zeitlin and of Saul Lieberman, is not one-sided. True, each lost his temper and published not merely fair criticism but a fair amount of spleen. But in the end, all of that is unimportant.

In the balance, viewed as the learned and creative masters that they were, both were great in their day. Each left a heritage of learning from which many generations will draw sustenance. Their great flaws -- and who is without them! -- lie buried with them in their graves. Their great achievements and even their models of human greatness attained in devotion to learning endure as goals and goads for the successor generation.

In only one way do we who now take over certainly improve upon their legacy. Some of us can engage in scholarly discourse, even disagreement, in a reasoned and mutually respectful way. This book is the proof.

Let me close by acknowledging that the idea for this book was not mine. It comes from two disparate sources, who meet only in my mind.

The first is William Scott Green, who saw the worth of the appendices my critical readers had generously created for my volumes of Yerushalmi-translation. He suggested I bring them together so as to give them the prominence they deserve. This book stands as a monument to the ongoing debate, the process of criticism, that scholarship at its best generates.

The second is Saul Lieberman, to whom the book is dedicated. At the end of a study conference in honor of his eightieth birthday, June 13-14, 1978, in Jerusalem, Lieberman stated (now in _Researches in Talmudic Literature. A Study Conference in Honour of the Eightieth Birthday of Shaul Lieberman. Held 13-14 June 1978_ [Jerusalem, 1983: Publications of the Israel Academy of Sciences and Humanities. Section of Humanities], pp. 225ff.) that he approved of only one kind of _festschrift_ or jubilee volume. He said, "It would be a _festschrift_ written by the honoree himself, and in it, the author would try to correct all the errors that he had made in all of his books and invite his colleagues and students to participate in the volume, so correcting the errors, both deliberate and otherwise, of the honoree." That would indeed be a memorable book, Lieberman added.

I did not wait for my eightieth birthday to publish this book. Indeed, in many of my other scholarly books, I have included the corrections and points of disagreement and controversy contributed by others. I see nothing out of the ordinary in such a procedure. It seems to me we have the duty to stand by our own views, unless they are shown to be absolutely in error, but equally to respect and listen to the views of others. At stake, after all, is learning. The reward will be a better grasp, a deeper understanding. As I said in the beginning, where the critical readers pointed to out-and-out errors, I corrected them without a murmur. Where they conceded I might have a point, but they nonetheless thought they had a better idea, I determined to give their views ample publicity.

I am honored to have won the friendship and loyalty of the authors of these chapters, who pay their tribute in the only meaningful way, that is, by taking up the task and sharing the burden.

Mr. Roger Brooks, completing his doctoral studies at Brown, served as my research assistant for this book. He did a good part of the work of detail and made many contributions to the project, for which I am grateful.

Jacob Neusner

Program in Judaic Studies
Brown University
Providence, Rhode Island, U.S.A.

29 Elul 5743
September 7, 1983

Chapter 1
YERUSHALMI SUKKAH
Irving Mandelbaum

1:1.I.B-E: PM explains the point of B-E as follows: If Judah derives the measurement of a sukkah by analogy to the measurement of the entrance to the Porch, then it would have been sufficient for him to rule that the sukkah may be up to forty cubits high (B). How, then, can Hiyya and Bar Qappara teach that Judah permits a sukkah fifty or even a hundred cubits in height (D-E)? It is this question which Abin then answers by saying that Judah is consistent with views held elsewhere (F-I).

1:1.III.K: The point of K requires some clarification. H-I argues that the sukkah of Helene described in E-G was a sukkah with sides that did not go up to the top. It is concerning such a sukkah that sages and Judah dispute at M.1:1A-B(J). E-G still poses a problem, however, for Judah's claim (G) that sages accepted his ruling is not challenged, and the story of E-G thus appears to support Judah against sages in the dispute of M.1:1A-B. K therefore refutes Judah's claim at G. Sages kept quiet about Helene's sukkah not because they agreed with Judah's ruling, but for a different reason. Like other wealthy people, Helene left an opening at the top of her sukkah for the purpose of ventilation, and such an opening did not invalidate the sukkah. E-G thus does not indicate that sages agreed with Judah's position at M.1:1A-B.

1:1.IV.A-C: The present translation is difficult, for it is not clear that Hoshayah means to say that the board projects beyond the sukkah-roofing (A), nor is it apparent how the airspace between such a board and the sukkah-roofing might be considered a sukkah at all (C). Alternatively, PM interprets A-C as follows. A man leaves a board at an angle on a piece of a column located in a sukkah over twenty cubits high. The board thus extends diagonally from the column to the roof of the sukkah. Since PM explicitly mentions that the board is fit for use as sukkah-roofing, he apparently takes the purpose of this action to be the creation of a "new" sukkah, with the column as its new floor and the board as its new sukkah-roofing. Now, Hoshaiah says, it is simple to determine whether the new sukkah is valid with respect to its height, for it depends as to how one measures this distance. The measure from the board at the roof of the sukkah downwards to the ground is still twenty cubits, but from the top of the piece of the column (which is the ground of the "new" sukkah) upwards there are less than twenty cubits. The "new" sukkah is thus a valid one. At the same time, however, there remains another question, for part of the board extending beyond the column to the roof of the sukkah is higher than twenty cubits from the ground, and so is not valid sukkah-roofing. The problem appears to be that the space between the column and the wall is now covered by invalid sukkah-roofing, so that the wall cannot serve the "new" sukkah at all (PM thus interprets B-C as referring to part of the board, rather than to the original sukkah-roofing). At issue, then, is whether to consider as invalid airspace or invalid sukkah-roofing that part of the board which is higher than twenty cubits above the ground. PM's explanation is also difficult, however, for it is not clear why one would place the board at an angle in order to create new sukkah-roofing. I therefore turn to consider yet another alternative, the interpretation of QH.

According to QH a man lays a board flat on the piece of a column, in order to create a platform for standing or sitting, and so to diminish the height of the sukkah. QH then emends the latter part of A to read as follows: "If one measures from the board [to the top of the sukkah] there is not a distance of twenty cubits. If, on the other hand, one measures from the ground [to the top of the sukkah] there is a distance of twenty cubits." If the sukkah is to be valid one must determine its height according to the former measurement. There is still a space, however, between the end of the board and the nearby wall, and the sukkah-roofing over this space is more than twenty cubits above the ground. This sukkah-roofing is invalid, and so serves to separate the platform from the nearby wall, and could possibly invalidate the sukkah (see a similar case at B. Suk. 4a). At issue, then, is how to rule concerning that part of the sukkah-roofing which is opposite the ground of the sukkah but not over the board. Do we say that this sukkah-roofing is too high to count as roofing at all? In that case the sukkah is deemed to be covered by airspace and such airspace invalidates the sukkah if it measures three handbreadths (M.1:10/I). Or do we regard this sukkah-roofing as if it were invalid sukkah-roofing? We regard such sukkah-roofing to form a "curved wall" (i.e., part of the adjacent wall, and not of the sukkah-roofing) provided that it measures less than four cubits (M.1:11A-B; see B. Suk. 4a). This is Hoshaiah's question, as interpreted by QH. Although this explanation of A-C requires an emendation at A, it nevertheless appears to be the most plausible explanation of a very difficult passage.

1:1.VI.L: Both PM (in Y. Shab. 1:1) and QH maintain that Eliezer bar Jacob refers here to Lev. 16:14: "[And he shall take some of the blood of the bull, and sprinkle it with his finger] on the front of the mercy seat, [and before the mercy seat he shall sprinkle the blood with his finger seven times]."

1:1.VI.N: Again, according to PM and QH the verse in question is Lev. 16:14.

1:1.IX.X: Alternatively, QH emends the second "R. Bun" (r'bwn) to "rabbis" (rbnn).

1:1.X.K-O: According to GRA (Y. Kil. 4:2) and PM Yohanan's point (K) is that the rule of H does not apply at all when the gap measures three to four handbreadths. For if one were to apply the rule of H in such a case, then one would have to permit carrying in a courtyard as long as the standing part of the fence were greater than the breached part, even if the standing section measured less than four handbreadths. Such a small standing section, however, is considered to be insignificant, and under ordinary circumstances one would not be permitted to carry in a courtyard surrounded by such little fencing (L). Mana then objects (M) that one is permitted to create an enclosure with reeds, even though each reed (= the standing part of a fence) measures less than four handbreadths. Hananiah answers, though, that in that instance the gaps between the reeds must measure less than three handbreadths, and so are regarded in any event as closed up (N). Finally, Yose b. Bun (O) disagrees with Hananiah and states that regardless of the size of the gap, one is permitted to carry in an area surrounded by more standing fence than broken fence.

1:2.III.A-B: Lieberman (TK, IV, p. 837, on LL. 8-9) notes that this version of T. appears to accord with House of Shammai, for it declares invalid any sukkah which was not constructed for the purpose of the festival. The readings which appear at B. Suk. 8b and Y. here, however, read "valid" at B (as does the editio princeps and Ms. London; cf. Lieberman, TM, p. 256, on L. 9), and so perhaps have been revised to agree with the view of the House of Hillel.

1:5.II.A: Lieberman (TK, IV, p. 838, n. 12) notes that "it is invalid" does not belong at A (since B distinguishes between valid and invalid wedges). This apodosis probably appears here by mistake because of a parallel passage at 1:7.I.D.

1:10.I.E.: PM (at Y. Erub. 8:8) and QH emend E to read "R. Yose b. Haninah said," instead of "R. Yohanan said," for, according to D, E-F is a statement of Yose b. Haninah.

1:11.III.A: According to PM Hezekiah seeks to distinguish between invalid sukkah-roofing at the side of the sukkah (M.1:11A-B) and invalid sukkah-roofing in the middle of a roof (Hiyya's rule at I.A). In the former instance one may allow up to four cubits of invalid sukkah-roofing because such sukkah-roofing "appears like a crooked wall," and so is not regarded as roofing at all. This consideration does not apply, however, in a case where the invalid sukkah-roofing is in the middle of a roof. In this case, therefore, even four handbreadths of invalid sukkah-roofing serves to invalidate the sukkah even if the sukkah is a large one. (PM here apparently assumes that Hezekiah follows Samuel's rule, cited in B. Suk. 17b: "R. Judah said in the name of Samuel, 'Invalid sukkah-roofing in the middle [of a sukkah] invalidates [the sukkah] if it measures four [handbreadths]. [Invalid sukkah-roofing] at the side [of a sukkah] invalidates [a sukkah] if it measures four cubits.'" By contrast, Rav maintains that "whether in the middle [of a sukkah] or at its side, [invalid sukkah-roofing] invalidates [the sukkah] if it measures four cubits.")

1:11.III.E: Jonah's point is that Yose can respond to the objections of the authorities at B-D by saying that in all cases invalid sukkah-roofing invalidates a sukkah only when it measures four cubits, and that this rule applies even in the middle of a large sukkah (PM).

1:12.I.F: The translation of F as a question follows the reading of PM (although PM appears to read the first part of F ["Is it not required"] in place of E, and not in addition to it). Alternatively, the printed text of Y. presents F as a statement, "[This ruling is required] to clarify the position of R. Eliezer." In any event, PM explains the point of F as follows. From M.1:12A-C one might conclude that Eliezer would declare invalid the sukkah of trees, for its walls, like those of the cone-shaped sukkah, are not clearly discernible. D therefore points out that Eliezer would not rule in such a manner. What invalidates the cone-shaped sukkah is not its walls but its roof, which is not clearly discernible. Since the roof of the sukkah of trees is easily recognizable, Eliezer would maintain that such a sukkah is in fact valid.

2:1.II.A-C: The point of A-B is not clear, for A maintains that it is Gamaliel who takes contradictory positions, while according to A-B it is sages who respond differently to Tabi's actions. QH resolves this problem by interpreting "sages" to refer primarily to Gamaliel. A-B thus points out that while Gamaliel did not object when Tabi put on tefillin, M.2:1D indicates that he would have objected had Tabi slept in the sukkah. C resolves this apparent contradiction of Gamaliel's views by saying that Tabi slept under the bed not in anticipation of an objection by Gamaliel, but simply in order to give the sages more room. Alternatively, PM takes "sages" to refer to sages themselves. Sages had objected to Tabi's sleeping in the sukkah, and therefore Gamaliel saw fit at M.2:10D publicly to praise his slave for obeying the sages' ruling. C then explains that sages did not actually object to Tabi's actions, but rather he himself volunteered to sleep under the bed in order not to make the sages squeeze together. According to this explanation, however, the point of A-B is that sages, rather than Gamaliel, objected to Tabi's sleeping in the sukkah (and Gamaliel in fact appears himself to approve of Tabi's action). It is difficult to see, therefore, how A-B illustrates that Gamaliel takes contradictory positions. For this reason I prefer the interpretation of QH given above.

2:6.II.D: The "other kinds of foods" to which Aha b. Jacob refers are those foods made from grains other than the five grains (viz., wheat, barley, rice-wheat, two-rowed barley, and spelt; cf. M. Hal. 1:1) from which one customarily makes bread (PM).

2:8.II.E-F: E-F is better translated as a single stich (following PM):

> "If you maintain that the House of Hillel accepted the position of the House of Shammai, [namely,] that the wine should not be neutralized, who taught here [in M. T.Y. 2:7E-F], 'It may be neutralized?' It is neither the House of Hillel nor the House of Shammai."

E-F thus states that if House of Hillel agrees with House of Shammai at M. Ter. 5:4 then M. T.Y. 2:7E-F cannot be attributed to either of the Houses.

2:8.II.G: The reading of the printed edition is difficult, for House of Hillel would have formulated M. T.Y. 2:7E-F the same way whether before or after House of Shammai's concession to them. QH therefore emends the end of G to read "prior to the [House of Hillel's] concession to the House of Shammai." Idi's point is thus that one cannot prove from M. T.Y. 2:7E-F that the House of Shammai accepted the views of House of Hillel (as E-F maintains), for House of Hillel could have formulated M. T.Y. 2:7E-F before it accepted House of Shammai's position. Since Idi's position makes sense only according to the reading of QH, I prefer this version to that of the printed text.

2:8.II.H-I: If my interpretation of II.G is correct, then H-I supports not Idi at G, but the view of E-F that it was House of Shammai who conceded to House of Hillel.

(Comment to Y. 2:8): If unit IV does refer to M.2:8 (as PM and QH, followed by the comments in square brackets, indicate), then this unit serves this pericope and not Y. Ter. 5:4 at all.

3:1.IV.H-I: PM and QH read H as a question (to which I provides an answer): "And is it possible that he will not tie them together [and so change their character]?" The point of H, then, is that one may surely derive the rule concerning the stolen palm branch, myrtle and willow from the case of the stolen sukkah-roofing (G). A sukkah made with stolen roofing is invalid, for even though one assumes that the thief binds the roofing together, he does not thereby change the character of the covering, and so does not effect ownership of it. Similarly, one who steals a palm branch, myrtle, and willow and binds them (A) does not become their owner, so that these items become invalid. I answers, however, that in the case of G one need not assume that the robber bound the sukkah-roofing, for he could have simply placed it on top of the sukkah. We therefore cannot deduce from G whether a thief who binds together stolen items, such as the palm branch, myrtle and willow of A, thereby effects ownership of them.

3:1.IV.J: Yohanan's statement at J is not clear, for the phrase byn zh wbyn zh ("whether this one or that one") could refer either to the two parties of the dispute of C-E, or to the two reasons mentioned by Joshua b. Levi at F-G. The present translation prefers the former interpretation, and so understands Yohanan to maintain that the authorities of C-E do not dispute at all, but in fact agree that the stolen sukkah (as defined at K-L) is invalid. This explanation of J is difficult, though, for it seems unlikely that Yohanan would reject outright the formulation of a tannaitic dispute. Moreover, C-E may refer to a dispute between Eleazer and sages concerning the same issue (B. Suk. 31a). If this is the case then it seems even less plausible to interpret Yohanan's statement at J as opposing C-E.

Alternatively, PM (following Nahman at B. Suk. 31a) explains that Yohanan glosses not C-E but Joshua b. Levi's explanation of this dispute at F-G. At F-G Joshua b. Levi maintains that the Tannaim of C-E do not actually dispute, but rather each interprets the case of C differently. One authority maintains that C refers to one who stole land, and then built a sukkah (which is then valid, for the reasons stated in F), while the other holds that C concerns a case in which one stole the sukkah-roofing (so that the sukkah is invalid, for the reasons stated at G). Yohanan disagrees, however, maintaining that the authority at E would declare the sukkah invalid even if the thief had stolen the land. This Tanna would maintain that even if land is never regarded as stolen, the sukkah would at the very least be considered a borrowed one, and a borrowed sukkah is also invalid (see B. Suk. 27a, where Eleazar derives this rule from Deut. 16:13). According to this interpretation, then, Yohanan does not reject the dispute of C-E but rather attempts to explain the question which stands behind it. For this reason PM's explanation appears to be the more plausible of the two offered (although, to be sure, this explanation assumes that unit IV is related to the materials at B. Suk. 31a, and this supposition remains to be examined).

3:2.I.C-D: Alternatively, C-D may be translated as follows (though with no change in meaning):

C. If you say [that such a tree is] an olive tree, it does resemble a chain, but its branches do cover the larger part of it.
D. If you say [that such a tree is] a zargunah tree, its branches do not cover the larger part of it, but it does not resemble a chain.

We also note that PM reverses the descriptions of the olive tree and the zargunah tree, based on a passage in B. Suk. 32b. Also, if the zargunah tree does correspond to the dwlb' mentioned there, then it may be identified as the oriental plane tree, Platanus orientalis ('rmwn of the Bible; see J. Feliks, The Plant World of the Bible (Ramat Gan: Massada, 1968), p. 120).

3:2.II.E-H: The present translation takes "green ones" in F to refer to "green boughs." A, however, speaks of "black ones," meaning "black berries," and it seems likely that F refers to berries as well. PM explains E-G accordingly. The point of E-G is that it is not the color of the berries which invalidates the myrtle branch of M.3:2D, for where the berries are green and the same color as the wood the myrtle branch is still invalid. This follows from the plain sense of M.3:2D, which does not mention the color of the berries (PM here also emends G to read "these are of the same color as the wood," taking 'ynn to be the third person plural demonstrative pronoun, rather than a suffixed form of the negative 'yn). H therefore concludes that the reason the myrtle branch of M.3:2D is invalid is because the fruit is ripe. It follows, then, even when the ripe berries are green rather than black. Now this interpretation also poses a problem, for according to it, F ignores Yohanan's statement that M.3:2D refers specifically to black berries. The interpretation of E-G, therefore, must remain uncertain.

3:4.I.F-G: PM explains the point of F-G as follows. Trained myrtle branches often are without tips. B could be taken to speak of three such myrtle branches, one without its tip cut off, and two with or without their tips. In that case, however, Ishmael appears to prefer that there be more than one complete myrtle branch. F therefore cites Tarfon's statement at C. By saying that even three myrtle branches without their tips are valid, Tarfon indicates that he understands B to refer to two trained myrtle branches, i.e., branches with their tips cut off, and one complete myrtle branch. Ishmael therefore does in fact require only one perfect myrtle branch.

3:7.I.E: PM explains that Yose here refers to Simeon's saying at M. Ma. 1:4E (trans. Martin Jaffe, Mishnah's Theology of Tithing, p. 40): R. Simeon exempts citrons which are immature (bqtnm).

3:7.I.H: According to PM, H reverts back to D-E, and so refers to the half-ripe etrog, and not to those listed at G.

3:10.VI.D: Tanhuma takes mkl h^{c}mym to mean not "above all peoples" (its literal sense) but "from all peoples." In this way the verse supports his statement in C.

4:3.III.B: PM explains that the question of Simeon b. Laqish is based on M. Kel. 1:9S-T (trans. Neusner, HMLP, I, p. 37): [The area] between the porch and the altar is more holy than it. For those [priests] who are blemished or whose hair is unloosed do not enter there.

4:3.IV.B: According to PM Abbahu here explains the repetition of "For the Lord and for you, O altar!" at M.4:3.I. The first utterance refers to the end of Ps. 80:2, wlkh lysw^{c}th lnw, here taking lkh to mean not "come" (its literal meaning), but "for you" (lk, the preposition l + the second person masculine singular pronominal suffix). The first "For the Lord and for you" thus means "For the Lord, for you are our salvation" (this exegesis may thus be related to unit V's theme that God shares in the condition of Israel; see QH). The second time this exclamation is said the word "for you" in it means "To you be all thanks," that is, for your salvation (but see QH for an alternate reading).

4:3.V.A: Ba's point is that w^{e} hosia, "and he will give victory," is written as whws^{c} (defectively, without the letter y). Ba perhaps reads whws^{c} as w^{e}hiwasa, "and he will be saved." In any event, he clearly takes the direct-object marker 't which immediately follows the verb as the preposition "with" (PM). Ba thus reads the beginning of the verse as "And the Lord will be saved with the tents of Judah first."

4:3.V.B: Zakkai here reads wsknt not as w^{e}sakanta, "and you shall dwell," but as us^{e}kinati, "my presence."

4:3.V.C: Hananiah's point is that hws'tk, "who brought you out," is written defectively. It is not clear, however, how he reads the verb as "you were brought out."

4:5.II.B: PM reads the last part of B as a statement, and appears to take it as part of the baraita: "With an animal designated as a festal offering which one slaughtered on the fourteenth, people carry out their obligation on the count of the offering of rejoicing, but do not carry out their obligation on the count of peace-offerings." According to Ba's point this reading of B is that people can carry out their obligation to bring an offering of rejoicing even though it is not yet the time of rejoicing, as opposed to Eleazar's statement in A. Zeira then answers in C that the baraita speaks of an offering which was in fact offered on the fifteenth, that is, at the time of rejoicing. Since the unit later (e.g., at F-I) discusses solely the problems of the time of rejoicing it would appear this reading of B is the more plausible one.

4:5.III.F: According to PM F follows the attribution of D found in Tosafot to B. Pes. 100b (s.v. ydy qydws ys'w): "R. Aha in the name of R. Hoshayyah: 'Said Rab...'"

4:6.I.F-Q: The discussion concerning the views of Eleazar may be summarized as follows. Eleazar states at C that one who pours a water libation outside of the Temple is liable. At G-H two Tannaim disagree as to whether this rule applies only when the water is drawn specifically for the purpose of the water libation (see B. Zeb. 100b; cited by RYD). I-J then attempts to explain this difference of opinion in terms of a disagreement as to whether Eleazar maintains that the rite of the water libation derives from the authority of Torah (the view of Aqiva) or the authority of sages (the view of sages). Now it is not clear how the latter dispute would generate that of G-H, although it appears most likely that I should read "rabbis" in place of "R. Aqiba," and vice-versa (QH). According to such a reading the more lenient position of G would follow from the view that the rite is derived from the authority of the rabbis, while the more stringent ruling at H would follow from Aqiva's position. K-L then opposes I-J's interpretation of G-H, maintaining that both positions must accord with the view of Aqiba. At N-Q Zeira supplies a different account of G-H, stating that the two Tannaim there discuss a case in which six logs of water are poured out, three inside and three outside of the Temple (N). At issue between these authorities is whether there is a maximum measure for the water libation (O). The Tanna at G holds that there is such a measure (namely, three logs), so that any water beyond that measure is not considered to be drawn for the purpose of the libation, and one is not liable for pouring it out outside of the Temple (P). By contrast, the Tanna of H maintains that there is no maximum measure, so that all of the water is considered to be part of the libation, and one who pours any part of it outside of the Temple is liable (Q).

5:1.IV.B-C: Levi here presupposes that Jonah the son of Amittai was the son of the widow of Zarepath (I Kings 17:9-24). From I Kings 17:9, which mentions that Zarepath belongs to Sidon, and Judges 1:31, which implies that Sidon was on the border of Asher's territory, it follows that Jonah the son of Amittai was a member of the tribe of Asher (PM).

5:1.IV.H: Levi here interpets yrktw ("his border") to be related to the word yrk, "thigh," or yws' yrk, "descendant."

5:1.IV.J: The fact that Jonah is said to have gone down to Joppa, rather than to the port of Acco (which was nearer to the territory of Asher) supports the view that Jonah did not belong to the tribe of Asher alone.

5:1.VI.A-H: The statement, "And the third time in the time of Tronianus," which appears at Mekilta Beshallah 3, is omitted here, probably because it is replaced by unit VII.

(Comment on Y. 5:1): QH proposes that unit IV was included because of IV.K-M, R. Jonah's statement that Jonah b. Ammittai received the Holy Spirit because he became happy at the rejoicing of bet hashshoebah. Unit IV may therefore serve to supplement M. 5:1D.

(Comment on Y. 5:3): Unit V describes how the sounds and smells of the Temple service reached as far as Jericho, and so serves to illustrate Joshua b. Levi's ruling at IV.D, "Smell, sight, sound -- they are not subject to the laws of sacrilege." If the law were otherwise, all of the inhabitants of the area around Jerusalem would be liable for sacrilege.

5:4.II.D: D takes n^{c}ym zmyrwt ysr'l to mean not "the sweet-psalmist of Israel" but "the psalms of Israel are sweet [to God]" (PM).

5:4.IV.N-P: For the identification of Michal with Eglah, which N-P here presupposes, see B. San. 21a.

5:4.V.E: A passage in Y. Ber. 1:1 interprets the verse "And you shall not go up by steps to my altar, that your nakedness be not exposed on it" (Ex. 20:26) to mean that the priests would walk up to the altar "heel to toe and toe to heel," so that they would in no way expose their private parts. It is possible, therefore, that the phrase, "neither heel nor toe were seen" may refer to such a manner of walking.

5:5.III.A: Hiyya bar Ba here explains the unusual form msthwytm as meaning "they made two acts of prostration." According to E. Kautsch, ed., Gesenius Hebrew Grammar, second English edition, ed. A. E. Cowley (Oxford: Clarendon Press, 1910), p. 215, msthwytm is in fact a scribal error for the masculine plural participle msthwym.

5:6.II.A-B: PM interprets Zeira's statement to apply solely to the case of a festival which falls on the eve of the Sabbath, for only then would one draw water for the following day (M.4:7B). Zeira's point, then, is that since M.5:6H mentions only three blasts for the drawing of the water on the eve of the Sabbath, it follows that these blasts occurred not at the drawing of the water but at its pouring out. We note also that Zeira must interpret the "three [blasts] on the altar" at M.5:6H to refer not to the pouring of the water (as the present translation of M. explains it) but to the throwing of the willow branches on the altar (M.4:3C; see PM and QH to M.5:6H).

5:6.III.A-D: QH (following B. Suk. 54a) explains unit III as follows. The discussion concerns M.5:6G-H: On the eve of the Sabbath which came during the Festival there were forty-eight [blasts] in all. A-B asks why M. does not mention other occasions on which one sounds forty-eight blasts, such as the New Year which occurred on the Sabbath. On such a day one would have twenty-one daily blasts (M.5:6C) and nine blasts for each of the Additional Offerings of the Sabbath, the New Moon, and the New Year. C answers that M.5:6G does not follow the opinion of the authority who interpreted Num. 10:8 to mean that "they sound the trumpet in accord with the number of Additional Offerings" (QH here emends C to read "the passage does not conform to the view of him who said, etc." This emendation is supported by D, as follows.) At D Rabbis of Caesarea explain that even according to the authority cited in C one does not sound the trumpet for each individual

Additional Offering. Hence one does not sound the trumpet forty-eight times on the New Year which occurs on the Sabbath, and M.5:6G therefore does not mention this occurrence.

Discussion of Y. 5:6: Unit V appears to be related not to M.5:6G itself, but to unit III's discussion of that rule.

5:7.I.D: Alternatively, PM and QH read D as follows: It was necessary to raise this question only in accord with that which was taught by R. Nathan.

5:7.I.G-H: Yohanan's citation of T.4:17A does not respond to the question of F, for that rule maintains that there is a drawing of lots on the eighth day, and so does not accord with the position of Nathan. Rather, Yohanan provides support for Yose at C (or possibly for M.5:7J itself). The question of F thus remains unanswered, or, alternatively, is to be read as a statement (PM): "[Thus] it was in accord with the position of R. Nathan [that the question was asked], 'What is the law as to beginning with them for the next festival?'"

5:8.III.C: PM explains that "that Tanna" is Judah (M.5:8H), for the exegesis of I Sam. 21:4 supports his rule that the outgoing priests received five loaves of bread.

5:8.V.N-Q: According to PM O reads the word 'mwntm not as 'emunatam, "their [office of] trust," but as 'umanutam, "their skilled work." We also note that the opening of Abbahu's statement at Q, hysbtym, may be translated as "I calculated concerning them."

Chapter 2
YERUSHALMI BESAH
Stuart S. Miller

1:1.V.E: R. Zeira reverted [to the statement in V.A-B] and said [in contrast to V.B, which he found objectionable]: "A calf was already fully formed the day before, while the egg was fully formed only on the day on which it was laid." [Accordingly, the reason why a calf born on the festival may be slaughtered on that day is not for the explanation given in V.B, but rather because the animal is ready for birth before the festival and the owner is well aware that such is the case. R. Zeira's intention is to indicate that he too distinguishes between the case of a calf and that of an egg but for a reason other than that given at V.B. See QH and cf. S. Lieberman, Tosefta Ki-Feshutah V (New York, 1962), 914.]

1:1.X.H: R. Abba bar Zamina in the name of R. Yosedeq: "On account of these two things R. Yohanan went down from Sepphoris to Tiberias. He [R. Yohanan] said, 'Why do you bring me this elder, for what I permit he prohibits, and what I prohibit, he permits.'"

1:1.XII.A: All parties [that is, the House of Shammai as well] concur in the case of produce that falls from the tree [on the festival] that it is forbidden [on the Sabbath immediately following, and vice versa]. [This statement seems to follow the line of thought established at Unit X and continued in XI and XIII.]

1:1.XII.B: R. Bun bar Hiyya asked before R. Zeirah, "What is the difference between fruit that falls from a tree and eggs? Is it possible that where the fruit are still bound to their 'mothers' (the trees) they are not forbidden? [Certainly, they are forbidden.] Alternatively, is it possible that eggs found in their mothers [during slaughter] are not permitted? [No, as I.G-I clearly indicates.] [The cases of fruit and eggs are seemingly different; eggs can be deemed ready by virtue of the preparation of their source, fruit obviously cannot be.]"

1:1.XII.C: "If that is the case [that the difference between fruit and eggs is that the status of the latter is dependent upon that of their 'mothers,' then, at least according to the House of Hillel,] if an egg was laid on the festival day it should not be eaten on the Sabbath [immediately following], and if an egg was laid on the Sabbath, it should not be eaten on the festival day. [This follows from the view maintained earlier by the House of Hillel that eggs laid on the festival day may not be eaten on that day itself since they are not considered to be in the status of their mothers who were prepared in advance (see I.A-D). Accordingly, both fruit and eggs would have the same law in the case described here.]"

1:1.XII.D: He [R. Zeirah] replied to him [R. Bun bar Hiyya], "Is it so? It is not enough for you that you have imposed a strict rule on the matter so that if it was laid on the festival, it may not be eaten on the festival, and if it was laid on the Sabbath it may not be eaten on the Sabbath.

1:3.III.R: Since a matter of certainty concerning it overrides the prohibitions of the festival nights, it surely is reasonable that a matter of doubt concerning it should override the prohibitions of the festival. [So the Yerushalmi and Ms. Erfurt of the Tosefta read. According to Lieberman, Tosefta' Ki-Feshutah V, 923, this is the preferred reading.]

1:5.III.B: But surely we have learned: But if there are only those particular birds there, these are permitted [M. 1:5]. [What then is the import of R. Yudan's words?]

1:6.I.C-E: R. Hananiah in the name of R. Yohanan: "They permitted the matter at the end because of the considerations at the outset. For if you tell someone that he may not put them back, then to begin with he will not open them [and if he will] not open he will diminish the pleasure of the festival day."

1:6.I.G: Said R. Yose b. R. Bun, "If there is no [other] opening [one may remove and put back shutters], but if there is an opening, he should use the way through that opening."

1:7.I.Y: There was the instance of R. Eliezer and R. Abba Mari and R. Mattenaiah, who gave instruction that it was permitted to bring bread for [the troops of] Ursicinus on the Sabbath, since the community may need him. [Cf. the discussion of S. Lieberman, "Palestine in the Third and Fourth Centuries," reprinted in idem., Texts and Studies (New York, 1974), p. 120.]

1:7.II.A: [Y:] It has been taught [in reference to M. 1:7]: They [also] do not take out a key.

1:9.II.A: R. Isaac, R. Eleazar in the name of R. Immi father of R. Abodema of Sepphoris, "Where there is a dispute, [it has to do with crushing salt] for roasting. But as [to crushing it] for the pot, it is permitted to do so." [Cf. PM.]

[Alternatively], R. Isaac, R. Eleazar in the name of R. Immi father of R. Abodema of Sepphoris, "Where there is a dispute [it has to do with crushing spices] for roasting. But as [to crushing them] for the pot, it is permitted to do so [even according to the House of Shammai for there is a more noticeable difference in the food. See the comments of R. Eleazar Azikri in I. Francus, Talmud Yerushalmi: Masekhet Besah (New York, 1967), pp. 112f. and especially Francus' note #346. If this interpretation is correct, Unit II would clarify the issue with regard to crushing spices in general in accordance with the subject of M. 1:9].

1:10.III.E: Is it permitted to grind but prohibited to select? [Would Rabban Gamaliel have permitted one but prohibited the other?]

1:10.III.H: R. Aha in the name of R. Simeon b. Laqish: "'No work shall be done on those days, [but what every one must eat, that only may be prepared by you.]' (Ex. 12:16) until '(And) you shall observe the (feast of) unleavened bread...'" (Ex. 12:17). [Some of the commentators explain that the intention here is that all the forms of work which precede the point at which the unleavened bread has to be "observed" are prohibited. Thus kneading is allowed, but the activities leading up to that point (e.g., selecting, grinding and sifting, as at III.G) are forbidden. See PM to Y. Shab. 7:2 and QH to our passage.]

2:1.V.N: Said R. Abba bar Zabedi, "R. Abbahu decided (horei) the law in accord with the view of R. Simeon b. Eleazar." [In the statements of R. Huna and R. Yohanan (V.J-K), the term darash (to interpret) is used. The usage of horei here may be (1) to indicate that the law had indeed been decided in accordance with R. Simeon b. Eleazar's view (cf. the statement of Raba in the Babylonian Talmud, Besah 17a), and/or (2) to emphasize that the practical application of R. Simeon b. Eleazar's view was accepted (as opposed to the theoretical understanding).]

2:1.VI.J: R. Hiyya taught: [If] he himself forgot and did not prepare an erub, he may fill a jug of water for himself and light a candle for himself. [See B. Ratner, 'Ahavat Ziyyon Vi-Yerushalayim (reprint ed., Jerusalem, 1967), Besah, p. 18 and Lieberman, Tosefta' Ki-Feshutah V, 944. This interpretation would make R. Hiyya's statement consistent with the three statements which precede it at VI.G-I. It could, however, be maintained that G-I should agree with J (as rendered by Prof. Neusner) and should be translated: "One may roast a little fish for him," etc. This is possible and seems to be the intention at B. Besah 21b. Note, however, that the Babylonian parallel uses different language (e.g., madliqin lo for madliq lo).]

2:1.VI.K: There was the case of a father who imposed an oath on his son [that he would not allow his son to benefit from him (or his possessions) unless the son studied Torah]. [Cf. PM to Y. Bikkurim 3:6 and Margolies' comments in his Mar'eh Ha-Pannim to our passage. Also see the remarks of Asher b. Yehiel (Rosh) to B. Nedarim 38b. Note, however, T. Bekhorot 2:11.]

2:1.VI.L: The case came before R. Yose b. Halapta who permitted him [the father] to fill a jug for him [the son] and to light a candle.

[Alternatively,] the case came before R. Yose b. Halapta who permitted him [the son] to fill a jug for himself and to light a candle. [This understanding would be consistent with VI.J as translated above. In J the person is permitted to do certain things despite the fact that he has not prepared an erub. Here the son would be permitted to benefit from his father's things (jug of water, light) despite the latter's oath (see K above). In both cases, the person's basic needs are allowed to be taken care of.]

2:5.IV.D: [Following V to Y. Shab. 3:4:] He said to him, "Yet does it actually do her any harm [since he cannot produce semen]?"

2:8.I.A: Following the version at Y. Shab. 5:4:] R. Ba and R. Samuel -- the two of them say, "In the view of sages, even [if the strap between the horns] is to lead [the cow], it is forbidden. [Cf. the reading of R. Hananel at B. Besah 23a: Rav and Samuel -- the two of them say... See Ratner, 'Ahavat Ziyyon Vi-Yerushalayim, Shabbat, p. 66ff.]

2:8.II.A: Genibah said, "It is merely a theoretical law that he [Eleazar] used to teach, and he would come [to report it in the name of his master]. [Cf. PM to Y. San. 11:3 and B. Yevamot 77a.]

3:1.II.A: [Azikri (Francus, Talmud Yerushalmi: Masekhet Besah, p. 164) offers a different explanation: The anonymous opinion at M. Bes. 3:1 A-D represents the view of R. Judah as well. However, we would expect Judah to maintain that on a festival, hunting for a beast or fowl in a vivarium (or a garden) would not be permitted since the assumption at I.B is that he considers such an act to be lacking some phase of the hunting process.]

3:1.IV.B: R. Yose b. R. Bun in the name of R. Immi, "This refers to a woven net [which does not hold the beast firmly. See Jastrow, p. 823 and cf. Lieberman, Tosefta Ki-Feshutah V, 964].

3:8.I.A: R. Huna said [that a person should say to a storekeeper: "Fill up this utensil] either less or more [than the usual measure]." [See PM and QH.]

4:3.IV.B: Rab was seated before R. Hiyya the elder, and he was eating [dates]. He appeared to toss [the pits] into the stove but [actually] he tossed them before the stove.

4:4.I.A: [Rabbenu Hananel to B. Bes. 32a and Sefer Ha-Ittur (see Ratner, 'Ahavat Ziyyon Vi-Yerushalayim, Besah, p. 36 and cf. Lieberman, Tosefta' Ki-Feshutah V, 982) add:] and Rabban Simeon b. Gamaliel permits. [Cf. T.Y.T. 3:13: They do not open sealed stew pots (on a festival day), but Rabban Simeon b. Gamaliel permits. The view of Rabban Simeon b. Gamaliel is necessary for the understanding of I.C presented below.]

4:4.I.B: [See B. Bes. 32a where Rav Judah explains Ironian to mean "provincial" and Abbaye defines the vessels referred to as "dishes of peasants." Cf. the comments of Azikri in Francus, Talmud Yerushalmi: Masekhet Besah, p. 205.]

4:4.I.C: The opinion of an individual here [Rabban Simeon b. Gamaliel at I.A, see above note] accords with the anonymous view there [at M. Ed. 2:5 as presented at I.B: Stew pots are susceptible to uncleanness when a Zab carries them. Thus this anonymous view and Simeon agree that the stew pots are completed utensils], and the opinion of an individual there [Eleazar's at I.B] accords with the anonymous view here [at I.A and T.Y.T. 3:13: Sealed stew pots should not be opened on a festival day because that act would constitute completion of a utensil for use, which is prohibited at M. 4:4A-B. Similarly, Eleazar maintains that stew-pots are insusceptible to uncleanness when carried by a Zab because they are not completed utensils. Cf. PM and QH].

4:5.IV.D: [Perhaps what is meant is that should the blind man be permitted to go out with his staff and the shepherd with his leather bag, as R. Simeon maintains, then the shepherd should also be permitted to "lead a domestic beast with a staff," as at M. 4:5I. See the discussion in Lieberman, Tosefta' Ki-Feshutah V, 987f. and cf. PM.]

5:1.I.A-B: The Mishnah speaks of [the hatchway] of that very roof but that of another roof is forbidden. [Produce cannot be let down through the hatchway of another house altogether.]

5:1.II.I: There were nets spread out and they were burning in the sun. They came and asked Rab, "What is the law about moving them?"

5:2.VI.G: R. Meir happened by and heard the noise. He said, "Have our rabbis declared [clapping of all sorts] permitted on the Sabbath?"

5:2.VII.K: Said R. Samuel bar Abodema, "The rabbis permitted a sick person to do so from the belly button upward, and if he is wearing his clothes, from the belly button downward." [See PM and QH.]

5:2.X.P: Said R. Shimi, "As for the one who maintains that they do consecrate, [he means] in the courtyard of the Temple, since they annulled the prohibitions pertaining to Sabbath rest where the Temple [court] was concerned. [Thus the restriction of M. 5:2F applied to acts of sanctification which occurred outside of the Temple court. See PM to Y. Pes. 8:3.]

5:3.I.C: [Or, following Azikri (Francus, Talmud Yerushalmi: Masekhet Besah, p. 235) or PM:] It applies, further, when there is another shepherd available. But if there is available only that one shepherd, then [the beast] is in the status of the shepherd [taking baqar to mean "shepherd" rather than "flock"].

5:4.II.A: R. Judah declares exempt in the case of water, for it is of no substance [M. 5:4D-E]. There is a tanna who teaches that it [R. Judah's exemption in the case of water] is because it is absorbed into the dough. [Azikri adds these words on the basis of manuscript evidence he claims to have had before him. See Francus, Talmud Yerushalmi: Masekhet Besah, p. 236 and Lieberman, Tosefta' Ki-Feshutah V, 1008. Cf. PM and Ratner, 'Ahavat Ziyyon Vi-Yerushalayim, Besah, p. 47, who suggest a similar reconstruction based on the Tosefta's version [T.Y.T. 4:6] of R. Judah's position: R. Judah declares exempt in the case of water because it is absorbed into the dough. Also see QH.]

5:4.II.B: What is the practical difference between the two positions [the two versions of R. Judah's position, see A above]?

5:4.II.C: [It is with regard to] hot water used in cooking [hamim instead of ha-mayim (water). Again see Francus, Talmud Yerushalmi: Masekhet Besah, p. 236 and Lieberman, Tosefta' Ki-Feshutah, p. 1008.]

5:4.II.D: He who said, "It is because it is of no substance" -- indeed, [is] it [hot water] a matter of substance?! [Cf. Francus, p. 236, n. 140, and Lieberman, p. 1008.] [Accordingly, if a woman borrows hot water for a cooked dish, R. Judah would still claim it is of no substance with regard to M. 5:4C.]

5:4.II.E: He who has said, "It is because it is absorbed into the dough" -- indeed, [where hot water is concerned] it is not absorbed into the cooked dish. [Hence, R. Judah would agree in the latter case with M. 5:4C.]

5:5.I.H: On Qesion/Qratsion see S. Klein, Sefer Ha-Yishuv I (Jerusalem, 1939), p. 151.

5:7.I.I: Since he [the host] assigned ownership of their portions to them [the guests] through another [i.e., via a proxy], the portions are no longer in the status of the person [that is, the host] with whom they have been left [as a bailment]. [Thus the resolution of the problem is that the portions or produce are in the status of the one who left the bailment, as originally stated in M. 5:7. If the portions had been in the status of the one with whom the bailment was left, the transfer of ownership would have been ineffective and the guests would not have been permitted to carry away their portions. See PM and QH.]

Chapter 3
YERUSHALMI TAANIT
Stuart S. Miller

1:1.I.A: The reason of R. Eliezer is that since the four species grow beside water, they serve as helpers [peraklitin from Greek parakletos. See W.F. Arndt and F.W. Gingrich, A Greek-English Lexicon of the New Testament (1979), p. 618.] for producing rain.

1:1.I.G-H: According to the view of this last [baraita], the original view of R. Eliezer [QH: in the Mishnah; PM: at I.A] and the other [presented here in the baraita] are one and the same. [Cf. QH and PM.]

[Alternatively,] both the earlier and the later explanations of R. Eliezer's position [at I.A and B] are in agreement with this [baraita] which has just been presented.

1:1.I.R: R. Simon in the name of R. Joshua b. Levi: "[Does] the matter depend upon the agent of the community?" [PM].

1:1.I.T: He said to him, "No. That which you have said, '[Does] the matter depend on the agent of the community?' refers to the prayer for dew where the individual, should he want to make mention, does so. And that which you have said, 'It is forbidden for an individual to make mention until the agent of the community does so,' refers to the prayer for rain." [See PM.]

1:1.II.L: [Cf. translation in The Prophets, Nevi'im: A New Translation, (Philadelphia: Jewish Publication Society, 1979):] "Oh let Your dead revive! Let corpses arise! Awake and shout for joy, You who dwell in the dust! -- For Your dew is like the dew on fresh growth; You make the land of the shades come to life."

1:1.II.M: What is the meaning of, "You make the land of the shades come to life?"

1:1.II.N: Said R. Tanhum of Adrayya, "The earth shall give forth her trust [the dead]." [Following Jastrow, p. 1179.]

1:1.V.B: [Cf. B. Ta. 4b:] Rav said, "One begins [to mention rain] in the additional service, stops in the afternoon, evening and morning services, and resumes again in the additional service [of the second day]." ...Samuel said, "One begins in the additional service, continues in the afternoon, stops in the evening and morning services and resumes again in the additional service." [See QH.]

1:1.VIII.C-G: [Cf. Rabbenu Hananel to B. Ta. 3a:] On account of five matters Israel was redeemed from Egypt. Because of oppression, as it is said, "And the people of Israel groaned under their bondage. Because of their outcry, as it is said, "And God heard their groaning." Because of the merit of the fathers, as it is said, "And God remembered His covenant etc. [with Abraham, Isaac and Jacob.]" Because of penitence as it is said, "And God saw the people of Israel etc." Because the end had come, as it is said, "And God knew their condition."

1:1.IX.C: Said R. Simeon b. Laqish, "'My God' [read eli instead of elai, "to me," in Is. 21:11]. From where will He join me? 'From Seir!'" [See QH.]

1:1.X.Z: And it says, 'You shall be saved by stillness [shuvah] and quiet nahat' -- By means of the Sabbath [Aramaic shubah] and [its] rest [neyah] you will be redeemed. [Cf. Jastrow, pp. 904 and 1509.]

1:3.I.H: [On the removal of two stars from Kimah, i.e., the constellation Pleiades, see L. Ginzberg, The Legends of the Jews (Phil., 1968) I, 162 and especially the sources referred to in V, 183, n.40.]

1:3.V.I-L: [The parallel in Y. Ber. 9:2 reads as follows:] [I:] It was taught: R. Simeon b. Eleazar says, "The earth drinks [the rains] only as far as its upper layer goes." [J:] If so, what should the roots of a carob or a sycamore do? [K:] Said R. Haninah, "Once every thirty days the great deep rises up and waters them." [L:] What is the Scriptural proof for that statement?: "I the Lord am its keeper; every moment I water it." (Is. 27:3)

1:3.VI.D: The views assigned to Rabbi are at variance with one another. There [at VI.B] he has said that [under all circumstances] they follow the proper order [of previous years], and here [at VI.C] he has said [that if the year was intercalated] they assign it its intercalated month. [PM]

1:5.I.A: Said R. Yohanan, "Any fast concerning which a court decrees "to cease" [eating and drinking while it is still day, i.e., a most difficult and critical fast like those of M.1:6 which begin at sunset] pregnant and nursing women do not fast on. [The understanding of "to cease" (le-hafsiq) presented here follows PM and QH. Prof. Neusner's interpretation suggests an entirely different meaning for le-hafsiq: "to interrupt" or "to suspend" a fast once it has been effective. This is in line with the understanding of the term at 1:3.II.G and J.]

1:5.I.B: Said R. Samuel bar R. Isaac, "This [the allowing of pregnant and nursing women not to fast at I.A above] is acceptable when the court already decreed not to cease [eating and drinking while it is still day; that is, a sequence of fasts of lesser importance had been proclaimed earlier], but if it decreed to cease at once [eating and drinking by sunset, because of the urgency of the situation] pregnant and nursing women do fast. [Thus R. Samuel disagrees with R. Yohanan, taking the opposite view that it is incumbent upon all to fast in the most critical instances.]

1:5.I.C: And so it has been taught: Pregnant and nursing women fast on the ninth of Ab, the Day of Atonement and the second sequence of the three public fasts. [On the second sequence of fasts see M. 1:6. Y. reads: the first and second sequences of the three public fasts. Cf., however, Rabbenu Hananel at B. Ta. 14a.]

1:5.I.F: This [the point of view at I.C] does not speak of a case in which they already decreed not to cease. [Rather, the baraita requires pregnant and nursing women to fast precisely on those days on which one is to eat one's final meal while it is still day. This includes the second sequence of fasts discussed in M. 1:6. Thus Samuel seems to have been correct; pregnant and nursing women fast on the more critical days. As for the final seven fasts mentioned in Y.'s version of E, these were imposed when all else failed (M. 1:7) and were apparently considered too difficult for pregnant and nursing women to observe (see PM). If Y.'s reading at C is accepted, then the intention would seem to be that the court could impose a decree to cease eating and drinking before sunset even where the first sequence of fasts (those of M. 1:5) are concerned. Pregnant and nursing women would then be obligated to fast as well (PM). Cf. B. Ta. 14a where it is concluded that these women fast the second sequence of fasts (M. 1:5) but not the first, as they are not critical enough, or the last (M. 1:7) which would endanger their lives. See Rashi's comment ad loc. and Lieberman, Tosefta' Ki-Feshutah V, 1098.]

1:5.I.G: R. Ba bar Zabeda, R. Isaac bar Tabelai in the name of R. Yohanan: "And even where they decreed to cease at once [eating and drinking while it is still day] pregnant and nursing women do not fast on them [the second sequence of fasts]." [Or, following PM who takes into consideration Y.'s reading at I.C, even if the court were to decree eating and drinking forbidden as of sunset during the first sequence of fasts, R. Yohanan would contend that pregnant and nursing women do not fast.]

1:6.VI.H: [Y. Yoma 8:1 has "What is the law?" (ma hu din) instead of "How about this?" (mahu hakhein).]

1:6.VI.K: [Y. Yoma 8:1 has the same reading here as it has at VI.H.]

1:6.VIII.N: It was taught in the name of R. Judah: "Those who want to have children may have sexual relations [i.e., in times of distress such as a drought.]" [Cf. B. Ta. 11a where people who have no children are permitted to have sexual relations during years of famine.]

1:7.I.A: R. Yudan son of R. Hama of Kefar Tahamin: "[The thirteen fast days span six weeks] which are [roughly] equivalent to the forty days that Moses spent on the mountain." [Following QH where it is explained that the days of ascent and descent of the mountain were not counted.]

2:1.VIII.B: "Now is it possible for a mortal to take his heart and put it into his hands? But what is the meaning of 'Let us lift up'? [Following Jastrow, p. 1533:] Let us make our hearts as even as the palm of our hand (remove all crookedness) and then (turn) to God in heaven."

[Alternatively, following QH:] "Let us consider what is in the palm(s) of our hands, [i.e., theft and violence] and then [after repenting, turn] to God in heaven." [Cf. the comments of S. Buber in his edition of Lamentations Rab., ad loc. Also see S. Lieberman, Tosefta' Mo^{c}ed, (1962), p. 326. In his Tosefta' Ki-Feshutah V, 1073, Lieberman, following Rabbenu Hananel at B. Ta. 16a, explains the passage as follows: "Let us liken our hearts to our hands to see whether the heart is like the hands which should not be soiled with theft."]

2:1.IX.M: "When the north wind blows, overlay the bricks [of your houses to strengthen them.] [See PM.]

2:1.X.F: "When there is a sigh from below, the rains fall immediately." [Cf. Jastrow, p. 1518 who renders shever as "broken tune."]

[Alternatively:] [When there is a breaking [of hearts] below, rains fall immediately." [Cf. PM and QH.]

2:1.X.H: "This means when they yield [literally, "incline their necks"] to repentance, the rains fall immediately."

2:1.X.AA: [The parallels to this text read:] "Perseverence in prayer conquers [even] the bad man, all the more so the Good One of the world." [See Ratner, 'Ahavat Ziyyon Vi-Yerushalayim, Taanit, p. 72.]

2:1.XI.P: "Even while He opens [the armory] and while He bolts it, His mercy is drawing near."

2:2.II.M: He said to him, "And has it not been taught: 'One includes the blessing against the apostates and against the transgressors in the blessing... 'Who humbles the proud.' The blessing for the elders and for proselytes is included in the blessing, '...for the righteous.' The blessing for David in, '...Who builds Jerusalem.' [If each of these were to be counted separately,] you would have to provide for each of them [the blessings] a reference to the Lord [from Ps. 29]. [Cf. the reading at Y. Ber. 4:3 which is followed in the commentaries, including PM, and see the remarks of Azikri, ad loc. The following rendering of this reading is also possible: ...You [certainly] have enough [blessings, from which to choose] to make correspondence of each of them with a reference [in Ps. 29] to the Lord [or 'God'] possible. Cf. Jastrow, p. 810 and L. Ginzberg, Perushim Ve-Hiddushim Ba-Yerushalmi III (New York, 1941), p. 277.]

2:2.II.Q: R. Samuel bar Nahman in the name of R. Jonathan: "They are for the eighteen commandments that are written in the second pericope of the tabernacle" [i.e., parashat pequdei (Ex. 38-40) as opposed to parashat terumah (Ex. 25-27) which is the first pericope dealing with the tabernacle. Some commentators, however, understand Jonathan's statement to be an allusion to the second Temple or to the repetition of the word "tabernacle" in Ex. 38:21. See Ginzberg, Perushim Ve-Hiddushim Ba-Yerushalmi III, 289, B.H. Epstein's comments in his Torah Temimah, and PM.]

2:2.V.B: R. Helbo and R. Samuel b. Nahman both say, "They are for the twenty-four times that it is written in the pericope of Solomon [words of] 'joy, prayer, supplication.'" [It is necessary to include the verbs "to pray" and "to supplicate" to arrive at the figure of twenty-four. See Ginzberg, Perushim Ve-Hiddushim Ba-Yerushalmi III, 292 and cf. the Yefeh Enayim of Aryeh Leib Yellin to B. Shabbat 30a.]

2:2.VI.H: [A Genizah fragment (L. Ginzberg, Seridei Ha-Yerushalmi, (New York, 1909), p. 174) and the parallel at Y. Ber. 4:3 read:] R. Jonah in the name of Rav: "Even an individual who decreed a fast upon himself has to make mention of the substance of the incident that has caused the fast." [The Genizah and Y. Ber. versions have, in addition, before the comment of R. Jonah, the following: R. Yannai son of R. Ishmael in the name of the House of Yannai says, "[The supplication, VI.E-G, is inserted] in 'Who hears prayer.'" -- This helps to explain the disagreement of Jeremiah and Yannai at VI.K.]

2:2.VI.I: And where does he say it [i.e., in which Prayer (tefillah) does he begin to recite it? Does he begin in the evening Prayer, though he is still permitted to eat, or in the following morning's Prayer]? [Following Azikri at Y. Ber. 4:3. Cf., however, Ginzberg, Perushim Ve-Hiddushim Ba-Yerushalmi, p. 301, who maintains that the question is unrelated to what follows.]

2:2.VI.J: R. Zeirah in the name of R. Hunah: "He says it like the night of the Sabbath and like its day [to wit, beginning with the evening prayer and continuing with the following morning and afternoon tefillot]." [Cf. the usage of the expression "like the night of the Sabbath and its day" in M. Nid. 4:4 and see Ginzberg, Perushim Ve-Hiddushim Ba-Yerushalmi III, 298f. and QH. The texts confuse b ('on') and k ('like'). See V., which appears to have the latter (V. to Y. Ta. 2:12 clearly reads "like the night of the Sabbath and like its day") and cf. Ratner, 'Ahavat Ziyyon Vi-Yerushalayim, Berakhot, pp. 107f.]

2:2.VI.L: [Following the emendation suggested by L. Ginzberg, Perushim Ve-Hiddushim Ba-Yerushalmi III, 303:] R. Yose answered, "And lo, the following Tannaitic teaching differs: Every day a person must say eighteen blessings, and on the night following the Sabbath and on the night following the Day of Atonement and on a public fast." [Apparently, the point is that the Havdalah is added to an existing blessing on the nights following the conclusion of both the Sabbath and the Day of Atonement. Similarly, the reference to the fast does not form an additional blessing in the tefillah of the public fast.] Now on the basis of what R. Yose has said that the Tannaitic tradition is at variance [with the view of Rab at VI.K] it follows that the question concerns the view that the passage is to be inserted between '...Who redeems Israel,' and '...Who heals the sick.' [Evidently, Rab maintains that the passage that the individual who assumes a personal fast must say (see K) should be inserted between '...Who redeems Israel' and '...Who heals the sick,' as maintained by R. Jeremiah (VI.A-C) with regard to the public fast. Rab would seem to have agreed with Jeremiah where the public fast was concerned so Yose's question with regard to Rab's view is appropriate. See Ginzberg, ibid.]

2:2.VII.A: [Following Mss. Amsterdam and Constantinople at Y. Ber. 4:3: What is the prayer that serves to summarize the eighteen blessings [of the Prayer]? [Or, following the reading of the text of R. Solomon Sirillo at Y. Ber. 4:3 and the crossed out version in Ms. Leiden there: R. Joshua says: The abstract of the eighteen (blessings)" (M. Ber. 4:3).] [Either reading would make sense in view of the following discussion in the gemara. See Ginzberg, Perushim Ve-Hiddushim Ba-Yerushalmi III, 315.]

2:9.IV.B: But why David? Because he sought to deal with [the consequences of] the census. See II Sam. 24:10 where David realizes his mistake and 24:25 where God accepts his plea. Cf. QH.]

2:11.III.E: "But his ordinance [that is, the law which applies to him] is his disgrace." [This can mean either (1) that the destruction of the Temple relieves him of the prohibition of drinking wine (Rashi to B. Ta. 17a and PM) or (2) his inability to identify his priestly watch and father's house is the disgrace which results in the non-observance of the prohibition. (Rabbenu Hananel to B. Taanit 17a, R. Samuel Edels (Maharsha), ad loc., and Lieberman, Tosefta' Ki-Feshutah V, 1081) Cf. the usage of the expression "his ordinance is his disgrace" in B. San. 22b and P. Meg 1:4.]

2:11.III.F: Will he be permitted as far as mourning is concerned [following Lieberman, Tosefta' Ki-Feshutah V, 1338]?

2:11.III.G: If you were to say [otherwise, i.e.,] that his disgrace is his ordinance, and he should be prohibited from mourning, then, in similar fashion, his disgrace is his ordinance in that he should not be permitted to work [since work too was prohibited on the day he would ordinarily serve. Thus he should be prohibited from working at all times because he is uncertain of his fixed day. Now this is unlikely so mourning must be permitted. See PM and Lieberman, Tosefta Ki-Feshutah V, 1338.]

2:12.I.H: Now this accords with that which R. Zeira said in the name of R. Huna: "He says it like the night of the Sabbath and like its day [that is, beginning with the evening Prayer prior to the day of the fast. This follows the reading in V. See note to 2:2.VI.J above.]"

2:12.II.P: [Megillat Taanit reads:] On the seventeenth day thereof the peoples rose up against the remnant of the scribes in the town of Chalcis and in Bet Zibdin, and there was salvation for the House of Israel.

3:2.I.D: It has been taught: They sound the shofar for the need of trees close (peras) to Passover, and for cisterns, ditches and caves close (peras) to Pentecost [T: Tabernacles. For this rendering of peras, see Lieberman, Tosefta' Ki-Feshutah IV, 674f. and V, 1092.]

3:3.V.F: [Following Jastrow, p. 443:] "Storm" (haziz) -- because He makes the sky full of irregular lumps (cumuli): '...the Lord Who makes the storm clouds (hazizim)...'

3:9.II.D: [Y actually reads:] And so it has been taught: On the twentieth all the people fasted and the rain fell for them. [See Ratner, 'Ahavat Ziyyon Vi-Yerushalayim, Taanit, p. 88, who claims that the emendation suggested in PM is incorrect as our reading agrees with that of Megillat Taanit. Ratner notes that in Megillat Taanit the "twentieth" refers to Adar (not Nisan). He suggests, therefore, that "the eve of Passover" at II.C be understood as "close" to Passover.]

3:9.IV.A: Said R. Yudan Giria, "This Honi the Circle-drawer was the grandson of Honi the Circle-drawer. Near the time of the destruction of the [first] Temple, he [the earlier Honi] went out to a mountain to his workers. Before he got there, it rained. He went into a cave. Once he sat down there, he tired and fell asleep.

3:9.IV.B: "He remained immersed in his sleep for seventy years until the Temple was destroyed and it was rebuilt a second time. [Perhaps what is meant is from the destruction of the first Temple in 586 B.C.E. to c. 515 B.C.E. when the Temple was rebuilt, which was about seventy years. For the view that the passage refers to the grandfather of the Honi in M. 3:9 see the comments of R. Isaiah di Trani in his Tosafot Rid to B. Ta. 23a and Ratner, 'Ahavat Ziyyon Vi-Yerushalayim, Taanit, p. 88.

3:9.VIII.E: "But go and bring me a bullock for confession." [See next note.]

3:9.VIII.F: They went and brought him a bullock for confession. [Following Rashi to B. Ta. 23a. Cf., however, A. Büchler, Types of Jewish Palestinian Piety from 70 B.C.E. to 70 C.E. (New York, 1968), p. 251, who contends that acknowledgment of God as Judge is intended.]

4:2.II.B: When would all of Israel go up to Jerusalem?

4:2.II.D: When could all of Israel sit idle?

4:2.VI.F: To produce twenty-three delegations is something that you cannot do, for it is written, "...David and Samuel the seer established them in their set office."

4:2.VI.G: "In their set office [be-'emunatam]" -- With their skill [be-'umanutam], were David and Samuel able to do so]. For it took great skill [to institute a system whereby] a delegation would not take another share, where the seizure of inherited fields was concerned, until its fellow took its share.

4:2.VIII.C: [Following the Genizah version:] "And appoint R. Hanina bar Hama at the head. [See L. Ginzberg, Ginzei Schechter (New York, 1928), I, 427 and cf. B. Ket. 103b.]

4:2.VIII.L: He said to him, "When you go down there tell him that I appointed you a sage." [Haninah] realized that he would not be appointed [until he went there, which meant that the appointment would not be made] in his [Rabbi's] lifetime. [PM]

4:4.I.M-P: [That not all parties agreed, despite Yose's claim to the contrary at I.L, is suggested by the fact that there were those who contended that mourning and fasting continued to be prohibited, on the days stipulated in M. 4:4, after the destruction. Evidently, those who maintained this view believed that the event described at I.B-C was always commemorated as a special, historical happening of the past after which individuals no longer contributed wood to the Temple. The destruction itself made no difference in the observance of these days. For Yose, who maintained that individuals could and did contribute their own wood (I.E-F), mourning and fasting on these days were allowed after the destruction precisely because individuals could no longer bring wood-offerings. Those who held that mourning and fasting continued to be prohibited obviously had no such concern, hence they did not concur, at least where the wood-offering was concerned, that it "may be shifted and used for the community as a whole." The statement at I.P which says that the fast of the ninth of Av was once, after the destruction, postponed to the tenth but was not completed indicates that the wood-offering days continued to be recognized after 70 C.E. as contended by those sages opposed to Yose's view. For the interpretation presented here, see Lieberman, Tosefta' Ki-Feshutah V, 1112f.]

4:5.III.I: [Following QH:] In a day and a night a courier can leave Jerusalem and arrive at Tyre. [The courier did not need until the first of Elul, he could have arrived at Tyre a whole lot sooner.]

4:5.III.L: R. Simeon b. Laqish said, "It may be compared to a king who was sitting and making calculations. They came and told him, 'Your son has been taken captive and has been condemned...'"

4:5.III.M: R. Mana asked, "It is possible that the calculations could have been confused [and incorrectly recorded] in the past [when they were constantly preoccupied with battles and were sorrowful], but is it so with what was to happen [that is, the destruction which was recorded later, once the catastrophe had occured]? [See PM. Note that Ezekiel's oracle concerning Tyre (ch. 26) takes the destruction for granted.]

4:5.VII.A: [As to the seventeenth of Tammuz,] why did they [the generation in which the statue of Manasseh was set up, V.C] not designate it as a fast day? [PM]

4:5.VII.B: Hinena, Abayye of Bar Yantah in the name of R. Benaiah: "Because the greater part of the community [PM: during the time of Manasseh, see VII.A] did not accept it."

4:5.VII.C: [PM gives two explanations:] Said R. Joshua b. Levi, "Whatever happened to that one [the first Temple] was repeated, but whatever happened to this one [the second Temple] did not reoccur." [Or alternatively,] "Whatever happened on that day [the seventeenth of Tammuz] was [eventually] retracted, but whatever happened on this day [the ninth of Av, specifically the destruction] was not retracted." [PM does not consider VII.D-E to be connected with Joshua b. Levi's statement and instead connects it with what follows in VIII.]

4:5.VIII.R: [Genizah version reads:] R. Levi in the name of R. Hama son of R. Hanina: "'But with the roar of a great tempest (hamullah)' -- But with the roar of the mighty word (ha-millah) which you said: 'For they are stronger than we' (Num. 13:31) -- 'He will set fire to it and its branches will be consumed.'" [See Ginzberg, Seridei Ha-Yerushalmi, p. 184.]

4:5.IX.U: [Genizah version reads:] "Mesarbai: "He handed over His house to His enemies." [See Ginzberg, Seridei Ha-Yerushalmi, p, 184.] [IX.S-W represents an aggadic interpretation of the first two entries in the so-called "Baraita of the Twenty-Four Mishmarot (priestly courses or 'watches')." This listing of the priestly courses has been fully reconstructed using archaeological evidence and the testimony of medieval piyyutim (liturgical poems). For bibliography and a discussion of the passage found here see S.S. Miller, Studies in the History and Traditions of Sepphoris (Leiden, 1983), pp. 123ff.]

4:5.X.E: But because Rabbi lived nearer to the destruction of the Temple, there were old men who remembered what had happened, and when he gave his exegesis they would weep and be quieted [by Rabbi, who interrupted the lesson] and [finally] stop crying. [Cf. PM.]

4:5.XI.K: "Men dogged [sadu] our steps" [The Five Megilloth and Jonah, A New Translation, (Jewish Publication Society, Phil., 1969): "Our steps were checked"] -- the path to that house [the Temple] was confounded ['asdu].

4:5.XIII.G: There is he who says, "It was because they would play ball [on the Sabbath." See the parallel in Lamentations Rab., ed. Buber, p. 53b. Also, Ratner, 'Ahavat Ziyyon Vi-Yerushalayim, Taanit, p. 106 and QH.]

4:6.IV.L: When the ninth of Ab ended, R. Isaac b. Eleazar would announce [that they should open the barber shops], and they would open the barber shops and whoever wanted got a haircut.

4:7.I.R: [Following the reading in Lamentations Rab., Proem 33, (ed. Buber):] They read a verse of Scripture and drew him near: "[And God said to him, 'I am God Almighty: be fruitful and multiply; a nation and a company of nations shall come from you [and kings shall spring from you]'" (Gen. 35:11).

4:7.I.S-T: [Again following Lamentations Rab. as at I.R. above:] They read a verse of Scripture and put him away: "[And now your two sons, who were born to you in the land of Egypt before I came to you in Egypt, are mine]; Ephraim and Manasseh shall be mine, as Reuben and Simeon are" (Gen. 48:5) -- They [the tribe of Benjamin] were not considered [in this verse] among their brothers [cf. PM and QH.]

Chapter 4

YERUSHALMI HAGIGAH

Yaakov Elman

Foreword

The following brief notes, which are intended to supplement Professor Neusner's translation of Yerushalmi tractates Hagiga and Mo'ed Qatan in Volume 20 of The Talmud of the Land of Israel, are not in any sense complete, or intended to constitute a commentary to those tractates. They originated as private notes, and to a large extent reflect my own interests and priorities; they are thus much fuller in passages touching on Purities (chiefly Chapter Three of Hagiga) than elsewhere.

In the main, these comments are designed to point out some alternative readings or interpretations, especially in difficult passages, or to call attention to some of the literature available on them, though, here too, no completeness is claimed. In some particularly difficult passages, in particular the supremely difficult Third Chapter mentioned above, they contain summaries of the discussions of two of the most sophisticated of the traditional commentaries, which, unfortunately for modern scholarship, are written in a somewhat arcane, pilpulistic style; these summaries extract the fine textual comments from the whole.

Ratner's indispensible work, while consulted, is rarely cited; it is not difficult of access, though his citations must always be checked, both because he did not have available to him the better editions of the work of the classical commentators which he cites, and because he did not distinguish between quotations, paraphrases, and sometimes, references to works other than Yerushalmi which were nevertheless referred to as "Yerushalmi."

I have in particular emphasized the work of two scholars of the "old school," R. Joshua Isaak Shapiro of Slonim in No^{c}am Yerushalmi, and R. Meir Marim of Kobrin, in his Sefer Nir; on both, see the brief comments of B.M. Bokser, The Study of Ancient Judaism, N.Y., 1981, Vol. II, pp. 106-7. These works are written in a difficult style, as noted. I have also singled out for attention the Sha^{c}arei Torat Erets Yisrael of R. Ze'ev Wolf Rabinowitz, which is rather difficult to find, even in libraries, and is always worthy of consideration; see Bokser, op. cit., p. 109.

I wish to thank Professor Jacob Neusner, without whose encouragement and stimulus these notes would never have been written, and, who, with a characteristic generosity of spirit, first suggested and then arranged for their publication: gādōl ham-m^{ec}aśśeh min ha-^{c}ośeh (B.M. 9a)!

My wife and family, who have borne and continue to bear the burden of my periods of inaccessibility, also have made their contribution to scholarship; may the results be worthy of the time taken from what is rightfully theirs!

My thanks to Professor Baruch Bokser for the copy of Sefer Nir which he graciously made available to me.

It is entirely fitting that this volume be dedicated to the late Professor Saul Lieberman, whose studies in Yerushalmi so often illuminate the text and are so often reflected, albeit dimly, in these notes, and who first opened the doors of Yerushalmi to me.

It is not inappropriate, I think, to take note of the date: the eve of the Ninth of Av, the traditional anniversary of the destruction of both Temples, for our difficulties with the text of Yerushalmi are but a consequence of persecution and exile.

Yaakov Elman

8 Av 5783
18 July 1983

Notes

Note: For reasons of clarity, the exact limits of proposed emendations are not always indicated, and a comparison with the original text is required.

1:1.A: Reʾiyāh can mean "appearance" or, elliptically, "appearance-offering." PM prefers the first, QE the second. It is this equivocal use which occasions Y.'s initial comment; see Ratner, p. 54, and Lieberman, p. 1265.

1:1.E: Ratner suggests that "the blind" was not in Y.'s version of Mishnah, since its Scriptural origin is not glossed.

1:1.I.A: The use of apilū would seem to support the interpretation of QE as against that of PM: that is, "Our Mishnah-passage['s listing of exemptions refers] to the [requirements of bringing] an appearance-offering. But as to, etc.," rather than "[When] the Mishnah [refers to a minor's exemption....]"

1:1.I.D: Interchange of b/p is common in Semitic languages from an early date: Beqi'in = the well-known Peqi'in. See C. Brockelmann, Grungriss der Vergleichenden Grammatik der Semitischen Spachen, Berlin, 1908, I, p. 234; compare Hebrew dᵉbaš = Akkadian dišpu.

1:1.I.G: "Who presided this week?" reflects T. and Bavli rather than Y.'s text, which is mī šabat šam, "who spent the Sabbath there?" The same phrase can be found in Mekilta, ed. Horovitz-Rabin, pp. 58-9; see also Lieberman, Tosefta Kifshuta, Vol. 8, p. 680.

The difference is not trivial, since Y. and its cognates indicate that the lecture was customarily given on the Sabbath, and that scholars came to visit from "out of town" to attend it.

1:1.IV.C: For hdr = ḥzr, "retract," see D. Sperling, Studies in Late Hebrew Lexicography in the Light of Akkadian (unpub. diss., Columbia University, 1973), p. 50f.

1:1.IV.I: STEI notes that this Amora's name should be Simeon b. Abba, not Samuel. Cmp. his comments ad Y. Ber. 2:7 (p. 8), in the course of which he speculates that this

Simeon (who was never ordained; see Y. Bikk. 3:3) was a brother of the famous Babylonian Amora Samuel, and thus of R. Hiya b. Abba.

1:1.V: The basic problem the commentators faced, whether implicitly or explicitly, is the relationship of this version of R. Yohanan's statement at E to that found in BT Hag. 9a, or, more precisely, the exact meaning of tašlūmīm, "completion [of a sacrificial obligation]." If taken in the usual way, R. Yohanan at E is expressing the same view as Hezekiah at D, and in agreement with his reported view in Bavli. But then R. Yohanan should be linked with Hezekiah at K, L, O and P. Thus, QE, NY and STEI emend accordingly. PM, as usual, takes the text as is, and admits (see MP s.v. ʾāmar R. Yohanan) that Y.'s version of R. Yohanan's remarks differs from Bavli's.

As noted, however, that is less of a problem that the strange use of tašlūmīm. Nir proposes an elegant solution which may be a shade too sophisticated, given the state of the text. He suggests that Hezekiah here is not R. Yohanan's well-known teacher, but one of the later Amoraim, who is mentioned in Y. Pes. 8:2 and elsewhere, and that he is here interpreting R. Yohanan's remarks; presumably Nir would reverse the order of D and E. According to this Hezekiah, then, R. Yohanan's opinion proceeds from Deut. 16:16, while R. Ila at F derives it from the law of the Second Passover. It is the former which is reported in Bavli, while the latter is reflected in K, L, O and P. However, as is noted in Bavli, the question raised at M-P represents a special case, inasmuch as the Second Passover was instituted primarily for those who were unclean during the first. Gilyon Hashas, basing himself in part on Tosafot Hag. 9a s.v. kēwan, reverses the views attributed to Hezekiah and R. Hoshaiah, and omits R. Yohanan from that context altogether.

1:1.V.D: QE omits the proof-text, which is actually yr'h yr'h, and is unclear. Nir, as we have seen, takes it as his point of departure. He explains that "even when one is exempt [on the first day], one must be fit to be "seen" [in the Temple in order to be allowed to fulfill his obligation on the succeeding days of the festival]; if not, the exemption remains in force throughout the festival even though one becomes fit on a later day. This seems to be based on the equivocal orthography of yr'h, which can be active or passive and includes within its semantic range the meaning "to be fit;" cmp. XV.D.

1:1.V.I: PM, QE and Nir find this question out of place since the sacrificial obligation itself constitutes a "practical difference." However, the preceding is really a preliminary review of positions rather than a list of "practical differences."

1:1.V.M-P: See NY, who explains R. Yohanan's position as follows: tašlūmīm implies that if one was liable on the first day, even if he subsequently became exempt, the obligation remains, in contrast to his understanding (apud Turé Even to BT Hag. 4b) of Bavli; see his discussion of Y. Taan. 4:5. According to R. Hoshaiah, however, even though his ostensible position is that "each day constitutes an obligation [unto itself]," he actually means that each day's obligation proceeds from that of the first day. Moreover, NY emends R. Hoshaiah's opinion at P to "exempt," an emendation which makes H impossible, a result which he does not seem to have taken into account.

All in all, STEI's reconstruction seems preferable as requiring the least amount of tampering with the text:

K. In the opinion of Hezekiah (and R. Yohanan) he is exempt [from the obligations of the Temple-appearance].
L. In the opinion of R. Hoshaiah he is liable.
M. So in the case of someone who became clean [on the later days of the festival]:
N. If someone became clean on the later days [of the festival],
O. In the view of Hezekiah (and R. Yohanan), he is exempt.
P. In the view of R. Hoshaiah, he is liable.

Six changes are required: the deletion of "R. Yohanan" from L and P and its addition to K and O, and the emendation of "unclean" in N to "clean;" last is the emendation of "became unclean" in M to "became clean."

XIV.A: See Nir, who provides contrasting analyses dependent on whether the one who sent the agent was himself exempt (cmp. NY) or not.

XIV.B-D, H-I: Nir (and STEI) reverse the proof-texts so that the more appropriate ones (Deut. 12:6 for the unclean and Deut. 31:11 for the unsightly) are to be implied in the conclusion at J.

XVI.H-I: QE omits the first "they do not" and understands Samuel as allowing a claim on land, but not its seizure as a pledge, this being (to him) the only position conceivable. According to QE, then, the dispute then concerns only movables.

This is too drastic for Nir and NY, not to mention PM, who see the essential disagreement as whether the heirs" responsibility for their parents" debts is Rabbinical and can in this case be disregarded since the debt is regarded as being undocumented (Samuel), or is Scriptural, and does not end with death (R. Yohanan). STEI (cmp. PM in MP) relates Samuel's view in B to that expressed in Y. B.K. 10:1 re a loan before witnesses [i.e., without documentary evidence] which can nevertheless be collected from the heirs, and R. Yohanan's view in C (that the obligation remains even without designation having taken place) to his in Y. Gittin 3:3 that the obligation cannot devolve on the heirs unless they inherit real property. (For a comprehensive discussion of all the legal issues involved, see PM s.v. R. Yôḥānān āmar.)

A subsidiary problem is whether the heirs are responsible for burnt and/or peace-offerings. The latter may be obligatory only on the father, since he eats of it during the festival: the obligation may not have been incurred at all (Nir). For our purposes, it is sufficient to note that Y. itself does not make this distinction.

1:2.II.E: STEI (see Ratner) restores: "For the rejoicing-offering applied to men and women and applied to all seven [days of the festival], which was not the case for the [other] two" on the basis of T. 1:5. This then serves as an introduction to R. Yose's remark at H.

1:2.II.F.a: STEI notes that "others" can refer to those who are invited as guests.

1:2.II.F.a: Translation follows PM; STEI provides an alternate interpretation: "and it applies both to those categories [of sacrifices] from which [festal-offerings] usually [come, i.e., animals previously unsanctified] and from which [festal-offerings] do not usually [come, i.e., vows and thank-offerings; see 1:4 below]." Cmp. Nir.

1:2.II.K: PM and Nir understand pāsuṭ in its sense of "small coin": "Rav Huna ate a small coin's [worth] of meat every festival-day."

1:2.III.C: Translation follows PM ad the parallel passage in Peah 1:1. QE here, Nir and Ratner suggest that this was R. Yohanan's standard response upon hearing a baraita unfamiliar to him and unfavorable to his views; see Y. Shab. 2:1, where, however, the reading is k'n, "here." Curr. eds., Ridvaz read k^{c}yn: "Is there indeed a case similar to this?" which would agree with PM, but this reading has no ms. support. Ms. Leiden and ed. Venice (in Hag.) and Sirillio (in Peah) read kn, "so."

Lieberman, Yerushalmi Kifshuto, pp. 64-5 points out that lyt k'n is the standard phrase used in Y. to introduce an emendation (see lit. there cited). The phrase wyš k'n zw expresses doubt as to the reliability of the quoted baraita.

1:2.III.J: "To make a record for himself" is based on the parallel in Peah: lršwm; cmp. BT Yoma 80a, šyktwb; the text here is obviously corrupt. See MP.

1:2.III.K-M: If Nir is correct (see below), M-R is quoted in support of K rather than L.

1:2.III.N-R: Tosafot (Hag. 7a s.v. tōplīn) relate R. Yohanan's view regarding the impermissibility of dividing up one's festal-obligation with his view regarding the prohibition of adding unconsecrated beasts: just as the festal-offering must not be divided among beasts, so too may one not add beasts. However, second-tithe money may be used (see BT Hag. 8a); this is linked with the prohibition against bringing free-will offerings on a festival day (though it is allowed on the intermediate days).

Nir points out that the positions taken by R. Yohanan and Hezekiah are not symmetric. According to Hezekiah, the prohibition of mixing tithe and unconsecrated coins in order to bring a supplementary festal sacrifice applies even on the intermediate days, while according to R. Yohanan the prohibition of adding unconsecrated beasts does not apply to those days. He therefore suggests (apud Rashi Hag. 8a s.v. Hezekiah) that R. Yohanan's prohibition is based on the need to bring festal-offerings from unconsecrated animals -- but all animals brought for sacrifice on the first festal day are considered as consecrated! R. Yohanan therefore suggests that it is preferable to add tithe money to buy a larger animal rather than an additional sacrifice, if the needs of the feast require it.

If so, the two positions taken by R. Yohanan are not related, as Tosafot would have it. The problem of R. Yohanan's reason for the prohibition of dividing one's obligation between two beasts remains, especially in light of the fact that, were the additional beast bought with a mixture of tithe and unconsecrated funds, the latter should be sufficient to allow it to be offered up. After discussing several solutions to this problem, Nir concludes that not only are the two opinions recorded to R. Yohanan's name not related, but that the authorities for the second issue, that of division of obligation (in Q and R) should be reversed. That is, R. Yohanan is the one who permits addition, because division is prohibited: the second beast would be a free-will offering which may be bought from tithe-money. Hezekiah, on the other hand, prohibits addition; since division is allowed, the second beast would be a festal-offering which cannot be bought with tithe-money.

This reversal of authorities is relatively common in Y., both within Y., and between Y. and Bavli. At any rate, if Nir is correct, M refers to K rather than L.

Whether the symmetry thus gained is sufficient to offset the lack of any textual support in Y. or Bavli for this reversal is difficult to determine. In addition, one result of his analysis is that the prohibition of adding animals applies primarily to tithe-money; buying additional animals from unconsecrated funds would be permitted. But such a distinction is not found in either Talmud.

NY connects the dispute at O and P with A and F. R. Yohanan's prohibition of addition stems, in his analysis, from the requirement that each animal be worth at least a māᶜāh, which minimum he holds is Scriptural; Hezekiah holds the minimum to be of Rabbinic origin, and thus each animal may be worth less than a māᶜāh. But again, if so, why is the discussion not cast in such terms?

1:2.III.S: QE prefers to omit S; Nir suggests his reason is that the case at T does not relate to the issue at hand: the question is one of adding beasts, the case concerns ten beasts which were all consecrated at the same time. In answer to this objection, Nir explains that the "left-overs" from the ten consecrated animals can be sacrificed on the festival itself, while additional beasts may not. BB then relates to the situation after the obligatory offering has been brought, even in a case of addition.

1:2.III.Z: Nir sees a contradiction between this analysis of R. Yohanan's view on addition, and that given above. He suggests that here the essential element is the consecration and not the sacrificial rite itself: it is that which determines the status of the sacrifice, since all peace-offerings -- festal and free-will -- are subject to the same procedures. Since it is the consecration which is determinative, money may be added at that point (there is a minimum for sacrifices but not a maximum), but not beasts. The sacrifices which result from that act of consecration of the funds allocated may thus be brought on the festival.

1:2.III.AA: To continue Nir's analysis: R. Simeon b. Laqish holds that the essential element is the bringing of the sacrifice, and not the consecration. The requirements of the sacrificial rite on the first festal day "overcome" the usual prohibition of unnecessary slaughtering on the festival, but the animals which remained for the last day (the "left-overs") are not considered as necessary, and may not be brought.

QE (in SQ s.v. leᶜôlām suggests reversing the authorities to at Z and AA to conform better with Bavli; Nir points out that the reasoning attributed to each position fits better as the text stands.

1:3.C: Bavli's version has "first day of Passover," which is decidedly not that of texts of Palestinian origin (see Ratner). Q emends Y. on the basis of Bavli, and Nir criticizes him roundly for it. Y.'s version is "the Festival," i.e., Sukkot, which precludes the analysis found in BT Hag. 7b-8a. Nevertheless, the passage is syntactically difficult, in both versions: C does not follow smoothly from A-B; and A itself, as Bavli points out, is difficult in its singling-out of burnt-offerings for the immediate days of the festival. PM and QE both accept Bavli's emendation:

A. Burnt-offerings, (vows and free-will offerings) are brought on intermediate days of the festival, (but not on the festival day [itself], and the burnt-offering [brought] for [the fulfillment of] appearance-obligations is brought even on the festival day,) and is brought (only) from [beasts bought with] unconsecrated money.

B. Peace-offerings [for festal obligations] derive even from money in the status of second tithe, etc.

1:3.I.J: QE reverses the thrust of R. Yose b. R. [A]bun's remark: "And are not festal-offerings equivalent to free-will peace-offerings?" though the gain in continuity is elusive. Presumably we know more about festal peace-offerings than about the other! Nir summarily rejects QE's emendation. He explains the question thus: why does Scripture deal with each type of peace-offering separately inasmuch as both require exactly the same ritual?

(Along these lines, the question might be translated: "And are not free-will peace-offerings equivalent to festal peace-offerings? Why [then] does Scripture include them as a secondary element in these verses [i.e., requiring Rabbinic exegesis, rather than proceding from the plain sense of the verse]?" Cmp. Nachmanides to Num. 27:9.)

Nir notes that III.T would fit better here than in its present position.

1:4.I.H: Curr. eds. contain "or the reverse?," which is lacking in the parallel passage in Y. Sukkah 4:5. Translation omits it, but NY takes it as raising the possibility of interpreting the verse as referring to the last festal day. It thus becomes a response to this interjection.

1:6.I: Nir seems concerned by the irrelevance of B-H to A. R. Yose's objection at D is well-taken: why raise the question of the overriding of the Sabbath-restrictions on slaughter in this context? The thrust of B should be in support of A. Nir therefore re-aligns this passage along that line. Thus:

B. Judah bar Safra in the name of R. Hoshaiah: "And you shall keep it as a feast [bringing a festal-offering] unto the Lord seven days in the year (Lev. 23:41)." And are there seven days? Is not the Sabbath excluded [from the number of days on which a festal-offering may be brought]?

C. But there are eight days [of the festival, inclusive of the Eighth Day of Gathering], making [with the exclusion of the Sabbath] seven [in all on which festal-offerings may be brought].

Nir thus reverses the order of Bb and Ca. The thrust of D is then that we cannot have it both ways: we cannot use Lev. 23:41 for the law of final-day compensatory offerings and for the rule that festal-offerings do not override Sabbath restrictions.

The response at E-H is that the verse comes essentially to teach the first, the second is only implied by the way.

Cmp. BT Pes. 70b.

1:6.I.G: NY notes the contradiction between R. Hoshaiah's views here and that in 1:1 V.H, where he states that each day of the festival constitutes an obligation on its own, and does not derive its fitness for bringing a sacrifice from the obligation of the first day. His solution is to re-interpret I.G here as not reflecting exactly R. Hoshaiah's views. What R. Hoshaiah actually meant is that if one could not perform his duty on the first day, he may do so on the second, and so on. It might have been better to emend I.G straight out!

It seems to me that a reconciliation can be effected rather easily, and, indeed, NY himself further on (p. 172 s.v ubazeh) gives something of the interpretation proposed here. 1:1 V.H refers explicitly to all seven days of the festival, while here R. Hoshaiah deals with the problem of the eighth day, which in the case of Tabernacles and the Eighth Day of Gathering constitutes a particular problem: the latter day is both related to Tabernacles and is considered in some respects a festival unto itself; see II.B. In 1:1 his concern is basically either with Passover or Passover and the seven days of Tabernacles in the strict sense.

1:7.III.D: QE emends to "the light which is in it" (m'wr from s'wr) on the basis of parallels; see Ratner and ziyyun Yerushalayim ad loc.

1:7.IV.I: "Alien" -- mgyr. Nachmanides takes it as "neighbor," see Ratner; both interpretations are possible from √gwr.

1:7.IV.B: STEI lists a number of variants of this name, including 'rym (Y. Pes. 3:7), lbzh (Y. Sheviit 4:1), ntzh (BT Kid. 40b and Sanh. 74a), ^{c}rwd (Sifre Deut. Eqeb 41 [= ed. Finkelstein, p. 85:13 and app. crit.]. Perhaps the best-known is Arzah ('rzh), quoted in Tur Y.D. 369.

1:7.IV.C: Ratner claims that several early authorities had in their texts of Y. a similar story told of Rav and his father. Whether this was an additional story or another version of the present one is unclear, however. See Ratner, p. 57 (bottom) and the lit. there cited.

1:8.V.M: "In his master's presence" -- deleted by PM and QE, presumably on the basis of the prohibition of a student's rendering decisions in his master's vicinity; see Y. Gittin 1:2. However, the parallels at Y. Meg. 4:1, Leviticus Rabbah 22:1, and Y. Peah 2:4 do contain that reading, though Eccles. Rabbah 1:9:2 does not.

Summary at the end of Chapter I: The connection would seem to be the following: having taken up the issue of oral traditions and their importance, it was deemed pertinent to delimit exactly their authority. This unit appears in much the same form in Y. Peah 2:4. In regard to Unit VIII, however, even Nir, whose ingenuity seldom failed him, confesses his puzzlement as to its placement.

2:1.D: For this expression, which goes back to high antiquity, see S. Loewenstamm, Y. Kaufman Jubilee Volume [Hebrew], Jerusalem, 1961, p. 117.

2:1.I.C: See Lieberman, Yerushalmi Kifshutah, p. 100 s.v. qōšeret: le^{c}ōvdāh means: "Is it the definitive law?," the equivalent of Bavli's halakah l^{e}ma^{c}aseh. See also Lieberman, p. 1287.

2:1.II.C: See ad I.C.

2:1.II.E: For the role of water in Creation, see U.M.D. Cassuto, Studies on the Bible and Ancient Orient [Hebrew], Jerusalem, 1972, I, pp. 70-85.

2:1.II.I: Ratner suggests that the original form of this midrash can be gauged from the adaptation found in Yalkut Hammakiri, London, 1909, II, p. 38:

R. Yose says: Woe to those creatures who see but know not what they see, who stand and know not on what they stand! On what does the earth stand? On the pillars, as Scripture states: "He who makes the earth shake from its place, and its pillars quake" (Job. 9:6). And the pillars [stand] on the waters, as Scripture states: "To Him who spread the earth over the waters," (Ps. 136:6)....

2:1.II.N-O: This passage appears in Midrash Echah, ed. S. Buber, Vilna, 1899, 3:29. A significant variant which shifts its Sitz im Leben is dōrēš ūmagī^{c}a lāhen, "would reach the[se verses] in preaching" in place of qōrē' 'ōtān, "read them."

2:1.III.G: See Lieberman, Yerushalmi Kifshutah, p. xvii (Introduction), and see Ratner. Rabad of Posquieres quotes our passage in his commentary to Sifra 74a

(Mesora^C 5): One is not permitted to decide [lit., "to say a word"] matters of ṣāra^Caṯ ("leprosy") unless etc. Cmp. ms. Leiden.

2:1.IV.E: See Lieberman, pp. 1287-8. In ms. Erfurt of T., [Hag. 2:1], the fire comes down before R. Eleazar's discourse begins, in Mekilta deRashbi, ed. Epstein-Melamed, Jerusalem, p. 158, R. Yohanan does not dismount until after the fire begins.

2:1.IV.G: Lieberman notes that "fulfill" refers to the proper performance of the Commandments, without which esoteric knowledge is not vouchsafed; see Avot deRabbi Nathan Ch. 39 [= ed. Schechter, p. 75a], and Canticles Rabbah 1:4.

2:1.V.A: "Where and whence?" See Lieberman, pp. 1292-3; cmp. esp. Genesis Rabbah, ed. Theodor-Albeck, p. 17: "He said to him: 'What is this, Ben Zoma, from whence the legs?' He said to him: '"Not" from "nothing" [play on 'ayin], Rabbi.' Said he to him: 'I swear by Heaven and Earth that I shall not stir from here until you tell me whence the legs!'" Lieberman stresses the importance to the Gnostics of the question of man's origin; see his nn. 16-18, and Deut. Rabbah, ed. Lieberman, Jerusalem, p. 119 n. 2. R. Joshua's original question had no gnostic connotation; see Lieberman, p. 1293 n. 21; Ben Zoma's response was an expression of humility, though one which avoided a direct answer to R. Joshua's query.

As to "went mad," there is a divergence in tradition, reflected in T. and elsewhere (see Lieberman, p. 1294 s.v. k^ebar, and Ginzé Qedem, V, p. 179). Lieberman posits a text (see ms. Oxford of Gen. Rabbah) which read "he was not in the world," which, in Palestinian usage had a double meaning: he had died, or gone mad.

2:1.VII.A: A Geonic tradition read Āḇōr, either because he had turned "back" from religion, or in the rare sense of one who visits prostitutes; see Yalon's Quntresim I, p. 48, and Lieberman, p. 1289 ad l. 16.

2:1.IX.FF: BT Kid. 39b has "the tongue of Huspit Ham-meturgaman."

2:1.XI.D: Ben Sira Hashalam, M.Z. Segal, 3:19-20 [Charles, 3:21-2]. See Segal's notes ad loc.; the problem of Ben Sira in Rabbinic literature has most recently been discussed by S.Z. Leiman, Canonization of Hebrew Scripture, Hamden, Connecticut, 1976, pp. 96-102.

2:1.XII.A: "Crushed," see Ratner: "tied" and K. Brockelmann, Lexicon Syriacum, p. 568b s.v. p^ekar.

2:1.XII.B: See Ratner, and add the sources given in Lieberman, p. 1293 n. 23.

2:1.XV.B-C: Referring to the worlds created before "this world," see Lieberman, p. 1296 (top) and Tos. Kif. I, p. 123 n. 86.

2:1.XV.E: Translation reflects QE's emendation. hskm means "agreement," not "contemplation." See Ben Jehuda Thesaurus V, p. 409b s.v. sakam.

2:1.XVI.J: QE takes byh as a metaphorical extension of biya', "Woe!," i.e., God is in charge of responding to mankind's supplications. PM takes byh as "what, that which" without explanation. The source of "gate" in the translation eludes me.

2:1.XVII.C: It is interesting to follow the interplay of Hebrew and Greek in this short statement. In the verse quoted, of course, "throne" and "footstool" are in Hebrew, while in the Amoraic observation itself, the Gr. loanword 'pypwryn [= 'pwpwdyn, an easy graphic error for Gr. ὑποπόδιον; see Levy Wörterbuch I, p. 138b] takes the place of

Heb. h^{a}dom; cmp. Howard Jacobson's suggested bilingual pun malkā' qāti'ā' = Caesar Caesor [A.Z. 10b] in AJS Review 6 (1981), pp. 39-42.

2:2.I.F: "Departed": see Lieberman, Ginze Qedem I, p. 178.

2:2.II.A: See Lieberman's important note on the use of r^{e}šūt in Y. to mean a "less severe obligation," and its elliptical use for š^{e}būt šel r^{e}šūt, as here. Laying-on of hands is hardly a matter of r^{e}šūt in the Babylonian sense of a matter of personal preference. (Tarbiz 5, p. 97)

2:2.III.C-D: See ad 2:2 F above, and cmp. BT 16b: Abaye said: "he came to a bad end [i.e., morally];" Raba said: "he went out on the king's work!"

2:2.V.Y: See Ratner for a summary of conjectures for the enigmatic 'wyyn. Add Levy Wörterbuch I, p. 38b: "comrade" from Gr. ὁμοια.

2:2.VI.C: Translation follows PM, but see Lieberman in Tarbiz 5, p. 99: zimzum means "rumor." The meaning is thus: courts may inflict punishment even on the basis of rumor when the times require it. For this meaning of zmzm Lieberman adduces Genesis Rabbah, ed. Theodor-Albeck, p. 969 and PT Sotah 1:7 (17a), as per his emendation in On the Yerushalmi (Hebrew), p. 57 n. 18.

2:2.VI: Some texts reverse the penalties in E and H; see Ratner.

2:3.II.A: The essential issue that exercised the comm. is whether Y. agrees with the opinion stated in Bavli (Zeb. 33a) that the guilt-offering of a meṣōrā^c is not of Biblical authority, and therefore the rule that the laying-on of hands must follow immediately upon the slaughter of the animal does not apply. Gilyon Hashas to Y. Bezah 2:4 holds that it must. Moreover, since that rule of immediate laying-on of hands is derived from Lev. 3:8, which refers to free-will peace-offerings, the ruling in N cannot be right. He therefore reverses the rulings in A and B, esp. in view of the fact that D differs from BT Bezah 20a in regard to the positions taken by the respective schools of Hillel and Shamai.

NY and STEI retain the current text and explain that Y. does not agree with Bavli in this; free-will peace-offerings would have been acceptable the day before, and so the laying-on of hands is considered as done in the "ordinary way;" the one who brings it has thus satisfied his obligation. This is not the case with the guilt-offering, which cannot be brought before the eighth day of the meṣōrā^c's purification period. The laying-on is therefore invalid if carried out prematurely, and the obligation has not been fulfilled.

2:3.III.A-D: Translation reflects both T. and Y. But Y.'s text of E differs from curr. ed. of T.; since it is the latter which appears in the translation, herewith is the former; For he who did not bring a festal offering on the first [day] of the festival may bring a festal offering on the second; if he did not bring a festal offering on the second, he may bring a festal offering on the third.

2:3.III.J-K: Translation reflects both T. and Y.

2:3.V.A-I: [In Y.'s version]: M^{c}SH B: Hillel the Elder brought his burnt offering to the Courtyard and laid hands on it. The disciples of Shamai surrounded him. He began to shake its tail, and said: "See, it is a female, and I have brought it as a peace-offering." He put them off and they went their way. After a time the power of the School of Shamai increased and they wanted to decide the law permanently in accord with their opinion. Now, Baba b. Buta was present; he was of the disciples of Shamai, [but] knew that the law was in accord with [the views] of the School of Hillel. Once, he entered the Courtyard and found it deserted. He said: "May the houses of those who made the temple of God desolate be [themselves] made desolate!" What did he do? He had 3,000 young sheep of Qedar brought; he examined them for blemishes, set them on the Temple Mount, and said: "Listen to me, my brothers of the House of Israel! All who wish to bring burnt-offerings may bring [them] and lay hands on them. [Whoever wishes to] bring peace-offerings may bring [them] and lay hands on them]." At that time the law was confirmed according [to the views] of the School of Hillel, and no one said a word [in protest].

2:4.II.D: The preceding ubilbăd še... insures that what follows is a verb; šyblym = šeyablīm is thus to be parsed as a hif. of blm "to bridle." This reading is confirmed by ms. Leiden and ed. princ., and by the parallel in Y. Demai 6:6, šyblyn. The parallel at Y. Meg. 1:4 (ed. Vilna), šeyablīᶜa, hif. from blᶜ "to swallow" in the sense of "to include" has no textual support. QE adopts the reading offered by Tosafot Hag. 18a s.v. 'elā, šyklm (šeyᵉkalem), piel of klh "to complete, to use up." Whatever reading we adopt, the meaning is reasonably clear: the dough must be prepared for use on that day only, or, alternately, dough may be made only if he has no bread for that day.

2:4.III.A: Ratner omits as a redundant repetition of III.A. QE understands it as a quote which introduces further analysis, similar to Bavli's gūpā', but the latter is resumptive, a use which is irrelevant to our passage, since no intrusive comments intervene between A and B. It seems to me that our text is a corruption of a quotation of 2:4 C-D, and should be emended accordingly.

2:4.III.C: Ratner seems to prefer the reading of ed. Constantinople, ᶜōrōt šelāmīm, "skins of peace-offerings," to curr. ed. ᶜōrōt šel mī, "to whom do the skins belong?" Although the former is not otherwise attested, it is easier to account for the misreading of an original šlmy′(abbreviated) to sl my than the reverse. QE (in SQ) quotes Mishnah Lamelekh ad Mishneh Torah, Hilkot Kle Hamiqdash 4:5 as preferring a more general term to "skins" as the subject of C: he suggests ᶜavōdāh, but this is hardly idiomatic, and "skins" is clearly pars pro toto.

2:4.III.G: QE emends "festival day" (yōm ṭōb) to "day of slaughtering" (yōm tebōaḥ); Nir explains that the error arose from a scribal misinterpretation of the acronym yw't, which usually stands for ywm twb. STEI emends G to refer directly to R. Simeon b. Laqish: "[If Pentecost falls on Friday, according] to the School of Shamai you say that its day of slaughtering is after the Sabbath."

2:4.V.A: STEI (ad parallel in Y. Yomah 1:2, p. 245) emends: "Every day the high priest puts on his [priestly] garments and offers [the daily burnt-offering], and [then] goes and eats in the Chamber of Counsellors; he comes and offers the twilight burnt-offering and comes and spends the night at home.

R. Uqbah's comment then serves to limit this procedure to Sabbaths and festivals during the period in which the Romans had custody of the vestments (Y. Pes. 7:8 (35a)). This obviates the need to explain how it was that the high priest came to spend all his nights in the Temple, according to A, or Sabbath and festival nights, according to B, a requirement nowhere stated.

2:5.I.C: Nir emends to "he will (not) separate himself from t^erūmāh; since the point here is to interpret 2:5 as in agreement with R. Simeon b. Eleazar, the Rabbis must hold that hands are generally at a first remove, because making them rabbinically in the second remove is not sufficient to insure that care would be taken in the handling of t^erūmāh. Actually, the same effect could be achieved by interpreting the phrase as a question.

2:5.I.G: Hy' is intrusive though supported by ms. Leiden; the original may perhaps have been krbnn [d]tmn hy'. STEI places the pause after hy' and interprets G as meaning that R. Simeon b. Eleazar agrees with the Rabbis of F. He then restores: tmn [ltrmh], that is, "there [in F] the issue concerns t^erūmāh," [brm] hk' [lḥwlyn], "while here the issue is one of unconsecrated food." Since you say that his hands are at a first remove, etc. STEI provides a smooth text at the cost of completely rewriting the passage.

2:5.II.F: STEI in his remarks on the parallel at Y. Bikk. 2:2 (p. 143) transposes and emends slightly: "Now how, etc. Will you maintain, etc. [Can you say that it refers to] one who wishes to touch [t^erūmāh], but did we not learn [the rule respecting] t^erūmāh [along with that regarding first-fruits, so that the same law applies to both?] Are not wanting to eat it, etc." G then continues: "[But the hand-washing is required] in order to make the washing of hands a habit [when touching t^erūmāh]?" The question is then asked regarding Hag. 2:5 which requires the washing of hands for unconsecrated foods (and not t^erūmāh), and the passage continues with I.

2:5.III.C: Text of T. and Y. do not contain the words "unconsecrated food prepared in accord with cleanness required" which anticipate the conclusion at F. See Tosefet Rishonim IV, p. 144 ad ll. 10/11.

2:5.IV.D-E: C-D reveals the reasoning behind B: the point of B is that the gatherer of the ashes must be absolutely clean, either from impurity which affects the hands only (STEI) or from the more serious impurity contracted by contact with a corpse (Nir), since in either case, even the gathering of the ashes by means of some utensil will cause further impurity either by "shifting" (STEI) or "carrying" (Nir); E is then an objection to D, for impurity can be contracted for reasons other than the peculiar status imposed on the participants in the ceremony of the red heifer. The problem with Nir's interpretation is that corpse-impurity is hardly considered as of lesser severity than most other forms of impurity; indeed, he must struggle to account for the dead creeping thing of V.C, which is classically considered a source of minor impurity.

2:5.IV.F: The actual basis for the impurity is unclear. PM understands ^{c}ōmēd mah^amat dāḇār tāmē' as referring to the well-known susceptibility to uncleanness of wooden vessels made as containers; STEI emends to ham-m^eqabbel dāḇār tāmē', "which accepts (i.e. contains) an unclean thing." QE's suggestion, that the wooden vessel is unclean because it is held by an unclean person is rejected categorically by STEI; Gilyon Hashas attempts to retrieve it by reference to M. Parah 10:3 q.v. Nir suggests that nails driven into the wood would convey impurity, but not all wooden utensils require metal nails, and this particular attribute is hardly implied by our text.

2:5.IV.I: STEI reverses the order of IV.I and V.A-B. IV.I thus forms the climax of the whole discussion: even a thick beam, which is not susceptible to impurity by "carrying" is susceptible to impurity by "shifting."

Because of Nir's awkward position regarding corpse-uncleanness (see above), and for other reasons, such as the apparent duplication of V.C and IV.D, he interprets IV.D as requiring that the gatherer be clean even of the minor impurity contracted by contact with a dead creeping thing. PM, who interprets IV.A-D in this way, takes V as a separate question, based on M. Parah 9:6.

2:6.I.I, II.E: Y.'s text is: [But] if one's feet are still in the water, he may confirm himself for whatever purity he wishes.

2:6.II.H: STEI neatly transfers "higher than that" to the end: "Once he has set his mind on achieving [any level of] purity, he does not require an intent higher than that."

2:7.A: "Ordinary folk," that is, the Am Haaretz, lit., "people of the land." In the First Commonwealth times it referred to the land-owning country aristocracy, but in later times it came to refer to uneducated peasants who were suspected of not adhering to all the laws of tithing; see most recently, Aharon Oppenheimer, The ᶜAm Ha-aretz, Leiden, 1977, pp. 1-10, 239-244.

"Abstainers," pᵉrūšîm, are of course those who were considered reliable in such matters.

2:7.F: Hasdé David ad loc. notes that our mishnah and its complementary baraita present a progression of pᵉrūšîm: a priest, a levite, a layman and a proselyte (the latter two being Rabban Gamliel the Elder and Aquila the Proselyte).

Lieberman ad loc. suggests "Gadgadah," equivalent to "Felix," "Lucky."

2:7.II.A: See Nir and STEI, who emend II.A to the following: Simeon bar Aba raised the [following] question before R. Zeirah:

A. "Just as you said there, '(Carrying [the source of uncleanness alone does not transfer uncleanness to]) unconsecrated food, but (carrying [the source of uncleanness transfers the uncleanness by]) actual contact with the food,'

B. "along these same lines [do we say that] (transfer of uncleanness through shifting [a source of uncleanness, without actual contact] does not apply to unconsecrated food, but transfer of uncleanness through shifting [the source of uncleanness] with actual contact with the food [does affect the transfer]?"

The difficulty they address is that we actually do know the answer to IIB from 2:7 A, but are in doubt as to the answer to IIA, rather than the reverse, as curr. ed. has it. Thus, PM, who does not amend the text, is constrained to comment (s.v. veyesh maśā': "'Whether something made unclean by carrying can make unconsecrated food unclean by touch, as we hold in regard to something made unclean through moving [without contact]' -- that is the question [posed]. And [the answer] is obvious... and can [easily] be derived from the general rules governing uncleanness which are stated in many places...."

2:7.III.B: The translation follows PM, who takes E-F as a unit. QE [in SQ] assumes that an Am Haaretz certainly is subject to the law of "shifting" as far as tᵉrūmāh is concerned, and takes E as an affirmation of that principle in regard to A. F he thus interprets as an objection to E, which is then redundant in view of R. Yohanan's statement in B. He therefore attributes B to R. Hanan and emends accordingly on the basis of the reading of R. Samson of Sens in his commentary to Toh. 7:5 [curr. ed. has erroneously: Parah]. (This reading may of course be correct in itself without reference to the interconnection of E-F.)

2:7.III.F: R. Samson of Sens ad M. Toh. 7:5 called attention to a scribal error in our text. His emendation is extended by STEI thusly: "There is no consideration of "interposition," nor of "shifting," nor of [the effect of] the private domain of an Am Haaretz as far as unconsecrated food is concerned, but [only for] t^{e}rūmāh." This is based on T. Hag. 3:21.

For the problem of whether "shifting" was decreed on the Am Haaretz, see Sens (loc. cit.) and Tosafot Hag. 19b s.v. bigdē, Lieberman, p. 1326-7, and the literature cited therein.

2:7.IV.A: According to QE, the question posed in IV.A does not concern the substance of t^{e}rūmāh, but the status of one who is conscientious in eating t^{e}rumah [i.e., a priestly haber] in regards Holy Things: is he treated as a Zab, even though he guards himself from uncleanness in the third degree? The question thus relates more directly to the concerns of the Mishnah than those of curr. eds., but Nir subjects this emendation to searching criticism, and ultimately rejects both it and the reading of curr. eds., neither of which are answered in any plain reading of B-E. See below.

2:7.V: This extremely difficult passage has been interpreted in various, often diametrically opposed, ways. Nir sees part of the problem in the transposition of IV.C to its present location. He interprets the passage as follows:

A. [As to] a substance which [is in the status] of Holy Things, what is the law on its functioning as does a Zab as far as the purification-rite [of the red heifer] is [concerned]?

B. Let us derive [the answer] from the following:

C. He who cuts off a reed -- he who cuts the reed and he who immerses it must undergo immersion [= current IV.C].

D. Now, it is not difficult [to understand why] the one who cuts off must immerse [before doing so. But as to] the one who immerses it, why can he not wrap it in bast and immerse it [= current IV.D]?

E. Let us derive the answer from the following:

F. Two flagons, one clean [for use] for Holy Things, and one clean [for use] for t^{e}rūmāh, which touched one another -- both of them are [deemed] clean [= current V.B, quoted from M. Parah 10:6].

G. Thus, if he wraps it in bast, [both] he and it are clean, [from the continuation of M. Parah 10:6, which states that if he carries t^{e}rumah in paper, it remains clean. For this sort of transposed quotation, see below.]

H. But interpret the rule [to apply to the case of] one who cuts it off with the stipulation that he will immerse it.

I. But, see, a Tannaitic teaching differs: They have treated one who was clean for the purification-rite [who went and] moved the spit or semen of one who was clean for [the purposes of] t^{e}rūmāh -- [= current V.C]

J. The same rule applies to one who was clean [for purposes of] t^{e}rūmāh as one who was clean for [purposes of] Holy Things [as far as the purification-rite is concerned] [= current V.D].

K. (Thus, since we are concerned with his spit or semen we consider eaters of t^{e}rūmāh as Zabim in respect of Holy Things.)

This complex re-arrangement may perhaps illustrate the lengths to which some commentators felt required to go in order to make sense of these few lines. If no other reason that simplicity, the suggestion of Gilyon Hashas commends itself: the proof intended comes not from the beginning of M. Parah 10:6, which is quoted in our passage, but from the next part, as noted above. This phenomenon is often to be met with in the Talmuds and Midrash Rabba, where while the first stich of a verse is quoted, it is actually the second stich which is intended, as the reader is considered knowledgeable enough to complete the text-proof for himself. [See ANRW II 19.2 Bokser VIII D c: "Pt may cite the beginning of a text and refer to its end, and do so even without including... WKW, 'etc.'"] As we have seen, Nir recognized this phenomenon but did not use it to re-interpret the basic question posed so as to make the latter part of Parah 10:6 an answer to it, without requiring a complex re-arrangement.

3:1.I.C: "Holding place," see Y. Brand, Klé Haḥeres Besifrut Hattalmud (Jerusalem, 1953), pp. 77-80. The "holding place" was apparently an inner rim around the mouth of the vessel.

3:1.II.A-B: This applies even for tᵉrūmāh; see QE s.v. kāḇed, and Lieberman, p. 1311 n. 15.

3:1.II.B: T.'s version reads: As for Holy Things, one may place [the unclean vessel] inside a basket or gurgathon [large wicker-work basket], and immerse [it]. Abba Saul says, "So would they do for tᵉrūmāh, but not for Holy Things." That is, they would not immerse one vessel inside another for tᵉrūmāh except in the case of large baskets.

3:1.II.H-I: See Lieberman, p. 1313 n. 20. Y. often gives a rapid reprise of comments on a mishnah before going into each point in greater detail.

3:1.III.B: "The Sandal-maker," "has-sandlār." See Ratner, p. 72, who suggests that his cognomen was a shortened form of "the Alexandrian," on the basis of H below. For the same phenomenon, see the Yiddish "Sender" from "Alexander."

3:1.III.H: On the attitude prevalent in the West (i.e., the Land of Israel) to Babylonian Jews, as perceived in Babylon, see BT Yoma 66b; see also M.A. Tannenblatt, New Chapters toward the History of the Land of Israel and Babylon in the Talmudic Era [Hebrew], Tel Aviv, 1966, pp. 198-211. The misunderstandings that arose between even the greatest of these respective Jewries are well-illustrated by the story told below of R. Yohanan and R. Eleazar the Babylonian; see M.Q. 3:7 XIX.

3:1.III.Q: Mī, rather than the more usual kad, "when." See Levy, Wörterbuch² III 96a s.v. mī II.

3:1.V: E does not follow from D, even if the latter is emended in accordance with T. Kelim B.B. 3:1, without a corresponding emendation of E. GRA ad. M. Kelim 25:1, and, following him, Gilyon Hashas and STEI emend "ground" in E to "at the holding place."

STEI's emended text would then read:

D.b.-E. [The baraita] stated [its ruling] precisely [in the case] of [uncleanness issuing from] a loaf [of bread], but not from a (hand [which would presumably remain clean]).

(The question is thus whether the deduction from liquids on the ground is more probable than that from liquids on the cup's holding place -- in answering the questions raised at C in accordance with Y.'s canons of logic. PM prefers the former; the latter is the preference of the authorities cited above.)

F-I is also problematic. The text as it stands seems to assume that the cup is unclean, in contradiction to the foregoing. With GRA's emendations, the passage reads:

F. But if there is liquid on the hand, and one took [the cup] by the holding place, even in such [a case], is the liquid made unclean (by the hand) to make (the cup) unclean [as well]?

G. Let us derive [the answer] from the following:

H. [If there was] unclean liquid on the ground, and a cup whose outer side is clean touched it at its holding place, it is unclean [T. ibid.].

I. [It is because] the [liquid] is on the ground, but not on the hand.

J. And in the view of R. Yose, if the hands were clean, and the outer side of the cup was unclean, with liquid located on the hand, and one held the cup by its holding place, it is self-evident that the liquid on the hand is not made unclean by the cup so as to impart uncleanness to the hand.

K. And just as the liquid is not made unclean by the cup to impart uncleanness to the hand, is the liquid not made unclean by the cup to impart uncleanness to a loaf in some other place?

L. Let us derive [the answer] from the following:

M. Clean liquids located on the ground which touched in its holding place a cup whose outer side is unclean -- the liquids are unclean.

N. In what regard have [the liquids] been made unclean? Not to impart uncleanness to a loaf in another place?

O. Is this not because they are on the ground, but not in the hand?

P. But [as to] liquid located on the cup, and one touched [the cup] at its holding place, even so, is the liquid not made unclean by the cup to impart uncleanness to the hand?

3:1.VI.C: "...[the thong of his] sandal": Gilyon Hashas ad loc. refers to Tosafot Hag. 23b s.v. w^e^nies^e^qāh, wherein Tosafot take Y.'s "sandal" and Bavli's "[thong of his] sandal" as constituting a real difference in cases. But Y.'s style here as elsewhere is a good deal more cryptic than Bavli's; indeed, the word "Holy Things" is not explicitly stated in this baraita.

3:1.VI.E: QE and Nir understand the subject of "those" not as "sages" (see translation) but as "cases": "These are [cases] of which they [the sages] said... unclean, etc." Ms. Leiden originally lacked the word mēhen, "of them," which was added between the lines; in addition, the second phrase "there are" was added in the margin. These additions support QE and Nir, while the translation reflects the original text.

The salient differences between these readings is that according to QE and Nir the seemingly contradictory decisions refer to different cases: the case of those who carry the ashes of the red heifer (which are of a higher degree of purity than Holy Things in general), and that of Holy Things themselves, so QE; Nir proposes his own differentiation based on BT Hag. 23a.

3:1.VI.F: STEI emends "R. Zeirah" to "R. Ezrah," since the latter studied principally with R. Mana (see Y. Erubin 2:1, Nidah, end of Chapter One, and esp. Pes. 2:4), while R. Zeirah was the teacher of R. Mana's father, R. Yonah! See STEI, p. 68 ad Shevi'it 5:9 for a complete discussion of this issue.

3:1.VII.C: "Loosen," so PM. QE understands ḥṣym as "they clean." However, see Lieberman, p. 1316 s.v. b^e^ram, who refers to R. Samson of Sens in his commentary to M. Miqva'ot 10:4, where he interprets ḥōṣēh = ōṣeh meaning "tightens." The idea is that if knots are tightened to the point of becoming permanent, they do not constitute an "interposition," and the immersion is valid even with the knots tied. See also J.N. Epstein, Der gaonische Kommentar zur Mischnaordung Teharoth, Berlin, 1924, p. 88 n. 17.

3:2.IV: QE, Nir and Lieberman in passing interpret this passage in light of the parallel Bavli (Hag. 23b-24a), that is, as a debate regarding whether the rule of "combination" or "unification" is of Biblical or Rabbinic origin. As Nir notes, if this is the case, then "the main issue has been omitted;" but this is hardly unknown in Y., given the state of our text.

R. Aqiva then holds that the rule is of Rabbinic origin, while R. Simeon b. Laqish disagrees. Even with this assumption, however, the debate does not proceed smoothly, and Nir proposes various additions.

Since Y. is here rather cryptic, it may help to quote the relevant Bavli:

> A vessel unifies that which is [contained] therein for [the purpose of] Holy Things, but not for t^e^rūmāh.
>
> Whence do we learn this rule?
>
> Said R. Hanin, since the verse states: "One spoon full of incense, eleven gold [sheqels its weight]" (Num. 7:14), Scripture made all within it [as] one.
>
> R. Kahana objected [quoting M. Eduyot 8:1]: "R. Aqiva added the fine flour and the incense, the frankincense and the coals [to those substances] which, if one who had immersed that day [whose purification is not complete till sunset] touched part of, he makes the whole invalid." Is that [rule] not of Rabbinic [origin]?
>
> Why? Is it because the first clause of [the mishnah] teaches: "R. Simeon b. Bathyra testified regarding the ashes of purification [of the red heifer] that if an unclean person touched a part of it, he makes the whole unclean," and [then] teaches [in addition]: "R. Aqiva added"?
>
> Resh Laqish [= R. Simeon b. Laqish] answered in the name of Bar Qappara: [R. Aqiva's testimony] was required only for the remains of the meal-offering, regarding which [we have] the Biblical [rule]: "that which requires a vessel, the vessel unites; that which does not require a vessel, the vessel does not unite," and the Rabbis came and decreed that even where the [substance] does not require a vessel, the vessel unites.

3:2.IV.G: See Tosafot Hag. 23b s.v. še'im, in which RI is quoted as interpreting the question so: "Why are coals then mentioned?" that is, "Why does the one who touches one of them invalidate all of them? Since many of the coals are not necessary, the principle that limits 'unification' to cases in which the material is required to be placed in a vessel will not operate." The debate then centers around the Day of Atonement, when all the coals are needed, and so too the vessel that contains them.

3:2.IV.H: STEI omits "fine flour," which does have a fixed measure.

3:2.IV.L: Translation follows QE in this case. PM would require: "...and here a utensil unites them [in regard to purity, but not the offering up]."

3:2.V.A: "Plate." Curr. ed. has b^e^gasä, "in a large one," corrupted from b^e^bisa, ; see Lieberman, pp. 1317-8. A bisā is a mixing bowl rather than a plate.

3:2.V.M: If V is a direct continuation of IV, V.M may be directed not only against V.K but may also refer back to IV.A-B.

3:2.VII.O-P: According to most commentators, O-P must be read together: "R. [E]leazar in the name of R. Hoshaiah: The cited Mishnah-passage speaks of unconsecrated food which is prepared in accord with the rules governing Holy Things, and is in accord with R. Joshua." This punctuation is confirmed by BT Hullin 33b, which quotes R. Hoshaiah with this significant difference: "...and is not in accord with R. Joshua." It is true that Tosafot Hullin 34a s.v. man does separate "is not in accord etc." from the rest of R. Hoshaiah's statement, and sees it as a "Stamaitic" addition, but even so the statement is to be interpreted as a whole. At any rate, QE emends Y. according to Bavli; as usual, PM refrains from emendation.

The question is broader than this, however. BT Hullin 33b-34a provides three distinct interpretations of M. Hullin 2:5, two of which are relevant to us. QE follows that of R. Hoshaiah as quoted in Bavli, since the statement at O is quoted in his name, after all. This assumes that R. Joshua at M. Toh. 2:2 refers only to unconsecrated food prepared in accordance with the rules governing Holy Things, and that such food is not subject to a third remove of uncleanness, while food prepared as though it were t^{e}rūmāh can be so affected. According to the alternate reading of M. Hullin 2:5 (BT Hullin 34a), given in the name of ^{c}Ula, the latter mishnah is in agreement with R. Joshua, as our reading in Y. has it, and his statement in M. Toh. 2:2 is interpreted as referring not exclusively to unconsecrated food prepared as t^{e}rūmāh, but also to such food as prepared as Holy Things; thus, a third remove of uncleanness is possible, even according to R. Joshua. This interpretation obviates the need of emending Y., but requires an explanation as to why R. Joshua apparently limits the rule at Toh. 2:2 regarding third removes to unconsecrated food prepared as t^{e}rūmāh. This PM does as per BT Hullin 34a, but is contradicted by CC below.

As far as the problem of what R. Hoshaiah really said goes, it should be noted that R. Eleazar was ^{c}Ula's teacher, and his statement in BT Hullin 34a (top) seems to be an expansion of R. Eleazar's comments on M. Hullin 2:5. There seem to be two traditions in Bavli regarding this matter, that of ^{c}Ula, which agrees with Y. here, and that of Rabbah bar Bar Hana, as quoted in BT Hullin 33b (bottom).

(Another solution presents itself, one which has not, to the present writer's knowledge, been proposed before. As Lieberman points out in Tosefet Rishonim, IV, p. 662, ad T. Toh. 2:1, the debate between R. Joshua and R. Eliezer (not to be confused with R. Eleazer quoted in O) in that baraita, is reversed in some mss., with the latter taking R. Joshua's view as to the impossibility of removes of uncleanness creating uncleanness in the same degree. This would seem to fit better R. Eliezer's view in Toh. 2:7 which limits the degrees of uncleanness in the case of unconsecrated foods prepared in accordance with stricter requirements than the law requires (see the concise enumeration of the points at issue in Tiferet Israel ad M. Toh. 2:7, n. 56).

(On the whole, nevertheless, PM's interpretation, which does least violence to the text, seems preferable, since the quotation of Toh. 2:2 at C corresponds to the standard reading, and R. Samuel's objection at B depends on that reading. Also, if emend we must, adding a "not" at O-P, with QE, seems preferable to reversing authorities at C.)

In sum: M. Hullin 2:5 agrees with R. Joshua if he extends application of the rule governing unconsecrated food, but not if he does not. PM refers the first possibility, QE the second.

3:2.VII.Q: The apparent repetition of A in Q troubles most commentators, and only PM takes the text as it stands. He explains that both R. Yanai here (Q) and R. Yonatan above (A), were concerned as to whether R. Joshua held that the stringencies enacted regarding t^{e}rūmāh (D above) were extended to unconsecrated food prepared as Holy Things. R. Yonatan derives this somewhat indirectly from M. Hullin 2:5, while R. Yanai would seek more direct evidence from M. Toh. 2:2. The problem, once again, is that the main point is not stated.

PM's alternate explanation is also not free from objection: he speculates that the authorities in Q are not certain that the statement there can really be attributed to Rabbi, while in A they are. But if so, why not juxtapose Q and A to make that point clear?

QE once again resorts to emendation -- t^erūmāh' to "Holy Things" -- and thus transfers the whole question to the realm of Holy Things in that way. Gilyon Hashas and Nir point out the impossibility of that option, since in M. Toh. 2:2 R. Joshua (whose opinion is of most concern to both Talmuds, since the law follows his view) speaks of t^erūmāh and not Holy Things, though to rehearse the details of their analyses would take us too far afield. Albeck (in his notes to Toh. 2:2 in Shisha Sidré Mishnah, VI, pp. 568-10) points to a variant which omits "unconsecrated food" in that mishnah, which consequently deals with true t^erūmāh, and not unconsecrated food prepared as t^erūmāh. The question at Q refers to whether (à la Gilyon Hashas) t^erūmāh at a third remove invalidates the eater from eating Holy Things. This provides a natural bridge between Q and R while distinguishing between A and Q.

Nir suggests: "He who eats... becomes unclean in the second remove in regard to t^erūmāh," but then faces problems similar to those of QE, and his ultimate reading of the flow of discussion involves more eisegesis than exigesis.

Finally, NY and STEI emend according to BT Hullin 34b: "He who eats unconsecrated food prepared as Holy Things becomes unclean in the second remove as regards Holy Things." In this case, though, little remains of the original!

On the whole, therefore, the reading of Gilyon Hashas seems preferable in making the text understandable with the least strain. Nevertheless, in a passage whose difficulty is such as to cause each commentator to go his own way, surety is impossible of attainment.

To summarize: PM: A t^erūmāh... Q t^erūmāh; QE and NY: Q Holy Things... A Holy Things; Nir: A Holy Things... Q t^erumah; Gilyon Hashas: A t^erumah... Q Holy Things; STEI: unconsecrated food prepared as A Holy Things... Q Holy Things.

3:2.VII.S: According to PM, the mishnah referred to is Hullin 2:5, and the translation here thus departs from his rendering. It follows QE, without however accepting his proposed emendation. Again, according to PM, the "new point" expressed here is that of R. Yanai in the name of Rabbi. STEI suggests that the mere presence of water in Holy Things (except for the water-libation, which was uncommon) argues for its state as unnconsecrated food prepared as Holy Things, and we thus can prove that such food has the stringency of Holy Things in this case. Presumably PM would assign this water the same status as "liquids of the Temple slaughter-house" (See IV.E above) which are clean.

3:2.VII.X: Again the translation follows QE without adopting his emendation. PM interprets: "From [the foregoing], some of the mishnah [Toh. 2:2] can be understood simply [i.e., according to its simple interpretation, pešaṭ,] and some must be reinterpreted." The emphasis is not on A and/or Q, but on C. If Toh. 2:2 is taken at face-value, then the question of unconsecrated food prepared as Holy Things remains open, since R. Joshua speaks only of such food prepared as t^erūmāh; PM takes Z as a question. If, however, Toh. 2:2 is re-interpreted in accordance with the (generally) greater stringency of Holy Things as compared to t^erūmāh, then we can conclude as does our text in CC.

This novel interpretation hardly conforms to the usage of either Bavli or Yerushalmi, and nearly all commentators take X and AA as translated, but do not (and cannot) stop there, for if they do, Z does not agree with A or Q!

Thus, STEI takes CC to refer to Toh. 2:7 (which is not otherwise referred to in our passage!) rather than to Toh. 2:2; he interprets it as a confirmation of Q rather than as a refutation, with the addition of "not" after "his body" making Y-Z refute Q.

QE understands X-CC to refer to Toh. 1:9, which does, according to Nir and QE *apud* GRA, show that a third remove in Holy Things can create a second (the loaf, as third, makes the liquid unclean in the first remove, according to the usual rule, and the liquid in turn makes the loaf a second). However, in order to make this refutation of Q convincing, he must interpret Rabbi's statement as restricted to *t^{e}rūmāh*. The refutation BB-CC then involves proof that Holy Things too are affected by thirds. The difficulties in this interpretation are manifest.

In general, the commentators interpret X-CC in the light of their understanding of Q, with each emending and/or re-arranging the text to do so. Albeck, whose suggestion we followed earlier, takes X and AA as referring to the two variants alluded to above. The "confirmation" at X is then based on the variant found in ms. Kaufman of Mishnah quoted above (and found in curr. eds. of Y.). This makes Toh. 2:2 apply to *t^{e}rūmāh* and not to unconsecrated food prepared as *t^{e}rūmāh*. The consequent "refutation" is based on the variant found in curr. eds. of Mishnah and in BT Hullin 33b. The only emendation required is the addition of "not" in CC (and not in Z as QE has it): "his body is (*not*) regarded as in the second remove of uncleanness as far as *t^{e}rūmāh* is concerned...."

The problem of whether the formula at X can refer to the use of such variants awaits further study.

3:2.VIII.C: See Lieberman, V, pp. 1319 *ad* ll. 21-2 and p. 1324 *ad* ll. 35-7.

3:2.IX.T: The use of the term "halakhah" here is peculiar to Y. Nir takes it to refer to a Rabbinic ordinance analogically derived from Scripture; QE identifies it with Bavli's usage, which refers to a non-Scriptural Sinaitic law -- *halakah leMoshe miSinai*. The one possibility which is definitely excluded is the concept embodied in the English abstract "the Law," or "Halakhah" with a capital "H."

3:2.XI.F: Since the principle cited hardly substantiates R. Yohanan's statement, which is otherwise untenable, the commentators perforce emend E and/or F. STEI emends E-F to: "What had he said *after* his retraction? He had said only that it *invalidates* [a loaf of bread] etc.," while QE emends F in a similar fashion but leaves E unchanged; PM takes E-G as proof positive that R. Yohanan did retract, inasmuch as E-F is so difficult an opinion to sustain, but surely so egregious an error cannot be attributed to him. Nir re-interprets D-F in light of A-B. The question is then whether a hand, which always has the status of a second remove, can impart a similar status to another's hand, or to a loaf, in contrast to the usual case, wherein a further remove is always of lesser degree. R. Simeon b. Laqish takes the lenient view, R. Yohanan the stricter; E-G attempts to understand R. Yohanan's position before his retraction, since it is inconceivable that he would extend his rule to the creation of equal removes of food by food, which flies in the face of all the rules of purities. The answer is that "hands" are singular in this regard. Of Nir's several suggested emendations, perhaps the most attractive is the addition of "not" at the end of C.

3:3.I.B: According to PM, following T., the "dried foods" are t^e^rūmāh; the point of our mishnah-passage is that one may eat dry t^e^rūmāh together with unconsecrated food. QE takes A itself to refer to unconsecrated food. I.B therefore refers also to the handling of unconsecrated food by means of a spit. PM understands the spit as one used for t^e^rūmāh exclusively; he notes that T.'s "and he eats with it an olive's bulk of meat" must refer to unconsecrated food, since there is no t^e^rūmāh taken from meat. This is a methodological point of no little weight: QE disregards T. in interpreting Y., where Y. itself is merely quoting T., albeit in a slightly different version than that found in our texts.

The analysis in BT Hag. 24b also quotes T., with, as usual, the same text as we have in our eds. of T.; that is, instead of the word "with meat," it has "with [unconsecrated] radishes and onions." The analysis is essentially identical to the one in Y., and leads to an understanding of "dried foods" in our mishnah as referring to t^e^rūmāh, but Rashi interprets it thus: "One may eat [unconsecrated] dried foods with unwashed hands with t^e^rūmāh." The natural understanding of bit^e^rūmāh is: "within [the matrix of rules governing the eating] of t^e^rūmāh."

Lieberman ad loc. points out that it is apparent from II.H-I that Y. understood our mishnah in its simple sense; he takes II as a direct continuation of I. He thus understands the comment of R. Hanina b. Antigonos at I.A-B as making a linguistic point -- that Holy Things cannot by definition be "dry" -- rather than differing with the law as stated in the mishnah. I.B-C is then a restatement of 3:3 B, and not A.

3:3.III.F: QE emends the somewhat awkward text slightly: "They have treated (him [the eater]) as one who eats...." Since "food" (ōkel) and "one who eats" (ōkēl) are orthographically identical, the present text may simply have come about by dittography.

3:4.I.C: The words lō'kak are intrusive, as Nir notes; the usage is also atypical of Y.'s style. But Nir's proposal: "not only [is the produce of Regeb inferior to that of Judah], but does not a strip of land belonging to the Samaritans intervene?" is eisogesis. It seems better to delete the offending phrase.

As to p^e^sikya, translated here "strip of land" in agreement with BT Hag. 25a, Levy Wörterbuch[2], IV, p. 81a takes it as the name of a market-town, which fits Y. Demai 5:9 (25a): "one who buys from Psikia of the Samaritans." If so, it seems unknown outside of Y. and does not fit particularly well here as a place-name. In defense of "strip of land" we might point to "fascia," "belt" in T. Ned. 4:3 and elsewhere, and compare "r^e^ṣū^c^āh," "strip of leather, strip of land," with the same semantic range. For the second meaning, see BT Hag. 25a, as noted, but also BT Gittin 7b, Zeb. 53b, 118b and elsewhere.

3:4.I.D: See M. Toh. 9:1.

3:4.I.E: Nir raises three points: 1) the statement regarding the status of wine is merely a reprise of M. 3:4 B (But this seems to emphasize the contrast between Judea and the Galilee -- Y.E.). 2) QE interprets the statement regarding jars in Judea in consonance with BT Hag. 25b [print. ed. has, erroneously, 27], that is, it refers to the jars after they are emptied. If so, the question at III.B is difficult. 3) M. 3:4 F is cited at 3:5 III.D as an objection to R. Simeon b. Laqish (at 3:5 III.B), who considers an Am Haaretz untrustworthy as far as liquids are concerned, but here (at 3:4 I.E) such an objection is not raised. Nir therefore emends our passage to read: "And in Judea they are believed as to the character of the jars, but not in the Galilee [after the time of pressing and crushing?]" He thus eliminates the (redundant?) mention of wine, and offers a cleaner structure which prepares the way for III.B. What we have already seen of the rather loose and open structure of Y.'s discussions makes the assumption upon which his reconstruction is based somewhat dubious. Objection n. 1 cannot therefore carry the weight of his suggested emendation, and n. 3, which the Tosafists deal with vis à vis BT, cannot always bear such weight even within the far tighter (but still relatively loose) structure characteristic of Bavli. As for n. 2, which is based on BT Hag. 25b (bottom), it assumes, with Bavli, that if the wine is considered clean, so too the jars. But the baraitot in both Bavli and Yerushalmi, as they stand, do not make that assumption.

3:4.I.F: "Southern" is usually synonymous with "Judean." Indeed, by interpreting "Southerner" as a "South-Galilean," F loses much of its force and becomes casuistry in the bad sense.

3:4.II.A: PM and QE understand R. Jeremiah's remark as emphasizing the untrustworthiness of the Am Haaretz' testimony during the balance of the year. NY takes the other track: even a ḥāḇer, one who is ordinarily trusted regarding t^e^rūmāh, is not believed regarding the contact of his t^e^rūmāh with Holy Things even during the time of "pressing and crushing."

3:4.II.H-I: STEI proposes:

H. Interpret the Mishnah-passage to speak of a time other than that of the (oil-pressing).

I. ([And even if you say [that the Mishnah speaks] of a time other than that of the oil-pressing [omission by homoioteleuton],]) may you [then] say that the reference is to a time other than that of the wine-pressing?

That is, you cannot separate wine-pressing from oil-pressing, since both are mentioned in tandem in D above.

3:4.II.J: "Either," without an accompanying alternative, is as difficult in the Hebrew and in English. Ridvaz ad. loc. sees it as a misinterpreted 'ema, which, while frequent in Bavli, appears only once in Y. -- and then in the mouth of R. Zeira, a Babylonian (see. Y.Kid. 1:2 (59a))! QE ignores or omits it, which may be the best course. What is expected is tiptor b..., "interpret it [as speaking of a case which...]."

3:4.III: Nir and NY interpret the recurrent phrase w^e^lēṯ kol īlēn milāyā' kēn, here translated "matters cannot be this way" (in C, E, G and I) as a rhetorical question, with the case at hand modified to support the principle enunciated. However, 'elā kēnî ("but this is the rule," lit., "but this is [how] it is") usually introduces an emendation rather than a re-interpretation. An alternate translation would be: "but this is [the correct reading]," with milaya' here in its basic meaning of "words": "these words cannot be so," i.e., "this reading is incorrect."

NY relates these rhetorical questions to 3:1 IV.C-J, a suggestion which, while providing a point to them, is not otherwise convincing, especially in view of the rather complex reasoning that must be supplied in order to make the text conform to 3:1 IV. Nir's proposal is subject to the same objection. However, NY's suggestion to relate III.F to 3:8 A provides a possible linkage of IV to III, a connection over which PM expresses perplexity in his comments. The point that all the questions have in common is that Holy Things (food, Temple vessels) can be declared clean for a time, despite possible contamination by the Am Haaretz -- and yet become unclean automatically thereafter.

3:4.III.C: QE and STEI emend: "...the things which were to have been prepared under conditions of purity are (unclean, but during the season of wine-pressing or olive-crushing, the things which have been prepared under conditions of purity) are [considered] clean.

3:4.IV.A: R. Yohanan's statements at A, D, K, Q and W are intended to resolve the ambiguity of the comments at C, H-J, O-P, V and BB, all of which may be taken either strictly or leniently.

3:4.IV.F-J: The point underlying the problem of the gourd is this: water which has been exploited for some purpose is unfit for use in the ceremony of the red heifer (Num. 19:17). Since a gourd absorbs some of the water poured into it, it may also release some of the absorption -- and that water would be unfit as not "free-flowing;" so PM on Y. Erub. 9:4. QE understands the danger as this: the released water may be unclean.

3:4.IV:T-AA: Once again the translation reflects curr. eds. of T. rather than Y.'s version. Y. interchanges T and U, and Z and AA.

3:4.VI.C: Lieberman, pp. 1331-2, suggests that dammēᶜa here is a polaric verb similar to saqqēl, "to stone" but also "to remove stones." Here dammēᶜa would mean, in contrast to its usual sense, "jugs... which protect wine or oil from becoming a mixture of tᵉrūmāh and common food."

3:4.VI.D: See Lieberman, pp. 1331-2 and the literature there cited. According to him (see also Tos. Kif. IV, p. 690 ad ll. 60-1), qōdē'ah means not "to pour" as the commentators have it (and as is here translated), but rather "to draw," i.e., these jars are used to divert the wine or oil from the press so that they do not enter the pit and become demai, mixed common food and tᵉrūmāh, but rather are separated as tᵉrūmāh.

3:5.II.A: As it stands, this statement is disjointed; its second half is cast in the form of a protasis rather than the apodesis to be expected. STEI therefore excises it as a gloss which stands isolated in its present context (lit., "[if] the liquid made the vessel unclean"), and he emends the rest:

If food preserved in a state of purity touched [a pot], if it is in Modiin inward [toward Jerusalem], (the food remains clean; from Modiin outward, the food is unclean).

3:6.I: As Neusner notes in the summary, our text is confused. The problems are chiefly, but not limited to, the intrusive mention of Jerusalem, and its relation to the effect of other witnesses. PM does his best with the text as it stands, and the translation reflects his interpretation. QE understands the role of the gentile supervisor as insuring the extensive and intensive search of the premises in question; the intervention of the gentile results in impurity as far as the house is concerned, and non-acceptance of the testimony. QE thus emends accordingly, "If a gentile is (not) with them, they are deemed trustworthy...."

Nir examines the problem of the relationship of the witnesses to the gentile. The gist of the interpretation offered is this: if there are witnesses, the tax-collectors are believed; in Jerusalem, they are believed even if it is only the presence of a gentile which is corraboratory. The second solution proposed by Y. he interprets thus: they are believed only when there are no witnesses, since if they are trusted in their admission of entry, they are believed in their denial of having handled purities; in Jerusalem, they are believed despite the availability of witnesses. The basic proposition is that the law is more lenient in Jerusalem. The statement in G, "therefore it is necessary to specify that there are witnesses" he takes as an intrusion.

STEI emends the entire discussion, and produces a smooth text (which may or may not coincide with the original).

A. Tax-collectors who enter a house, the house is unclean.
B. But if there is a gentile with them, they are trusted to say: "We entered but did not touch [these objects]."
C. But here you say so [i.e., without the presence of a gentile]!
D. Two solutions can be offered:
They are believed when they say: "We entered, but did not touch," (when there are no) witnesses who know [that they entered]. Tax-collectors who entered a house, the house is unclean [when there are] witnesses who know [that they entered].
A second solution can be offered:
They are trusted when they say: "We entered but did not touch," therefore it is necessary [to state] that this applies to a case in which witnesses are present, [and there is a gentile with them].
(Tax collectors who entered a house, the house is unclean when there are witnesses who know that they entered, but no gentile was with them.)
The first solution restates our mishnah; the second, that of M. Toh. 7:6 (and not T.).

STEI's reconstruction is indicative of the lengths to which a commentator must sometimes go to produce a satisfactory text!

3:7.II.A: See STEI, whose emendation yields a smooth text and eliminates the doubtful tsbwt as a noun, though the meaning remains the same.

3:8.I.A: The basic principle at issue is that vessels can be made unclean only by a "Father of uncleanness," and not by someone or something at one or more removes from the source of impurity. Since even an Am Haaretz (during the festival) is not considered as being in that state, what could have happened to the Temple vessels to require their immersion?

3:8.I.B: Vessels may be immersed when new or unclean, but "sprinkling" is one of the requirements of the ceremony of the red heifer -- the purification of one who has come in contact with the dead (or even "corpse-matter"). Indeed, degrees of impurity at one remove or more do not make vessels or utensils unclean. It is presumably the difficulty of envisaging a situation in which Temple vessels will come into contact with a corpse or one who has had contact with one (by touch or "over-shadowing") and has not undergone purification -- since handling the vessels is the prerogative of the priesthood -- which impels QE and Nir to emend "utensils" (klym) to "priests" (khnym), graphically rather simple. Whether much is gained thereby, however, is problematic; once our concern is with priests who have come into the contact just described, they themselves can make vessels unclean, but that is a situation which is again hard to imagine, for priests are considered "conscientious." Thus, PM and NY take the text as is, since in the end it all comes to the same thing.

The distinction, which these commentators do not make explicit, may be that if we must fear possible impurity of such a serious nature in some vessels (i.e., those in use), we must likewise purify the substitute vessels in 3:8 B (see Ridvaz s.v. v[e]kēlīm), while if our concern is primarily with priests, only vessels which were in use and might have been touched by a priest would require attention.

3:8.I.C: There are various opinions as to what the word "all of them" refers. Ridvaz takes it to refer to the duplicate and triplicate sets of Temple vessels. QE understands "all of them" to refer to priests (as per his emendation) all year round.

NY addresses the critical point: if the problem is one of sprinkling (as B has it), why is immersion alone sufficient as a substitute? (See NY p. 178a s.v. [c]al ken). He roundly criticizes PM and QE for their rather forced interpretations. Unfortunately, he does not make his own position altogether clear, at least on this point. Once R. Abba's interpretation at B runs afoul of this objection, the next proposal is that of R. Abun b. Hiyya (at C); if so, "then" refers to "all means of purification," an interpretation no less forced than that of PM and QE.

Nir's interpretation is more natural -- "them" refers to all entities which might require immersion, that is, vessels and priests both. Elsewhere (p. 150a s.v. upārīk, end) he suggests that the reference is to "all the strictures of the law, that is, the danger of corpse-impurity as well as the milder forms of impurity possible," but this makes C a restatement of B which does not materially carry the discussion any further.

A possible solution to the critical problem noted above might be along the lines suggested by Kesef Mishnah ad Mishnah Torah Hilkhot Parah Adumah 11:2: "one requiring purification for corpse-uncleanness who was not sprinkled on the seventh day may immerse whenever he wishes without regard for when the sprinkling takes place." This is in contradiction to BT Kid. 62, but is supported by Palestinian sources (see, for example, Sifre Numbers, ed. Horovitz, p. 167 s.v. bayōm).

3:8.I.D: According to Nir, the difference between the danger envisaged at A and that of D inheres in this: at A the greatest concern imaginable is that the priest may become impure by midras at home through his menstruant wife, a degree of impurity which does not affect vessels, which, as already noted, are affected by "Fathers" and not removes. At D, however, the moist spit of a Zabah causes its bearer to become a "Father of Uncleanness," and thus makes utensils unclean.

Nir understands the "chatting" priest to be an Am Haaretz; the thrust of E is that we ought to extend the requirement of immersion to all priests, hāberīm included, since all priests may speak to visitors at times.

3:8.I.E: Nir interprets: since we do not require such wholesale immersion of all priests, we may assume that both visitors and priests will be careful in their observance of the purity-laws, at least in the Temple and with regard to their entrance into the Temple. The danger of contamination of Temple-vessels is therefore only a Rabbinical degree -- that described in F-G.

3:8.II.A: STEI points out the redundancy of "even [on the Sabbath]" inasmuch as the Sabbath is the proper time for the removal of the bread. Nir and NY take "even" as emphasizing the fact that, in contrast to the prohibition of immersion of vessels on the

Sabbath outside the Temple precincts, within it is permitted for purposes of the Temple service.

3:8.II.C: Interpretation rightly follows NY, Nir (in large part) and STEI; see Lieberman, p. 1335 s.v. šulḳān.

3:8.III.A: Texts of Y. omits "on the festival day," as do some mss. of T.; see Lieberman ad loc.

3:8.V.H-T: Nir made a start in the understanding of this extremely difficult passage, though he ultimately confessed himself at a loss. STEI, apparently independently, made further progress, and Lieberman, in his notes on Y. published in Tarbiz 5, pp. 104-5, finally provided a satisfactory solution, which the translation reflects. The key point, which the commentators lost sight of, is that the discussion revolves around the fact of the Altar's insusceptibility to impurity, and the Table's susceptibility.

Various reasons are adduced for this state of affairs. First, the Rabbis' explicit linkage of the plating to the Altar's insusceptibility requires re-interpretation, since it is the plating, which, if substantial, causes susceptibility. (That is the point which led the commentators astray.) The answer given is that the plating was either insubstantial or irrelevant.

Another line of reasoning depends on the movability of the Altar and Table; a plain wooden utensil which is not moved around is usually insusceptible. Once this distinction re the two pieces of Temple furniture is made, the discussion turns to the problem posed by the Table. It is with this brilliant stroke that Lieberman cuts the Gordian knot, and allows an unforced understanding of Q-T.

Selected Bibliography and Table of Abbreviations

Note: Works consulted but not cited, and works for which bibliographical information is provided in the notes, are not included in this listing.

Albeck, C.	Shisha Sidré Mishnah (6 vols.), Jerusalem, 1952-1959
ANRW	See Bokser, B.M.
Aruch Completum	See Kohut
Ben-Jehuda, E.	Dictionary and Thesaurus of the Hebrew Language (8 vols.), N.Y., 1960
Bokser, B.M.	"An Annotated Bibliographical Guide to the Study of the Palestinian Talmud" in Aufstieg und Niedergang der römischen Welt, II 19.2, Berlin, 1979
BT	Babylonian Talmud
Fardo, D.	Hasdé David, Livorno, 1776
Frankel, D.	Qorban Ha-edah, in Vilna Romm ed. of Y
-----	Sheyaré Qorban, in Vilna Romm ed. of Y
Genesis Rabbah	See Theodor, J.

Gilyon Hashas	See Nathansohn, J.S.
GRA	Elijah of Vilna, notes in Vilna Romm ed. of Y
Kohut, A.	Aruch Completum (9 vols.), repr. Jerusalem, 1970
Levy Wörterbuch	See Levy, J.
Levy, J.	Wörterbuch über die Talmudim und Midraschim, 2nd ed. (4 vols.), repr. Darmstadt, 1963
Lieberman, S.	[Tosefta Kifshuta], Vol. V, N.Y., 1962
-----	Al Hayerushalmi, Jerusalem, 1931
-----	Tosefta Kifshuta (13 vols.), N.Y., 1955-73
-----	Tosefet Rishonim (4 vols.), Jerusalem, 1970
M.	Mishnah
Margaliot, M.	Pené Moshe, in Vilna Romm ed. of Y
-----	Mar'eh Hapenim, in Vilna Romm ed. of Y
Marim, M.	Sefer Nir, Vilna, 1890
MH	Mar'eh Hapenim, in Vilna Romm ed. of Y
Nathansohn, J.S.	Gilyon Hashas, in Vilna Romm ed. of Y
-----	Ziyun Yerushalmi, in Vilna Romm ed. of Y
Nir	See Marim, M.
NY	See Shapiro, J.I.
PM	Pené Moshe; see Margaliot, M.
QE	Qorban Ha-edah; see Frankel, D.
Rabinowitz, Z.W.	Shaaré Torat Eretz Israel, Jerusalem, 1940
Ratner, B.	Ahavat Zion Viyerushalayim (10 vols.), repr. Jerusalem, 1967
Ridvaz	Comm. of Jacob David of Slotz, , in Vilna Romm ed. of Y
Shapiro, J.I.	No^{c}am Yerushalmi, repr. Jerusalem, 1968
SQ	Sheyaré Qorban; see Frankel, D.
STEI	See Rabinowitz, Z.W.
T	Tosefta
Theodor, J. and Albeck	Ch. Midrash Bereshit Rabba, 2nd. ed. (3 vols.), Jerusalem, 1965
Tiferet Israel	Comm. of R. Israel Lifshütz in Romm Mishnah
Y	Yerushalmi
Ziyun Yerushalmi	See Nathansohn, J.S.

Chapter 5

YERUSHALMI MOED QATAN

Yaakov Elman

1:1.C: See Feliks, Agriculture in the Period of the Mishnah and Talmud [Hebrew], Jerusalem, 1963, pp. 328-33. Qilōn, here translated as "swape-well," is probably what is called a shaduf in Arabic, i.e., a levered pail which is used to transfer water to a field which lies beyond the regular irrigation system.

1:1.I.B: Y.'s text of T. is: R. Meir said that they irrigate even a field which depends upon the rain.

1:1.I.E-F: Y.'s text of T. agrees with curr. ed. of T.

1:1.I.B: See Lieberman, 1325-6. The interpretation of I.B-L which follows is based on Lieberman's superb reconstruction:

B. Is it [then] in accord with R. Meir?
C. Does R. Meir [emend dr = h' r] not hold that one may water a field which is rain-fed? [i.e., he is even more permissive!]

Further on, H is to be understood as a question.

1:1.I.P: Translation "shaded field" follows PM. Levy Wörterbuch^2 III, p. 228a s.v. m^{e}qērtā connects mqrt with Biblical mqrh in Jud. 3:20 and 3:24, and interprets it as "Kühlingsort." The context would seem to require a place-name, however, though its identification is unknown. Perhaps we have the ancient equivalent of the real-estate agents' "Shady Acres"!

1:1.I.O: Translation follows PM, but QE is closer to the truth with his interpretation of ḫbryh as hpyrh, "a ditch." STEI proposed ḫbryy as the name of a river, but did not elaborate. Lieberman, is a brilliant stroke (Samuel Kraus Jubilee Volume, Jerusalem, 1937, p. 305) noted that the Leiden ms. reads not ḫbryh but qbryyl, and associates this with qbry'l which appears in a number of mss. of Genesis Rabbah 13:6, ed. Theodor-Albeck, p. 118:7f. qbryyl/qbry'l is thus a river in the Galilee which shared some features with the Nile.

1:1.II.A: Translation follows PM. An alternate is: "[May one employ] collected rain-water?"

1:1.II.H: The continuation is to be found at the end of Y. Sheviit Chapter 2: "[A tannaitic teaching] was found which taught: [it is permitted] to irrigate a field whose crops have not yet sprouted..., the words of R. Simeon; R. Eliezer b. Yaakov prohibits."

See Tractate Sheviit, ed. Y. Feliks, Jerusalem, 1980, pp. 162-4 for other interpretations; also, his Agriculture, pp. 314-6.

1:1.III.C: Y. omits "they are like waters of a spring."

1:1.III.E: Ḫbryt: PM reads hkryt, with kryt as a place-name, unlikely in view of the definite article, though perhaps not impossible. Levy, Wörterbuch^2, II, p. 418a likewise reads hkryt, but interprets kryt as "storm-surge," and ʿd šṭprḫ hkryṭ as "until the storm-surge passes." D-E recur in Y. Ter. 8:6 (46a): ᶜd kdy šhpwḥ hkryṯ, but šhpwḥ is easily a graphic corruption of šṭprḥ, as Lieberman points out (Tos. Kif. I, p. 415), though this interpretation hardly fits the context there, which concerns the point at which ditch water may be considered safe from snake-venom. Lieberman prefers the reading of ms. Vat. -- ᶜd šṭprḥ hbryṯ, and interprets it both here in M.Q. and in Ter. as referring to the flowering of the bōrīṯ, as in Jer. 2:22 and Mal. 3:2. He follows Loew in his identification of the plant (idem., p. 416 n. 117), but see Feliks, Plant World of the Bible[2] [Hebrew], Ramat Gan, 1968, pp. 298-300, especially p. 300, where he details his objections to it. He suggests one of a number of "soda-bearing" plants other than Mesembryanthemum -- Salsola, Salicornia, Statice or Atriplex.

1:2.II.G: STEI proposes the addition found in Asheri's quotation of this text (M.Q. Chapter 1: Section 6): "on the basis of [the following]: one may repair damaged waterways in the public domain."

1:2.IV.B-I: The actual order and content of the passage in Y. differs from that given in T., and translated here. The actual text reads:

C. They judge property cases, capital cases and cases involving stripes,
D. And they attend to the redemption of captives, [cases of] personal valuation, [both] for things declared ḥerem and for things declared consecrated.
E. And they attend to the trial by ordeal of a suspected adulteress [Num. 5:11-31].
F. And they attend to the burning of a red heifer [Num. 19],
G. and they attend to the ceremony of breaking the neck of a heifer [in the case of a derelict corpse] [= E].
H. They pierce the ear of a Hebrew slave [who wishes to remain with his master] [= F],
I. and they attend to the purification rite of a "leper."

For the difference between the two texts, see Lieberman.

1:4: on the problem posed by the proper identification of 'ašuṯ and ḥūldāh in the light of M. Kel. 15:6, see Ben-Jehuda, Thesaurus, I, p. 413b n. 2.

1:5.I.I: STEI emends "eve of the festival" to "the [intermediate] days of a festival," in accord with the parallel at III.A below. Moreover, the point at issue is the permissibility/advisability of inspecting nega's on those days and not the eve of the festival, and nothing in the discussion requires that the question of a festival-eve be investigated.

1:5.I.L: The text as it stands is awkward; also, while from J-K it seems that R. Yohanan addressed his remarks to the mishnah in Neg. (4:10), so that the reference in L to our mishnah in M.Q. -- "[the position] not to rule strictly" -- is out of place. Furthermore, the interpretation of the Rabbis' position in M contradicts R. Yohanan in K-L: according to the latter the Rabbis forbid inspecting the second nega' whether leniently or strictly, while R. Yose in M understands the Rabbis to allow inspection for leniency. For all these reasons, all unstated, STEI emends as follows:

I. R. Yohanan said, "[An inspection] (on the [intermediate] days of) the festival is at issue between them." [Ridvaz however understands R. Yohanan as extending the purity-requirements of the festival to the eve thereof.]
J. R. Aqiba says, "This [negaᶜ] is [a new manifestation of] the original diseased spot, and you are not required to examine him, either to make a lenient ruling or to make a stringent one."

K. The Rabbis say that this [spot] is another [that is, a new] one, and you thereby declare him exempt from [uncleanness on account of] the original spot.

L. (And you release him [from the ordeal of] the first one, and do not declare him unclean [in regard to] the second one, for you are obligated to examine him to present a lenient ruling but not a strict one.)

STEI similarly emends the description of the Rabbis' position in M by adding: "and do not declare him unclean [in regard to] the second one."

One further emendation is not without interest. The use of "here" and "there" indicates that R. Yose was primarily concerned with explicating the passage from Negaim; since there is no evidence of such a commentary attached to the relevant mishnas in Purities, STEI and NY reverse these terms.

QE understands the last part of M (And we have learnt) as an objection -- "Have we not learnt here, etc.," which would indicate that R. Meir's position is not identical with that of the Rabbis in Negaim. This paves the way for the alternate interpretation of the relationship of M.Q. 1:5 to Neg. 4:10 in N.

Another occurence of the confusion of "here" and "there" is the use, noted by Ridvaz, of "here" to designate M.Q. in the latter part of M as opposed to the use of "there" for the same purpose in the rest of M.

1:5.I.N: Translation follows PM, who emends: "not to render a lenient decision and not a strict one;" curr. ed. does not reflect the Rabbis position in M.Q. QE re-interprets "here" to refer to M.Q. and "there" to Negaim; but then we must assume that "let it be inspected as at the outset" = "not carrying out any examination of the second nega^{c} at all" in order to avoid the need of emendation. PM's emendation -- one of his few -- seems on the whole preferable.

1:5.II.A: The actual text of the passage as Y. gives it reverses Rabbi's opinion -- he concurs with R. Yose in the case of one shut-up and with R. Meir in the case of one certified. This version corresponds to the one alluded to in BT M.Q. 7b, while the one given in the translation is not that of Y. at all, but that of T. and given in BT M.Q. 7b. For a discussion of the two versions, see Lieberman.

1:5.III.A: Translation reflects the emendation of PM and QE: "not" is transferred from the Rabbis' opinion to that of R. Aqiva.

R. Aqiva's position may be rendered more simply: "It is the original [sign], and he may [thus] not enter the Temple courtyard."

1:5.III.F-I: As PM points out, the question that lies behind F-I is this: what exactly is the difference between D and E as far as the proper understanding of the debate between R. Aqiva and the Rabbis is concerned. Beyond that is the question of the exact nature of the suggestions presented in the first place.

Gilyon Hashas, in a lengthy comment, explains that it inheres in the matter of timing: whether the dripping boil (which does not impede the effect of "blossoming") became active (as ṣārebet) before or after the blossoming was completed (see M. Neg. 6:8 and 8:5). He applies this to the dispute between R. Aqiva and the Rabbis, with the original mark replacing the dripping boil. R. Aqiva thus holds that the blossoming was indeed complete. The one afflicted is clean, until the original mark disappears, thus impairing the blossoming and making him unclean; this is in accord with R. Simeon b. Laqish. R. Aqiva's remark in D must then be emended, however: "It is the original [mark], [Hence we deal with a case] similar to the blossoming forth from a (clean) person, so he is (unclean)."

STEI proposes another analysis which does not require emendation of our text. He interprets "blossoming from an unclean state" as applying here to one who is shut up for inspection. Blossoming takes place before he can be declared unclean. According to R. Aqiva, he is now clean because his isolation is equivalent to impurity. Blossoming has thus transformed his impurity to purity (Neg. 8:1). The Rabbis, who hold this mark to be a second nega^{c}, would declare him unclean, since the blossoming had come at a time when he was clean (i.e., clear of the first nega^{c} and not yet declared unclean on account of the second) by the operation of the same rule of transformation.

R. Aqiva thus agrees with the position set forth in the name of R. Yohanan, and the Rabbis with R. Simeon b. Laqish. STEI further identifies the latter two positions with the alternative interpretation of M. Neg. 8:1 set forth in the commentary of R. Samson of Sens s.v. miṭāhōr ṭāmē'. That is, R. Yohanan holds that the logic of blossoming from clean to unclean is a case of "spreading" (see I.F), and since the original mark is gone, there can be no spreading. R. Simeon considers it as a special Divine decree, and the impurity remains.

1:5.IV.B: "Cedar chests." See Lieberman, p. 1235, where he identifies b'ryzym with nibreḵeṯ, beqi^{c}a and mahamōreṯ, all referring to temporary grave-sites, pits and niches of varying sizes; see esp. n. 24.

1:5.IV.C: STEI emends: "[the bones] of his ancestors" to "the bones of his father" based on Nachmanides' Torat Haadam [ed. Chavel, in Kitvé Ramban, Jerusalem, 1964, II, p. 117].

1:5.IV.E: Apkarīsīn, see Levy Wörterbuch^{2}, I, p. 148a; from the Syriac apkorsō̄, a type of kafiyeh which covers the body as well.

1:5.V.O-P: Ed. princ. and ms. Leiden omit; text is restored from parallel in Y. Pes. 8:8 (36b).

1:5.V.T: See Lieberman, Tarbiz 3, pp. 453-4.

1:5.VII.I: The bracketed explanation is that of PM ad loc. In his comments on M. 1:5, however, he follows BT M.Q. 8a: it once happened that a man who had saved money for his pilgrimage to Jerusalem used the money instead to hire mourners, and thus remained home.

1:6.I.E: Y.'s text has: One may make it broader or longer, either on one side or both sides, and one may make a burial-niche on the intermediate days of the festival.

1:6.I.G: See Lieberman, 1234-6, and our note above to 1:5 IV.B.

1:6.II.C: Nachmanides (op. cit., pp. 124, 127) interprets tošāḇ as a temporary, movable addition to a tomb (see T. Sheviith 3:4 and Tos. Kif., I, p. 175:7.

1:7.III.B: STEI takes kly ḥrs, "clay utensil" as a gloss to and emends it to šrq, in accordance with BT. M.Q. 9b. Levy Wörterbuch^{2}, IV, p. 614a takes it as some sort of make-up ("Schminke"), perhaps "rouge;" see also the parallel in T. Shab. 9(10):13, ed. Lieberman, p. 39:42 and Tos. Kif. III, p. 146 n. 68, and p. 141 ad l. 42.

1:8.II.B: STEI emends: "Anyone who can sew an even hem -- (such a one is skilled. Anyone who cannot sew an even hem) -- such a one is unskilled.

1:9.I.B: This refers to the festival day; see T. Yom Yov 3:16 and BT Bezah 34a (STEI).

1:10.I.A: STEI reverses the heights: 10 handbreadths for a roof, in accordance with Sifre Deut. [ed. Finkelstein, p. 229], and three handbreadths for a porch.

1:10.III.B: ᶜWq': PM has "rung," QE, "socket." STEI cites Y. B.B. 3:8 (74c), Leviticus Rabbah 29:2, BT Erub. 77b in support of "rungs."

2:2.II.A: The parallel story in BT M.Q. 12b concerns R. Yanai.

2:3.II.A: QE and Ratner cite Asheri M.Q. Chapter 2 no. 17 who reads: "may be sold on the intermediate days of the festival."

2:3.II.A: Praqmatya might better be rendered "merchandise." If so, the movement is for sale rather than to keep to produce fresh; translation follows QE, see also Gilyon Hashas and Ratner.

2:3.III.D: Translation follows PM, but STEI emends: "It is necessary to rule when there are no witnesses who know about the transaction. If, however, there are witnesses to support the claim, etc." D thus follows C, and there is no need to interpret these statements as questions. (See BT B.M. 104b, B.B. 70b, Or Zaruᶜa B.M. par 342.)

2:3.III.F: STEI emends mšty, "enjoy the proceeds," lit., "drink," to mšhy "stay with [us], stay over."

2:3.IV.A: PM interprets R. Yohanan's statement in the context of the interdiction of unnecessary labor on the intermediate days of the festival. Moving one's household is ordinarily forbidden; the loss entailed by service on the Roman boulé with its commensurate taxes was such as to permit such movements.

2:4.II.B: STEI emends in accordance with Genesis Rabbah, end Lekh Lekha [= ed. Theodor-Albeck, p. 477:1-2] where a similar question is asked: When Rabbi asked [regarding the festival].... It was taught: it is permitted even on the Sabbath.

2:5.I.A: This indicates some emendation of 2:5, but exactly what is unclear. R. Judah ought to express the stricter opinion, as he does at 2:1 I.J, but the text as it stands has him taking the lenient side of the dispute, i.e., allowing more labor. PM suggests two possibilities: either the Tanna at A allows the piling up and R. Judah only allows covering up, i.e., a reversal of A and B, or perhaps the emendation proposed is the excision of "also." A thus allows covering, B allows heaping, but not both. The first possibility seems more likely.

3:1.II.A: See BT A.Z. 13a.

3:1.II.F: See parallel in BT Ket. 111a.

3:1.II.G: Cmp. Y. Hag. 1:8 III.K, see Ratner, p. 60.

3:1.IV.B: STEI emends: let him (not) cut his hair before....

3:1.VI.W: The teachings of R. Eliezer are often attributed to the Rabbis in order that the law be determined in accordance with his opinion, see QE ad loc. and cmp. BT Nidda 7a-b.

3:1.IX.C-D: See Albeck's notes on this passage in his Mishnah, IV, pp. 482-3. The commonly accepted interpretation of dkmh, dkwwth is "like them," i.e., she was a convert as were Shmaia and Abtalion themselves.

3:1.X.I: Barbarit, here translated "garden," based on the parallel in BT M.Q. 17a; see Levy Wörterbuch[2], I, p. 261b, and comm., who take it as a place-name.

3:1.XI.I: That is, the ark containing the fragments of the tablets which Moses shattered (QE).

3:1.XI.J: STEI emends to R. Tanhum bar Hiyya on the basis of Y. Tann. 2:1 (65b) and BT M.Q. 16b.

3:1.XII.B-E: See above to IV.B-D.

3:1.XII.K: "I was R. Meir's servant bbrḥw šnym." QE understands the last words as "during his second flight." Whatever is hidden in these words (perhaps a place-name?), it cannot be "many years ago;" "while the years fled" may be orthographically possible, but is un-idiomatic in the extreme.

3:1.XIII.D-G: Translation follows PM; the problem is that F is equivocal: some hair-cutting is permitted, some not, depending on the means. The proof can thus "cut" both ways. The explanatory remarks at G contradict D, and thus catch nicely the problematical nature of this passage. QE and NY emend p^eliḡā, "stands at variance with" to m^esayē^ca, "is in aid of." Y's position seems to be that once hair-cutting is permitted during the intermediate days of the festival, so too is the prohibition of shaving during the thirty-day period of mourning suspended. For details, see the interesting discussion in NY, esp. p. 184, and Lieberman ad T. 2:1.

3:1.XIII.I: The relation of I to the preceding is unclear. NY sees it as contradicting the proof provided at E -- as per his emendation -- by raising an alternate possibility: perhaps, just as the Rabbis permitted hair-cutting on the intermediate days to one who was unable to cut his hair before the holiday, so too did they permit one prevented from hair-cutting by the onset of a (30-day) period of mourning before a festival, even though this case is not enumerated in our Mishnah. (The initial seven-day period would be governed by F; see Qeren Orah ad BT M.Q. 17b.)

NY transposes interprets I as a response to J-K. It was necessary to state the law regarding the prohibition of hair-cutting during the seven-day period of mourning.

PM, on the other hand, takes I as an alternate response to the problem presented at C: those who forbid do so by means of the use of scissors; those who permit, do so with knife or razor.

STEI reverses "seven" and "thirty":

> I. R. Samuel b. R. Isaac raised the question: there is no difficulty [regarding the law that obtains] during the (thirty) day [period of mourning, that is, he is permitted to trim his hair with a razor], but [what about] the (seven)-day [period]? [J.] R. Hananiah, friend of the rabbis, assumed, did we not learn.... This informs us that it is (forbidden) for him [to trim his hair during the seven-day period]....

3:1.XIV.J: STEI and Ratner register variants of place-names in Shibbole Haleqet Hilkhot Semakhot, par. 33: Hamaton [= BT M.Q. 19a] and Ded^calah.

3:1.XIV.K: STEI corrects to R. Simeon bar Abba; see his notes to Y. Ber. 1:7 (p. 8).

3:1.XIV.C-D: QE emends: he who holds regarding a (mourner) [that he] is permitted, [holds that view] when there is a festival [approaching]; [he who holds the view] regarding a mourner [that he] is forbidden, [holds that view] when there is no festival [approaching]. He who holds that [even with] a festival [approaching], that [hair-cutting] is forbidden [does so in a case of] deception, [and he who holds that] with a festival [approaching] it is permitted [does so] when there is no deception.

NY ingeniously accomplishes the same end without emendation by asssuming that the subject of these comments is "a mourner," even though he is not mentioned explicitly.

3:2.I.A: Balg^e^re, balnearia, see Levy Wörterbuch I, p. 235a.

3:2.I.D: 'Ontina, see Levy Wörterbuch I, p. 109a, "ein Stuck feiner Leinwand, bes. die daraus verfertigte Wasche zur Benutzung im Bade." Aruch Completum I, p. 146b s.v. antinaya confused it with "buntfarbiges Kleid", for which see Levy Wörterbuch I, p. 110a.

3:4.I.A: Y.'s version is:

A. They may not prepare deeds for share-cropping or land-tenancy on the intermediate days of the festival.

B. One may appraise [property] as long as one does not measure, weigh or count.

Y then continues with E and II.A.

3:5.I.A: The comm. take SNDL ("sandal") and SPR ("barber") as acronyms used as mneumonics: PM emends SPN to SPR and interprets: SPR = sīkāh ("anointing"), pūryā ("bed," i.e., sleeping in a completely equipped bed rather than subjecting oneself to the discomfort of a bed not altogether set up), r^e^ḥīṣāh ("washing"). QE's emendation yields: sīkāh, ne^c^īlat has-sandāl ("wearing leather sandals"), tašmīš ham-mitāh ("marital intercourse"), spr ("hair-cutting"), kibūs ("clothes-washing"), tōrāh ("study of Torah").

3:5.III.A: STEI emends "Rab" to "R. Ammi," but see Lieberman's note in Tarbiz 3, p. 455, where he proposes "a certain rabbi" in place of "Rab," and observes that on occasion prominent Amoraim are juxtaposed with otherwise unknown ones.

3:5.III.C: STEI emends: "...cuts his hair on the thirty-first day, but if he cuts it on the thirtieth day, he has [nevertheless] fulfilled his obligation," as quoted in Tosafot BT M.Q. 19b s.v. t^e^lātīn.

3:5.IV.H: STEI restores: "[The Rabbis say:] if one has gotten a haircut on the eve of the festival, etc."

3:5.IV.K: STEI: "or whether it was in accord with the view of the Rabbis, [in a case in which he cut his hair before the festival, thus] representing the view of all parties."

3:5.IV.M: Translation follows PM's first interpretation, but he, QE and NY provide an alternate one, to take M as a statement, not a question or objection. See NY, p. 93a col. II s.v. w^e^'im ken and p. 93b col. I s.v. ubazeh ff. Abba Saul holds that the thirty-day mourning period does not begin until the eighth day; if so, if its onset is delayed for some reason (the Sabbath, or the cases enumerated in 3:1), it is cancelled. The Rabbis, on the other hand, hold that only when the burial precedes the festival by eight days is the thirty-day period postponed, thus showing that the period begins on the seventh day; it is not therefore postponed indefinitely.

3:5.V.D-H: QE and STEI emend in accordance with T. Curr. eds. have: [E] "For the first three.... For the other four...." and omit F.

PM retains the text. According to him, mourning began on the first intermediate day, which is the third day of the festival; however, in the Land of Israel it would be the second day, since the institution of an Exilic festival-day is not in effect!

3:5.V.J-K: See Lieberman, 1252-3 ad l. 13.

3:5.VIII.G: STEI omits "to him," since the two could not have met face to face.

3:5.X.H-L: For the various interpretations of "saying a blessing" in this context, see Tosafot M.Q. 23b s.v. w^{e}en.

3:5.XI.B: Gilyon Hashas and STEI emend "fourth" to "seventh" with BT M.Q. 20a and T; see esp. Tosafot M.Q. 22a s.v. d^{e}ātā.

3:5.XI.E: STEI notes that the correct reading is "R. Jacob the Armenian" as quoted by Or Zaru^{c}a, II, p. 424, and again in Y. Gittin 6:7.

3:5.XI.F: See note to XI.B, the case is when the eldest son came on the seventh day.

3:5.XII.A-B: STEI notes that here too a word has fallen out (through pseudo-correction and partial dittography?): in Nachmanides' Torat Haadam, ed. Chavel, p. 146, our passage is quoted in the name of Rabad of Posquieres as: "those of Caesaria who bury [their dead] in Beth Shean." Asheri (M.Q. chapter 3:6) had yet another reading: "those of Caesaria who bury [their dead] in Beth Berai."

According to S. Klein, in Land of Galilee [Hebrew], Jerusalem, 1967, p. 125, the correct name is Beth Berai (see Y. Pes. 29c), and he locates it about 1-1/2 km north of Safed. Cmp. the discussion in Encyclopedia of Talmudic Geography [Hebrew], Tel Aviv, 1972, I, p. 239f; correct the reference to Klein on p. 242b (top) as here. But according to Lieberman (Tarbiz 2, p. 108), it should be locted near Caesaria.

3:5.XII.J: Translation follows PM; for alternate readings and understanding of this story, see QE and STEI.

3:5.XX.D-E: "Covering the head," i.e., the mouth, somewhat in the manner of an Arab headdress. See STEI and the sources quoted therein, esp. BT. M.Q. 24a and Aruch s.v. gav [= Aruch Completum II, 222a s.v. gub].

3:5.XXI.F: BT M.Q. 28a reports this of R. Hisda himself.

3:5.XXI.L: STEI emends the strange "first." According to him, the original text read: qdmwy, "before him" rather than qdmyy': Bar Qappara sent two disciples before him. However, our text already contains the preposition lyh, "to him," though that may have entered as a consequence of the initial error.

3:5.XXIII: For the construction of beds in the Talmudic period, see S. Krauss, Talmudische Archaeologie, Leipzig, 1910, I, pp. 62-6.

3:5.XXV.A: PM and QE would join XXIV and XXV together, and take XXV.A as a contradiction of XXIV.J.

3:5.XXV.J: See the ingenious emendation of Lieberman, p. 1255 n. 34; translation should be: (not) to turn it over even if [he had done so] for one day [already].

3:5.XXVI.B: Gilyon Hashas emends as in Semakhot [= ed. Higger, p. 192 (11:18) in crit. app. -- Higger emends according to our passage!]: [B] [If the bereavement is at] twilight... six days. [C] If it is on Friday at twilight... five, etc. Y. (in contrast to BT 19b) holds that only if three days of mourning have passed before the festival will the remaining four of the seven days of mourning after the festival be cancelled (see V.B.

above) and therefore the festival counts in the period of mourning, while if less than three days of mourning have passed, the festival does not count. But see Lieberman, p. 1255 n. 34 (esp. the end of n. on p. 1256), where Lieberman emends Semakhot 11:18 on the basis of our text, since it is clear that if the burial took place at twilight on a weekday, the mourner is required to turn over his bed immediately -- he has no right to defer that obligation as opposed to the twilight preceding the Sabbath, see BT M.Q. 27a (top). Thus Y.'s text is superior to that of Semakhot.

3:5.XXIII.L-M: Dargaš/darguš, see Rashi ad M.Q. 27a s.v. ^{c}arsa d^{e}gada: "a bed used (kept?) solely for good luck and no other purpose...." Maimonides takes it as a low bed placed next to a higher one, a sort of footstool; see also his comments to M. Ned. 7:4. See also Levy Wörterbuch[2] I, p. 423a s.v. dargaš and I, p. 14b s.v. 'abaqtā', Aruch Completum IV, p. 142b sv. darguš and II, p. 234a s.v. gad. Krauss, Talmudische Archaeologie I, p. 65-6, describes it as part-bed, part-sofa, part sedan-chair, and notes that its exact function was a matter of dispute even in Talmudic times.

3:5.XVIII.H-I: STEI omits this as intrusive from XXII.K-L above.

3:5.XXIX.F: It seems to me that a slight emendation is necessary here: 'yn 'ḇl brgl 'l' šhrbym nwhgyn bw bṣn^c' is a slight corruption of 'yn 'ḇl brgl brbym 'l' nwhgyn bw bṣn^c': laws of public mourning do not apply during a festival, but only those in private.

3:6.I.C: QE emends "rather" to "or."

3:6.I.D: STEI restores: R. Yose b. R. [Bun].

3:7.I.C: STEI cites Y. Sheq. 5:4 as evidence of the bad relations between R. Abun and R. Mana.

3:7.VIII.C-D: STEI reverses C and D.

3:7.XIX.M: "What benefit?" is based on the parallel at Y. Sheq. 2:5, where the tradent is Bar Nezirah; see Y. Ber. 2:1, where the name is given as R. Levi b. Nezirah.

3:7.XIX.N: Kmr, see Ben Jehuda, Thesaurus III, p. 2426a; QE takes it as a vessel for storing grapes.

3:8.I.A: Curr. eds. omit "or on the Sabbath eve" and place the "praiseworthy" clause at the end.

3:8.III.B: Parallel text in Y. Sanh. 2:1 has "...he heard that he had died. He said: 'Send [home] and have my good Sabbath clothes brought' -- and he tore them." Y. Hor. 3:3 omits "He said."

3:8.III.G: QE suggests that the question might be: if R. Eleazar agrees with R. Judah perhaps rending the garment from the bottom might constitute a worthless tear, as above (II.B).

3:8.VIII.B: STEI (Addendum, p. 619) emends on the basis of Torat Haadam, p. 57: R. Samuel b. Abodemi in the name of R. Tanhum: one whose mother, etc.

3:9.I.C: STEI emends: "They did (not) prepare a funeral meal..." and so too in D. Their actions were thus in conflict with the law as set forth above at 3:7 I.D.

3:9.II.C: STEI understand ^{c}nyyn as "spoke at length" in line with Y. Shab. 1:2 (4a); see STEI, p. 152 ad Y. Shabb. 1:2, but cmp. Lieberman, Tarbiz 3, p. 453-454. Dibbūrā' is simply a technical term for certain praises of the dead..

3:9.III.B: Curr. eds. of Y. omit the last phrase: "in the place...."

Chapter 6
YERUSHALMI KETUBOT
Baruch M. Bokser

1:1.VII.E: See Lieberman, TK 6:193-94.

1:2.I.A: See Lieberman, TK 6:390.

1:2.II.J: Cp. Lieberman, TK 6:225

1:5.I.D: PM's emendation to NGDRT is supported by medieval citations; Lieberman, HY p. 44 n. 40.

1:5.I.I: Lieberman, HY p. 44 nn. 50-60.

1:9.I.E: See Halivni p. 143 and, on the whole sugya, Lieberman, TK 8:96, 970.

1:9.I.X: Lieberman (TK 8:965) suggests that Samuel bar Isaac apparently read in M. Qid. 4:3 "R. Eliezer" in place of "R. Eleazar."

1:10.I.A: See Halivni pp. 146-51, which suggests that the attribution should read...BSM RB, BHN...

1:10.II.A: See Halivni pp. 146-51.

2:3.II.B: "Not," 'YN, is found in the citations; Lieberman, TK 8:782.

2:4.IV.G: Assis (p. 115), noting the parallels elsewhere in PT, the reference in the text of the L MS to a gloss (GRS), and the citation of G-Z only on the margin of L MS, suggests that the question in F is left unanswered and G-Z has been transferred from Y. Sotah due to the pericope's similar theme concerning validating a document.

2:7.II.E: As Lieberman (TK 1:181; 6:218) suggests, read "Levite," as found in T., and not "priest," as found in L MS to Y., which has apparently been corrected on the basis of the BT.

2:9.III.B: Cp. the reading in the Y. Git. 3:4 parallel.

2:9.III.C: See Lieberman, HY p. 45 n. 400, and p. 46 n. 1.

2:9.IV.F: Lieberman (HY p. 46 n. 4) prefers the reading Qartiganiah (QRTYGNYH).

2:10.III.A: Lieberman, HY p. 46 n. 6.

2:10.III.D: On the significance of the unripe produce, see Lieberman, HY pp. 46-47 n. 9.

2:10.IV.D: IV relates to and originates at M. Qid. 1:5 and is cited here due to the relevance of [D]; Lieberman, TK 6:220-21.

3:1.I.E: Lieberman's (TK 3:43 n. 93) reading KMWHRYWT as KMWHR Y'WT would produce the rendering: "If it were written here, '...virgins like marriage-present,' matters would have been as you say. But written here is '...the marriage-present of the virgins,'...

3:3.I.B: See Lieberman HY p. 47 n. 40.

3:5.II.B: I.e., the father; Halivni p. 180. Cp. Lieberman, TK 6:221-22.

3:5.III.A: = Lieberman (HY p. 48 and nn.) offers the following reconstruction and explanation of this difficult pericope, A-G:

[A] R. Eleazar asked, "As to the daughters of a woman who has been raped or the sons of one seduced, what is the law about their enjoying the stipulation of the normal marriage contract [which provides for their upkeep]?

[B] "It is obvious to me in regard to a woman married after being raped that she lacks the clause for male heirs [that they inherit the marriage-settlement, should the mother die, since she does not enjoy such a normal settlement anyhow, and the husband, former rapist, has already paid the financial penalty. Perhaps, however, he is required to provide food for the daughters].

[C] "[And in regard to a woman married after being seduced [it is obvious] that she lacks the clause for female heirs [that they receive support, for she lacks stipulations of a marriage-settlement and the financial penalty that the former seducer-husband had paid her would not be inherited by them, the females, but by the sons]."

[D] If you say that both sorts of women should present problems to him [sons and daughters of both the raped and the seduced women], then we should ask [in A] concerning the daughters of the one who has been raped and the daughters of the one who has been seduced, what is the law about their enjoying the stipulation of the normal marriage contract? [The variation, in referring to "sons" in one and to "daughters" in the other, however, must be intentional, indicating that only those cases are problematic.]

[E] It is in accord with rabbis that the question must be raised [for according to them the institution of the stipulation of a marriage-settlement may have originally applied even to the woman who has been raped].

[F] ...[F-G as printed in the text].

<u>3:6.III.K</u>: A clause delineating additional cases is missing in the L MS and printed editions but found in medieval citations; Lieberman, <u>HY</u> p. 49 and n. 1.

<u>3:7.I.K</u>: Lieberman (<u>HY</u> pp. 49-50 and nn.), drawing on medieval citations, corrects the text and demonstrates that K-O consists of Hisdas's statement (K) and its divergent interpretations by R. Mana and R. Abin. Thus:

[K] ...[as printed, reading WHY' for WH'].

[L] R. Mana said, "What is the meaning of [the statement] <u>he who rapes her is liable and he who seduces her is exempt</u>? He who rapes her is liable on all counts and he who seduces her is exempt on all counts."

[M] R. Abin said, "Shimi proposed the following,..." [as printed].

[N] And it [the Mishnah] follows R. Aqiba. [Thus the law of the priest and the seducer, both liable for monetary penalty, differ only in regard to shame and injury.]

[O] Or the one who seduces her is exempt from shame and the one who raped her is liable. And it [the Mishnah] follows R. Yose the Galilean. [While both exempt from monetary penalty they do differ in regard to shame and injury.]

<u>4:1.II.C</u>: See Lieberman, <u>HY</u> p. 50 and nn. 40-50.

<u>4:2.I.A</u>: On I and its interpretation in II, see Lieberman, <u>HY</u> p. 51 nn.

<u>4:4.II.R</u>: For II.R to III.D, see Halivni pp. 187-89 and nn.

<u>4:5-6.II.B</u>: Lieberman (<u>HY</u> p. 52 n. 3) suggests an emendation for L MS's awkward usage: SLH S'L, "sent and asked."

<u>4:5-6.III.B</u>: For an alternative reading "or to redeem," see Lieberman, <u>HY</u> p. 52 n. 6.

4:8.I.B: See Halivni pp. 192-93.

4:8.II.A: Halivni p. 195 emends to "Judah b. Haninah."

4:8.III.A: Halivni p. 195 emends to "Judah b. Haninah."

4:8.III.C: Halivni (pp. 194-96) believes the responses in C, E, and F purport to describe what had been enacted in Usha. Taking, in E and F, the word 'TTBT not as "asked" but as "challenged," he renders E as, "That matter [was also enacted and] challenged but not explained," and F as, "It was challenged and explained."

4:8.IV.A: "Insulted" = BMPQYR; see Lieberman, HY p. 52 n. 20 and fn. 48

4:8.V.E: See Lieberman, HY p. 53 n. 40.

4:8.X.A-B: See Lieberman, TK 6:250f.

4:8.XIV.I: See Lieberman, TK 6:254.

4:10.I.C: If we reverse the clauses in B, following QE, the present clause becomes even more apropos; Lieberman, TK 6:240 n. 52.

4:12.I.D: See Lieberman, TK 6:354, 355.

4:12.III.A: I.e., on entering the husband's house; Lieberman, TK 6:233 n. 19.

4:13.I.A: Following Lieberman, HY p. 53 n. 50.

5:1.IV.F-G: The text of F-G is difficult. Lieberman (HY p. 54 and nn.) reads:

[F] "...Even if the girl is mature?"

[G] They say, let us derive the answer from the following: The father...or a brother for his sister, [Lieberman supplying:] and even if she is a minor. All the more so a third party. All the more so if she is mature.

5:2.IV.A: See Lieberman, HY p. 54 n. 300, and TK 6:244; and Bokser, SC, pp. 71-72, 196.

5:3.III.A: See Lieberman, HY, p. 54 nn. 5-6

5:6.II.CC: Alt., "R. Hezekiah the Great in the name of Rab;" Lieberman, HY p. 55 n. 50.

5:6.III.C: Cp. Lieberman, HY p. 55 n. 80.

5:8.II.A: The printed editions have ^{C}D, "to what extent" instead of "ass driver." The L MS originally had [H]MR, which a subsequent had changed to ^{C}R, the reading that was misread as ^{C}D; Lieberman, HY p. 56 n. 4.

5:8.II.G: See Lieberman, HY p. 56 n. 6.

5:10.II.A: See Lieberman, TK 6:267.

6:1.III: Cp. Lieberman, Caesasrea, pp. 44-45.

6:2.I.B: Delete a marginal gloss that has entered the text in a corrupted fashion: "for the sake of the marriage-document;" Lieberman, HY p. 57 n. 30. On the pericope as a whole, see Lieberman, TK 6:379.

M.6:4.B: Alt. to "for each and every maneh": "for pocket money [lit., a basket] no more than a maneh": see n. to III.A, below.

6:4.I.N: See Lieberman (TK 6:279), who emends BNTLH to BBTLH, and NTLH to BTLH.

6:4.III.A: Lieberman (TK 6:276-77 and n. 26) takes III.A as an explanation of M. 6:4B, to the effect that the woman is not to be given more than a maneh for the basket of perfumes [= pocket money], even if she brought in thousands of denarim. Lieberman alternatively slightly emends the text, reading instead of MNH the word KMNH', a shortened form of KMNHG, a word found in M. 6:4C. He believes III.A is an abbreviated citation of this M. clause: "all follows the local custom," on which Yohanan, in B, comments. Then Abin, in C, explains Yohanan's statement. For C, Lieberman supplies three missing letters, reading: "They treated their value [=the value of perfume, i.e., the pocket money] in Syria and Arabia as equivalent to the value of the utilization of the ready cash." IV.A [which we would reletter as III.D] deals with the question whether or not for a childless woman the value of perfume is equivalent to that of ready cash.

6:7.I.C: See Lieberman, TK 6:282-83.

6:7.I.H: Cp. Halivni pp. 210-12.

M.7:2.A: Halivni (pp. 212-15) suggests that the phrase HMDYR Sis used when the vower, here the husband, prohibits himself from deriving benefit from another person, here his wife, if that other person does not act in accord with the stipulated condition.

M.7:2.C-D: Concerning texts reading "month" instead of "day," in C, and "months," instead of "days," in D, see Lieberman, TK 6:285-86.

7:4.I.B: Follow the citations in reading "days" instead of "months," a mistake in the printed editions; Lieberman, HY p. 58 n. 400.

M.7:6.G: G, an addition to the Mishnah, accords with Samuel's interpretation, below in III; Lieberman, TK 6:292.

7:6.III.D: Halivni (p. 217) suggests that Rab refers to a woman who raises her voice when speaking of sexual matters.

7:6.IV.A-B: For the textual reconstruction of A-B, see Lieberman, TK 6:292-93.

7:6.V.D: On the reading, "If she was [seen]," see Lieberman, HY, p. 60 n. 9.

7:6.V.H: As Lieberman (HY p. 61 n. 90) notes, the context requires the alternative reading of "...one-half" instead of "without."

7:6.V.J: See Lieberman, HY p. 61 nn. 100, 200.

7:6.V.K: V and L MS read SL' KM'N, "is it not," Lieberman, HY p. 61 n. 400.

7:7.VII.A: See Lieberman, TK 6:302.

7:7.II.C: Cp. Lieberman (TK 8:832f.) who explains: Since in uprooting a vow one acknowledges that the vow had once existed, the condition that there had never been a vow on the woman is violated.

7:7.VII.B: See Lieberman, TK 6:302.

7:8.I.D: See Lieberman, HY p. 63 n. 20, on the reading "with Rabbis" instead of "with Rab" and on the pericope's exegesis.

7:8.I.I: For this clause and the rest of the pericope through N, see Lieberman, HY p. 63 n. 20. Explaining that the idiom SLQT MTNYTYN means "finishing the Mishnah," Lieberman explains:

[J-K] Does the Mishnah end [close] with the opinion of R. Simeon ben Gamaliel? Is then the following Mishnah in accord with rabbis? But the coming Mishnah appears to explain R. Simeon ben Gamaliel, and R. Meir there is in dispute. Consequently, how can you say that R. Simeon ben Gamaliel accords with R. Meir in the latter Mishnah. The baraita in [M] provides the basis for the answer in [N], to wit, the next Mishnah does not explain the opinion of R. Simeon ben Gamaliel but provides a new dispute between sages and Meir. We therefore may say that R. Simeon ben Gamaliel is in accord with R. Meir in the latter Mishnah.

7:9.I.D: See Lieberman, TK 6:303.

8:1.I.A: "And she then became betrothed" is found in HY; see Lieberman p. 63 n. 30.

8:8.I.B-F: On B-F, see Lieberman, HY pp. 64-65 and nn., and TK 6:316-17, 323.

8:9.I.C: We follow PM and citations, which reverse the second-half of each clause; Lieberman, HY p. 65 n. 1.

8:9.III.F: Lieberman (HY p. 66 n. 3) explains: Since the requirement imposed by the sages that a woman in all situations be accorded a burial applies only to the husband of the woman and not to the heirs, the levir would be responsible only if he inherits the marriage-settlement.

8:10.I.C: Cp. Halivni pp. 224-25.

8:10.I.D: Lieberman (TK 6:26-27) suggests reading, "...they do not retrieve it..."

8:11.I.G: Lieberman (TK 6:324-25) explains: if the levir is an Israelite, he consummates the marriage, divorces her, and remarries her; if, however, he is a priest, since he is prohibited from marrying a divorcee, he should convince her to give him a quittance for her marriage-contract.

8:11.IV.A: The lack of the clause "Simeon B. Shetah..." in this version of the baraita reflects a distinct perspective concerning the history of the marriage-contract; Halivni p. 226.

9:1.VII.B: See Lieberman, TK 6:326 n. 10.

9:3.II: Cp. Lieberman, TK 6:328.

9:8.III.C: R. Simeon in M. 9:8P is thus making a general rule; Lieberman, TK 6:334 and Halivni pp. 229-30.

9:9.II.H: Halivni (p. 233) believes that Rab, pointing to the role of the ketubah as part of the special enactment to protect a woman, distinguishes between the case of a loan, where keeping a receipt may become a burden on the borrower, and the case of a ketubah, where the husband may not refuse to accept a receipt. Emending an 'YT to a LYT, Halivni reads the second-half of H through J thus:

[H] Is there no receipt [written out...-settlement]?

[I] ...Rab does not accept the requirement for a receipt [see b. B.B. 171a].

[J] Rab does not accept the requirement for a receipt in regard to one who said, "If one's document..." [the case of a loan]. But he accepts the requirement in regard to one who said, "If her marriage-contract..."

10:1.III.D: Lieberman (TK 6:324) reconstructs the last line thus: "But the second wife and her heirs take precedence over the marriage-settlement of the first. The second one and her heirs take precedence over the heirs of the first.

10:1.IV: The context requires the reading "Ben Nannos;" Halivni p. 236.

10:1.IV.B: Cp. Halivni pp. 236-38.

10:4.III.D: On Y. Ketubot and the Y. B.Q. parallel, see Lieberman, TK 6:346-48.

11:2.I.A: See Lieberman, TK 6:358.

11:3.I.F: Lieberman (TK 6:357 n. 16) suggests reading, "...should not come along."

11:6.V.A-D: On Simeon ben Gamaliel's view and V.A-D, see Lieberman (TK 6:361-63) and Halivni (pp. 243-45), who suggest that when an error is greater than a sixth and an inspection document was issued, sages consider the sale invalid (a position reflected in V.A), while Simeon ben Gamaliel declares it valid (as reflected in V.B).

12:1.II.C: Cp. n. to Y. 5:6 III.C, above.

12:3.II.G: Lieberman (TK 6:365-66) suggests Eleazar b. Yose comments directly on M. 12:3C-D and [F] should follow the reading of PT: "She dwells in a house as she would dwell when her husband is overseas." On the meaning of II.A-D see ibid. and n. 56.

12:5.I.B: Following Lieberman (TK 6:374-75 and n. 16), who reads SNSLTH Binstead of SNHLTH. Cp. Halivni p. 252.

12:5.II.A: Halivni (p. 251) aptly notes we should read: "R. Hiyya bar Ashi in the name of Rab, R. Hiyya raised the question [or: "said"] before Rabbi."

12:5.II.D: Cp. Lieberman, TK 6:377f.

12:5.III.A: Lieberman (TK 6:374-75 and n. 13) explains: When her deceased husband's children do not support her, out of a desire not to go to her in-laws she may relinquish not only her maintenance but also her marriage-settlement.

13:1.V.B: They still listen to him because he may rightly claim that she should have been more economical; Lieberman, TK 6:367.

13:3: See Lieberman, Caesarea, pp. 75, 76, and esp. nn. 159-160.

M.13:5.A: The idiom in full may have been: stretching out the leg and going overseas -- i.e., being no longer present; Lieberman, TK 6:379.

13:10.I.H: Y.'s version of the baraita accords with the Erfurt MS of T. in reading "from a town which is totally Israelite."

13:11.I.B: Y., like the Erfurt MS of T., reads, "they do not force him to come;" see Lieberman, TK 6:386, and Halivni pp. 259-61.

13:11.III: III, referring to M. 13:1H, is found in citations; Lieberman, TK 6:389-91, esp. 390 and n. 81.

ABBREVIATIONS

Assis — Moshe Assis. Parallel Sugyot in the Jerusalem Talmud (Ph.D. dissertation, Hebrew University, 1976).

Bokser, SC — Baruch M. Bokser. Samuel's Commentary on the Mishnah: Its Nature, Forms, and Content (Leiden, 1975: E.J. Brill).

Halivni — David Weiss Halivni. Meqorot UMesorot [= Sources and Traditions]. 4 vols. to date. (Tel Aviv, 1968: Dvir; and Jerusalem, 1975, 1982: Jewish Theological Seminary). References without a volume number are to vol. 1: Seder Nashim.

Lieberman, Caesarea	Saul Lieberman. The Talmud of Caesarea. Jerusalem, 1931.
Lieberman, HY	Saul Lieberman. Hilkoth Ha-Yerushalmi (The Laws of the Palestinian Talmud) of Rabbi Moses Ben Maimon. With Introduction, Commentary and Notes. (New York, 1947: Jewish Theological Seminary of America).
Lieberman, TK	Saul Lieberman. Tosefta Ki-Fshutah. A Comprehensive Commentary to the Tosefta. 8 vols. to date. (New York, 1955-73: Jewish Theological Seminary of America).
PM	Moses Margaliot. "Pene Moshe." In Talmud Yerushalmi. Reprint of Vilna, 1922 edition.
QE	David Frankel of Berlin. "Qorban HaEdah." In Talmud Yerushalmi. Reprint of Vilna, 1922 edition.

Chapter 7
YERUSHALMI QIDDUSHIN
David Goldenberg

1:1.I.M-N: M. San 7:9 does not provide "the besought proof for H," but proves the immediately preceding statement in L: "Even someone else [than the husband] may render her a woman who has had sexual relations." Therefore M should be translated: "As that which we have learned there."

Therefore also the bracketed explanation in N must be changed to: "[The latter has had sexual relations with a non-virgin who has the legal status of one 'who has had sexual relations with her husband' although it is not her husband. See M. San. 11:1]."

1:1.III.D: [If so] -- A highly interpretive remark (it implies some logical relationship in the argument between A-C and D-G such that A-C is some way negated). I would therefore delete it or substitute the innocuous "[Similarly]."

1:1.IV.A: You assume that A is a quote from the Mishnah. Although it is deliberately imitative of Mishnah's language it is not a quote but an interpretation, since 'w ("or") is substituted for the ambiguous w-.

1:1.IV.I: I would add in brackets: "['ys 'ys, 'man' appearing twice in the verse]" since the exegesis turns on the repetition.

1:1.IV.J: Replace "prohibited connections who are gentiles" and "prohibited connections who are Israelites" with: "connections prohibited to gentiles" and "connections prohibited to Israelites" respectively.

1:1.IV.Q: I'd add to your explanation: 'By interpreting b'dm as "in man" rather than "by man."'

1:1.IV.R-S: My changes follow PM.

1:1.IV.U: Your bracketed explanation is not technically correct -- see my remarks on IV.J and the text below IV.W. Therefore, I'd omit your explanation -- the line reads fine without it and doesn't imply that Jews and gentiles have the same set of prohibited connections which is not true (see PM).

1:1.IV.EE-FF: Rewrite as follows (following PM): (EE) Said R. Mana, "Is it not from [the exegesis of the following verse?] 'And he will cleave to his wife' -- and not to the wife of his fellow. [That is, 'cleaving'] in any manner. (FF) Similarly, [the prohibition of any sexual contact obtains] for a male or an animal.

1:1.V.C: R. Yohanan of Sepphoris -- See TY 2, p. 5 [= Tarbiz, 2, p. 239] and B. Lieberman Yerushalmi K.

1:1.V.H: Rather: For R. Hiyya taught, "A gentile... who divorced her, and the both of them [the first husband and the woman] converted to Judaism, I do not invoke the rule, 'Then her former husband, who sent her away, may not take her again [to be his wife]' (Deut. 24:4). [The rule is not applied because she is not regarded...]."

1:1.VI.E-F: Your translation is based on Tos. Ms. V, but I don't know if sryk lwmr can have interrogative force. I'd rather go with the variants and parallels -- including PT -- cited by Lieberman TK ad loc., to wit, "One must say that it is a writ worth a perutah. But a woman is consecrated with anything worth a perutah? Rather, even if one wrote it on a sherd or on a waste paper [both of which have a value less than perutah] and gave it to her."

1:1.VI.L,M: One -- (in L and M) should be "the one" the phrase is definite with an antecedent "he" understood.

1:1.VI.N: Rabbis -- rather "the colleagues." hbryyh is used distinctly from rbnyn and I should keep the difference in translation. Also, it is in determined state.

1:1.VI.S: Rabbis -- rather "The Rabbis" rbnyn being determined by the construct state.

1:1.VI.S-T: (Following PM) (S) The one who said that she may be divorced is of the opinion that it is permitted to betroth with a document written on material from which the Scribes prohibited benefit. (T) The one who said that she may not be divorced is of the opinion that it is prohibited to betroth with a document, written on material from which the Torah prohibited benefit, but the Scribes permitted such betrothal.

1:1.VII.C,D,F,G,O,P,T,CC,EE,MM; IX.Y,Z,AA,BB,CC: I'd rather translate m^{c}h simply as ma^{c}ah (as you do with dynr = dinar and prwth = perutah) since it does not mean "silver coin" although it may be such. The confusion of your translation becomes apparent at O and EE which should be translated: "The smallest silver coin is a ma^{c}ah." (You do translate m^{c}h thus at IX F-G.)

1:1.VII.EE: So let it be... should be a new line.

1:1.VII.LL-MM: The first part of MM belongs to the end of LL. The rest of MM can constitute a new line.

1:1.VIII.F: Instead of your bracketed explanation I'd say (the following PM at Yeb. end ch. 1): '[illustrating a case of illegitimate children between them]."

1:1.VIII.I: I'd accept the reading in Yeb.: "The House of Shammai concede to the House of Hillel as to the stringent side of things." See Qorban Edah here.

1:1.VIII.P: Rather (following PM at Yeb. ibid.): Said R. Abba Mari, "And that is right. What do we learn? That they declared unclean all the clean things prepared relying on the purification-power of the trough in the past. But not from this time onward [that is, once the case came to the House of Hillel]."

1:1.IX.L,R: See above on VII.C. etc.

1:1.IX.S-T: My corrections follow PM. Or you can be as ambiguous as the text and translate "silver [coins]" and "copper [coins]."

1:1.IX.W: A more literal transalation of the text: Hilpai said, "Set me down at the shore of the river if I cannot demonstrate that whatever is said in the mishnah of R. Hiyya [T.] may in fact be derived from our Mishnah, then throw me into the river."

1:1.XI.B: That is, declaring his intention to take her as his wife -- "Bespeaking" is more than a declaration of intention. It is the very act of "betrothal," for he gives the money or its equivalent and then says to her, "Behold you are sanctified to me," as below at R-S.

1:1.XI.L-M: R. Simeon's doubt turns on the interpretation of "And take her as a wife." Does this phrase constitute a new act ("bespeaking") distinct from the act of sexual relations or does it merely state the result of the act of sexual relations? The translation in M should reflect this and I would, therefore, translate: Or, "her husband's brother shall go into her" and lo, "he takes her as a wife." (I do not think R. Simeon means to base his exegesis on a different reading of lqhh i.e. lequhah or leqahah.)

1:1.XII.F: I believe PM reads F interrogatively: "Why did R. Isaac ask about a case of two surviving childless widows when our Mishnah deals with only one?" So also Qorban Edah, first interpretation.

1:1.XIII.A: An inquiry shall be held -- The traditional explanation of bqrt in Lev. 19:20 (= flogging) should somehow be mentioned, else the question in A makes no sense.

1:1.XIII.F,H: You have the wrong part of the verse quoted. I'd put in the Hebrew word (hrpwt), since the exegesis cannot be understood without it.

1:1.III.L: Bn (hwryn) and bt (hwryn) do not mean (slave-) boy and (slave-) girl. I'd translate: "...she is half slave and half free, betrothed to a free man."

1:2.I.J: Do you want to note where you do not follow PM, as here, where instead you follow QE?

1:2.I.L: Rather: It [= J] was taught in the name of an [anonymous] sage. (L1) How does R. Ishmael prove [that a writ is applicable to the Hebrew man servant]?

1:2.II.D: Rather: Said R. Abba... Scripture itself twice mentioned "price" (Lev. 25:51, 52).

1:2.III.C: Your bracketed explanations are, I believe, incorrect. The point is who will want to retract. Therefore (following PM, QE): [What was said at A was actually,] "Perhaps... purchase."

1:2.V.R: My correction is based on PM and QE who understand mpqyn as referring to the argument and not to the slaves.

1:2.VII.M,N,P: His hand is on top -- I'd prefer a less literal, more understandable, translation such as, "He has the advantage." But if you want literalness, how about preserving the idiom with: "He has the upper hand."

1:2.VIII.E-F: Corrections follow PM.

1:2.VIII.N: Corrections follow PM.

1:2.XI.B-C: Corrections follow PM.

1:2.XI.K: See on 1:1, V.S.

1:2.XII.I: This should begin a new unit (cf. XII A and XIII A).

1:2.XII.E: For the son... to act -- Rather, following PM: "For cannot the son be a minor [who has no legal right of knowledge and consent, since the verse simply says 'son' with no qualifications]."

1:2.XIV.C: Corrections follow PM.

1:2.XIV.J: Two pubic hairs -- Better: "two pubic hairs or two hairs under the arm."

1:2.XIV.Q: Do you want to note where you disagree with both PM and QE as you do here? If you change your wording slightly you would be in line with QE's first explanation. Thus: "Now in this case, it poses no problem as to his turning his wife into a widow, but how can he turn her into a divorcee [for a minor may not give a writ of divorce]?"

However, I'd prefer an explanation (as QE, second explanation, and PM) which take nyh' 'lmnh wqrwsh and hlysh as questions posed to R. Yohanan.

1:2.XIV.Q: One may interpret... -- Rather, following QE, "One may interpret the case to be one in which he had sexual relations with her [while a minor] and gave her a writ of divorce when be became an adult." PM: "...and he had sexual relations and gave her a writ of divorce when he became an adult."

(You would prefer PM since your translation of sec. S presupposes PM here.)

1:2.XIV.T: My brackets make it clear that we read t^{c}nah and not tanah.

1:2.XV.B: (et passim) Sages -- Rather: the sages reading wahakhamim and not w^{c}hakhamim.

1:2.XVI.O: Rather: "But has it not been taught [in a passage which can only speak of the status of betrothal, not of a fully consummated marriage]: 'A man may sell his daughter for marriage [and if she became widowed or divorced] he may do so again [provided she is still a minor]. Similarly, he may sell her as a slave-girl [and if she was a minor when receiving her freedom through the end of the six-year period, or the Jubilee year or her master's death] he may do so again. He may sell her for a slave-girl [and if she became free] he may sell her for marriage. However, he may not sell her as a slave-girl after he had already sold her for marriage.

1:2.XVIII.H: I would either emend the text on the basis of BT Qid. 17b as does QE (i.e., "A Hebrew slave-girl serves neither the daughter nor the son.") or I would refer to the BT variant in a note, for the text as it stands now in PT is impossible.

1:2.XXI.D: I struck out "in the earlap" despite the fact that Jastrow has it, because "earlap" has two meanings according to OED: the lobe and the outside ear as a whole. In our section, which distinguishes between the lobe and the rest of the ear, the term "earlap" would be ambiguous and confusing.

1:2.XXIII.B: Spit -- I'd prefer another translation, since "spit" for piercing animals is what comes to mind and this may not be the meaning. How about a deliberately vague "borer" as Jastrow?

1:2.XXV.D-E: In view of the fact that "I will not go out free" follows "I love my master..." in MT, whereas in our PT text it precedes it, and in view of the fact that the teaching in E is based entirely on "I love my master..." and not on "I will not go out free," I would therefore agree with the interpretation of PM and QE which sees "I will not go out free" as the proof-text for the end of D. Thus: "...and one at the beginning of the seventh year -- 'I will not go out free' [supposes that he could if he wishes and that occurs only at the beginning of the seventh year]."

1:3.XXV.A: Somewhere [perhaps in brackets] you should make it clear that "Canaanite" here means "non-Jewish."

1:3.III.D: I think you ought to note that your text is an emendation suggested by QE.

1:3.VIII.K: Rather: "For we have learned that he who led a cow, or drew it, or called it and it came after him, he is liable for what happens to the cow just as if he had borrowed it." Your translation is based on a printer's error, kmsykh. Ed. Venice has: hmsykh. See PM and QE.

1:3.VIII.P: Rather: "And has it not been taught: 'He may impart ownership of a meal of commingling by means of...] his wife' [ibid.]. [It cannot therefore be R. Meir] for R. Meir treats..."

1:3.IX.B: The point is not "issuing a writ" but receiving one. At any rate, I've rephrased the words to follow both the text here and in BT Git. 23b.

1:3.IX.G-H: Corrections follow PM. If you wish to follow QE and strike out my addition at G, you must insert it at H.

1:4.VII.CCC: Deleted because the interpretation also follows PM.

1:5.I.C.: tmn does not necessarily refer to Babylonia; see Frankel, Mabo HaYerushalmi, p. 12b.

1:5.II.I: Changes based on text here; not in the parallel, Qid 1.3. Between I and J insert as at 1:3, I N-O.

1:5.II.L: In the parallel (p. 74) you have this beginning a new section.

1:5.IV.E: And below it -- See Jastrow, s.v. sr^{c}: b^{c}'... wsr^{c} mynyh = he argued and he gave it up (pace PM).

1:5.VI.K: Your translation is an amalgamation of the text of T and of PT. I'd rather go with the one or the other, but not create a new text.

1:5.VI.P: Emigre -- Bad translation, since "emigre" connotes one whose emigration is usually permanent, while the nhwt' was a regular traveller between Babylonia and Palestine. But I can't think of a good translation.

1:6.I.C: Rather: "Said to him R. Eleazar, 'We have learned only: Whatever is used as payment for something else, and this implies something which is subject to assessment.'"

1:6.III.G: Add: "[without it being drawn, i.e. do we now view the ass as an exchange for the cow]?"

1:6.IV.C-D: Rather: If one sold him a cow for money, and he left [the money] with a money changer.

(D) on the next day he found him standing [to collect the money] [Translation follows Ms. Leiden and J.N. Epstein, Tarbiz, 6..1, p. 38.]

1:6.V.L: This section is not in the text.

1:7.I.C: Omitted, since, for example, sisith is dependent upon time of day, not year.

1:7.I.V: Omitted, since the question in Q does not refer to marriage above, but to all the father-son obligations.

1:7.II.K: My change is because, pace PM, I could find no definition of "ugly" for ^{c}zyb.

1:7.VI.U: Rather (following PM and Jastrow) "'Everyone's merit is in his own basket.' [That is, there is a different way of doing good for every man.]"

1:7.IX.B: You do not follow PM (and QE) here and your translation is startling... but technically correct. I therefore did not change it.

1:7.XI.A: My change is based on the PT text. If you mean to follow the emendation of QE then retain your translation, but I think you ought to note somewhere that the text behind the translation is emended.

1:7.XIII.B: Rather: Issi says, "[Women are also not liable for transgressing the prohibition of] 'They shall not make tonsures upon their heads.'"

1:7.XIII.C: What is the Scriptural basis for this? 'They shall not make tonsures upon their heads nor shave off the edges of their beards' [Lev. 21:5].

1:7.XIII.M: "Ahi' follows QE (there is no known Ati, while Ahi = Aha) which you've adopted, while PM takes 'ty as a verb not a proper noun.

1:8.I.JJ: Changes follow Jastrow.

1:8.II.C: Rather: "[And you shall eat neither bread nor grain parched or fresh until this same day, until you have brought the offering of your God: it is a statute for ever throughout your generations] in all your dwellings" [Lev. 23:14] -- whether in the land or abroad.

1:9.II.S: Rather: "If there be for him an angel one of the thousand [m'lp]" is not written, but rather, "one part of the thousand [mny 'lp]," meaning...

1:9.III.D: Add: The wise will inherit honor, but fools exalt disgrace (Prov. 3:34-35).

1:9.III.J-K: Rather: It is written n's' [i.e., forgetting sin, a play on nsh/y].

(K) And so David said, "You did forgive [ns't] the iniquity of your people; you did pardon all their sin. Selah" (Ps. 85:2).

2:1.I.E-J: following PM and QE:

2:1.I.E: And from which [verse] do you know this?

2:1.I.F: "They shall take every man a lamb according to their father's houses, a lamb for a household" (Ex. 12:3).

2:1.I.G: Now did all of them take a lamb? And is it not so that only one of them takes it in behalf of all of them?

2:1.I.H: But on this basis we learn that a man's agent is equivalent to himself.

2:1.I.I: Said R. Yose, "[A second prooftext, Ex. 12:3, is necessary, for the first prooftext given above, Ex. 12:6, is not acceptable, since] that case is different. For a man may slaughter the Passover-offering of his fellow without the latter's knowledge of consent."

2:1.I.J: If you say that a man may designate a lamb as a Passover for his fellow without the latter's knowledge and consent, [that is not so, for] he may not do this.

2:1.I.K: For R. Zeira said...

2:1.III.E: The changes are in line with QE's interpretation since it is that which you are following here.

2:1.III.J: I would delete your parenthetical explanation since I do not know your source.

2:1.IV.E: Add: [i.e., she is not yet at the legal age of consent to betrothe herself].

2:1.IV.H: Yohanan's view does not concern her status.

2:1.IV.J: Change follows PM.

2:1.V.I: Rather: "It was clear to R. Jacob bar Aha in the name of R. Joshua that R. Joshua b. Levi differs..."

-- so PM which I prefer over your translation which makes no sense.

2:1.VI.M: Rather (following PM; I do not understand your translation in context): "[Nevertheless] R. Yose b. R. Bun came [and declared that] according to Rab, if she should die, her husband will inherit her."

2:1.IX.D: Rather (following PM and QE; your translation in context makes no sense): "She wants to be betrothed [with the benefit she derives] by seeing him doing a good deed to the poor man [on account of her]."

2:2.II.C-III B: I would not begin a new section where you do (at III A), since III A-B is the proof for the statement at II C. The Mishnah citation at II C is only the lemma cited to introduce the proof (as below at III E the lemma is cited before nyh' phrase). Thus, my addition of "etc."

2:2.III.H: Changes follow PM and QE. I'd put all of H in brackets, since it does not appear in our text, but in the parallel in Ket.

2:2.IV.C: Either delete, or add: "...this woman if she would do so."

2:2.V.M: Hbryy' is determined, "the associates."

2:2.V.Q: See above 1:1, VI.S.

2:2.VI.A: Here you've translated the lemma of the Mishnah as found in the PT text ("For all...") whereas at the Mishnah itself you do not use the PT text but another text ("All..."). I would be consistent.

2:7.II.L: Add: "second tithe and residue of the meal offerings are in the same category." (see II.E)

2:7.II.P: Rather: "...in which she was betrothed through an agent" [the text supports your translation, but the context does not. I've therefore followed QE and PM.]

2:7.III.B: Rather: [He who bethrothes a woman] with food in the status of second-tithe -- R. Abbahu...

2:8.II.b: I believe your interpretation is wrong but if you wish to keep it, insert the brackets as I've done to show that your remarks are interpretive.

3.1.IV.D: Rather: It is doubtful whether the laws of sacrilege apply to it.

3:1.IX.E: PM and QE: "And can you use the argument of 'what do you prefer' [to make a lenient ruling] in a case..."

3:2.IV: As in II A.

3:3.II.F-H: Omit underlining. It is neither a Mishnah nor (pace PM) a Tosephtah.

3:3.II.M: Rather (following PM and QE: "...the Sabbath rest, for he did not make acquisition of his erub. He is also not in the status of the other townsfolk where he lives, for he...

3:3.II.O: Rather (following PM... R. Yose, "That [clause] 'And if they will not' [Num. 32:30] is actually the same as the clause 'For we will not [inherit with them...' Num. 32:19] [Therefore there was no need for Moses to make the statement unless for purposes of repeating the condition in both its positive and negative form.]

3:4.I.C,D: Should be preceded by elipses as is B.

3:4.II.D: Rather: ...People who make a circuit and buy on credit and assigned the merchant to pay the creditor --

3:4.II.E: The merchant got up early and fled --

3:4.II. I-M: Flax -- Thus you follow PM. Why? qytwn' has a perfectly understandable and common translation -- "ladle." So Jastrow s.v.

3:4.II.FF: Change follows Jastrow.

3:5.I.I-J: I would put this section in parantheses and note that it is not part of the Mishnah (see Albeck ad loc.) and indeed does not appear in the PT Mishnah text.

3:5.II.I: Rather: Interpret it to mean that once they are cut down they are not subject to redemption [that is, they do not require it].

3:6.I.D: 'b' may mean my father. See A.S. Rosenthal article to BT San beginning re the story of Rabbi and R. Hiyya.

3:6.II.B-C: Between B and C you omitted: B^1 -- If the father died, lo, this woman is betrothed. B^2 -- If there is no explicit statement on the father's part, the father is assumed to concur. (You'll have to remember C - N.)

3:9.II.C: Rather: There [at M. Qid. 3:9A-C] [Yose's opinion is that one does not use language which subjects his own situation to doubt, therefore he meant] to exclude all the older daughters [except for the very oldest] or [at E-G] to exclude all the youngest daughters [except for the very youngest]. Yet here he has said this... -- (I prefer my translation for not only does it conform to PM, but your translation takes ${}^{c}d$ "up to" as a key element in M. Qid where in fact it does not occur.)

3:9.II.J: Rather: Said R. Zeia, "[The dispute really does deal with how language is used, for R. Yose understands 'D LPNY PSH not to mean 'up to before Passover' but] in the Nabatean language 'until Passover will pass.'"

3:10.I.C: Rather [following PM; your interpretation makes no sense to me]: If there [at M. 3:9] [in which there are several doubts concerning who is considered older and younger, for] in each group there are "younger" and "older" [and there is thus ample reason why a man would not use language which places himself in a situation of doubt], R. Meir differs...

3:12.III.F: My change is due to the ambiguity of "to weave it into wool" which may mean "so that it becomes wool" which is incorrect.

3:12.VI.K: My rewording allows your translation to be seen as interpretive (following QE).

3:12.VIII.E: This section makes no sense. Therefore, I'd follow Lieverman [TY 1, p. 8 = Tarbiz 2, p. 113] who emends mwzhrym to nyzhrm and follows the reading of SY, nykryn instead of mbdyn. Thus, "it appears that you are not careful about holy Israelite girls."

3:13.I.C: Kepar Saporayya -- See TY 1, p. 8.

4:1.IV.C-F: I've kept the transliteration consistent. In F I've followed Jastrow which reads more smoothly.

4:1.IV.G-H: Rather: "...kept silence for them [and the place was known as Tel harsha [HRS = silence]." H. [Netins]: R. Imi...

4:1.IV.J: Or: "Joshua hung them on the Delphic oracle." See TY 5, p. 6 (= Tarbiz 3, p. 457).

4:1.IV.U: Rather (following PM and QE : "That he simultaneously judges while [seeking his good] works."

4:1.IV.BB: RSC here follows LXX. MT: "...before the Lord at Gibah of Saul, the chosen of the Lord."

4:1.IV.CC: Between CC and DD insert: CC,. And they said, "We have no claim of silver against Saul and his house."

Change following numbering sequence.

4:1.V.A,J: Cordyenians, Gobaya, Habel Yamma, Shunya, Sosraya -- following Jastrow.

4:1.VI.B: Rather: ...language, "tenth" and "tenth" [as the basis for analogy between the two cases. That is, Deut....]

4:1.VI.V-VII.A: The first part of A, "R. Yose... to come," should be VI.W. See PM and QE.

4:2.I.C,II.C: mwslk = abandoned; see forthcoming article by S. Lachs.

4:4.II.J: Change based on parallel PT Sotah 1:7 'mryn (the text of ed. Zhitomir - 'mr is valueless; ed. Venice has '"l).

4:5.I.B: It is unclear what the law is but it is not "that geneological searches are required." This section (A-D) is cited to prove that public officials and charity-collectors are of the select and therefore inquiry into their family is unnecessary as stated in the Mishnah (D). Further, since A-D is not topically related to our Mishnah, I would omit underlining in B.

4:6.I.I: In regard to her son makes no sense given your [= PM] interpretation. If you accept PM's interpretation, you must also accept his emendation: ...an impaired priestly woman [not born so, but became so via marriage with the] priesthood.

4:6.IV.H: Your interpretation is apparently wrong, since what you say would probably appear as 'd stkns lqdwst ysr'l kshy' btwlh or some such. Furthermore, btwlym does not mean virgin, but virginity. Therefore, I'd stay with PM and QE to wit: "The requirement is that her [age of] virginity [= three years] occur within the sanctity of Israel.

4:11.H-J: Changes follow Albeck which interpretation is substantially that of Rashi followed by QE and PM. On the other hand, your interpretation of ylmd and tlmd as piel is the reading of Ms. Kaufmann and Ms. Paris of the Mishnah. It is also accepted by Tosaphot ad loc. who translate soferim as "students."

4:11.III.A: He is carried [to the grave] in the bosom. And he may be buried by a single woman and two men...

For this change and that of II B see BT 80b and Semahot 3:2.

Chapter 8

YERUSHALMI BABA MESIA

Michael Chernick

1:1,II.B: Though Pene Moshe tried to relate this material to the surrounding discussion, most other commentators have treated it as an independent unit situated in this passage because it raises the question of whether an oath may be administered to a suspect individual. In M. and T., the parties present claims which appear untrue, given the situation. In M. both parties possess a garment, yet both claim they own all of it. In T. witnesses cast doubt on the debtor's veracity.

1:5, IV.C: It is possible to read R. Yose's statement as a question: "Does the Mishnah make the same statement?" That is, does B.M. 1:5 support the idea that an unpaid ketubah maintains the marital relationship in regard to finances? After all, the Mishnah grants the woman her finds even if her ketubah is not fully paid. This implies that divorce severed all financial relations between her ex-husband and herself. R. Hoshaiah responds that B.M. 1:5, which deals with a woman's finds, is consonant with the principle of the continued financial responsibility of the ex-husband. It merely clarifies that though the ex-husband must support his ex-wife as if he were married until he pays the ketubah, she need not cede her finds to him as if she were still married.

1:6, I.A: PM's revision receives added weight from B.B.M. 13a, which he cites. There the preferred reading is attributed to Samuel. Also, the continuation of the passage in Y. is paralleled almost exactly at B.B.M. 13a. If Samuel was indeed the author of this tradition at I.A, the question of contradictions within Samuel's views raised at I.C is more readily understandable. PM's connection of I to II is also strengthened in view of the above.

1:8, III.A: R. Jeremiah said in the name of Rab: "A codicil [receipt of payment] which is found in the possession of the creditor [along with the bond, see M1:8L], in the handwriting of the creditor, is invalid. For I say that the creditor was merely fooling inadvertently with his bonds." See B.B.M. 20a. Also possible: "... the creditor was in error regarding his bonds [and connected a codicil indicating payment to the wrong bond]." See B. Keritot 19a.

In regard to Neusner's comment at the end of B.M. 1:8, units D-E are related to both B. and C. B expresses that a codicil in the creditor's writing is invalid. C expresses that unless the creditor himself presents a receipt in the debtor's writing, the codicil is invalid. D-E then indicate that if a "bond among his bonds" was found which indicated that the debtor had paid, then the debt would be considered paid. The "bond among his bonds" is not specific and may mean a bond in the creditor's possession. If so, "how shall we interpret M. in light of B-C, or B-C in light of M.?" (=F). R. Yose b. Bun answers at G.: M. is a special case. A will, unlike a bond, would be valid even if it included a written statement by the creditor that the debtor had paid his debt. Rab (B) and Samuel (C), who would reject such a codicil in a bond, accept it here because "a person will not act in such a way as to injure his will." See Y Shebu'ot 7:7. There the text is: "R. Yose b. Bun said, 'Interpret it (M.), in accordance with everyone's opinion, as applicable to a will.'" "Everyone" refers to the opinions of Rab and Samuel.

2:2, I.E: R. Jacob David of Slutzk suggests that "placement" in a public place is always suspect and, therefore, is never regarded as an identifying mark. See comments of RIDBZ ad loc.

2:2, II.F-G: PM's understanding of this section is unconvincing, while the comments of R. Joshua Eisik Shapiro in No'am Yerushalmi and those of Z. W. Rabinowitz in Sha'are torat Erez-Israel are superior. They both hold that R. Yohanan's referent is T. B.M. 2:2, "... and one who finds an object in a public road or in a large highway (piazza), the objects are his because the owners have despaired (of retrieving them)." This tradition is attributed to R. Simeon b. Elazar. R. Isaac b. Tabelai responded on the basis of R. Simeon b. Elazar;s tradition in M., and R. Yohanan on the basis of R. Simeon b. Elazar's T. tradition (=II.E). All of pericope II, then, is based on two T. traditions of R. Simeon b. Elazar.

2:4, F-Y.'s text is: "[If] one found [an object] in a pile [of debris] or in an old wall, these things are his because I say they belonged to the Amorites [i.e., they no longer have owners]."

2:4, II.G-H: Neusner combines the text of T. and Y. Y.'s text is: "If he found [an object] between the boards [of the house threshold], from the door-jamb and inward is considered inside [the house, and the object belongs to the householder]. If [the object is found] from the door-jamb and outward, it is considered outside [the house, and belongs to the finder]."

2:4, III.A: While PM makes Y.'s material dependent on T. B.M. 2:1-2, this is in order to make Y. conform to B.B.M. 26a. This is not necessary. See the strictures of R. Aryeh Leib Yellin in Yefeh 'Enaim, B.B.M. 26a.

R. Jeremiah simply meant that the case of an inn might be a point of contention from the standpoint of the Mishnah. The law governing a rented house is clear, but the law governing an inn may not be the same even though space is rented in it. This is because of the impermanent nature of the rental. Because the inn is basically private property supervised by its owner, the traveler does not necessarily despair of retrieving his lost goods. On the other hand, the transience of the clientele at an inn means that many people pass through it. This increases the likelihood of theft and, with it, "despair."

A courtyard, however, is totally unlike a rented house. Even though it belongs to the householder, others come there. Because they may lose things there, and because it is highly supervised, they do not "despair." This is so even in the case of a rented courtyard.

R. Yose demurred. A rented courtyard may be private property, but this status is mitigated because others use it. Hence, one might argue as to whether the renter must announce objects found there or whether he may keep them. On the other hand, all agree that an inn is a public place which engenders "despair of retrieval." Hence, the finder owns the object found in an inn.

Unit III may not be out of place at all. Rather, it investigates possible extensions of the "rented house" case.

2:5, I: The Mishnah is interesting because it includes a fragment of halakhic midrash: cf. Sifre Deut. 224. The translation conforms to typical halakhic midrash usage.

2:5, I.A: PM, Yefeh 'Enaim, and Sh'are Torat Erez-Israel understand R. Elazar's statement as it is understood at B.B.M. 26b. Hence, they would translate thus: "... it also means to state that if money is found on the stool itself, it belongs to him [the finder]; if it is found on the counter, it belongs to him [the finder]."

2:5, I.D: Neusner inserts T. Y. includes only "relatives and neighbors."

2:9, I.Q: Y.'s text is: "And just as you specify these rules in regard to one who finds [an object], so these rules apply to one who is a bailee."

2:10, I-J: The rule is apparently based on the repetition of the word "return" in the biblical text. This repetition is translated as "surely."

2:10, L: "The rate paid to an unemployed worker" gives the impression of the society paying a fixed rate of unemployment compensation. This was not the case. Rather, an employer who, having hired workers, could not use them, had to compensate them if they could not get equally lucrative work as a result of honoring their commitment to him. Similarly, if a worker who was unemployed worked at a less lucrative labor than his/her normal work in order to gain sustenance, s/he was considered a "po'el batel," unemployed worker. Compensation to a professional finder for time lost at work was according to the normal payments to a "po'el batel" who worked as a recoverer of lost objects.

2:10, V-Y: See my comment on B.M. 2:10, I-J. Here the word "help" is repeated.

3:2, I.G: This section of T. B.M. 3:1 is not in the Y. texts before us. Prof. Neusner has reconstructed this passage on the basis of Y. Ketubot 9:4, where it is found.

3:3, J: Y.'s Mishnah does not have this clause in the Leiden MS or in the Venice or Vilna editions.

3:5, II.A: PM's comments, which serve as the basis of the translation here, read into Oshaiah's statement concerns and opinions which are difficult to find in the original formulation of that statement. Oshaiah seems to have commented on R. Judah's opinion alone, as follows: "[R. Judah's opinion at B.M. 3:5, R-S] applies when the seller did not say [specifically], 'I am supplying refined oil to you throughout the year.' If, however, he did say this, then he must supply [the full amount] of refined oil [without reduction for less even according to R. Judah]."

3:8, I.A-D: The Hebrew term zerurim usually means wrapped in a cloth or tied up in a pouch. The cloth or pouch would then be sealed with a wax or clay seal which would show whether the wrapping of cloth or the pouch had been opened. Jeremiah asks whether the wrapped coins referred to at 3:8B are considered wrapped only if they possess a seal, or whether simply bundling them is sufficient to prohibit their use.

3:9, I.D: R. Oshaiah's comment refers back to section I.B, "The law follows Aqiba even though the House of Hillel contests his view." Thus, the Hillelite position would reject Aqiba's view in a case where there were no witnesses and demand that the bailee pay according to the object's value at the time the bailee accepted responsibility for it

(PM). If, however, there were witnesses, even the House of Hillel would accept Aqiba's view according to Oshaiah.

4:1, II: PM's assumptions about the text, derived from material in B.T., lead to reading this section as a question, "Shall we learn that gold is a commodity from the case of R. Hiyya's daughter?" Y., however, may not share these assumptions, and it is just as reasonable to read section I.I as a statement: "We learn from the case of R. Hiyya's daughter [that the collection of debts in this manner is permissible and does not constitute interest-taking]." This is supported by sections I.J-K.

4:1, I.L: The implication of this passage is that weights of gold which are lent may be returned to the creditor in equal measure, but coin must be returned only to the exact amount of the loan. If the coin has increased or decreased in value, only the amount equal to the loan is returned, otherwise problems related to interest-taking arise. Qarat is probably carat, a gold weight, rather than a coin. Laqan is, most likely, a coin. At issue, then, is the difference between lending an object or goods and lending "value"/money. The latter raises issues of ribbit, interest.

4:1, II.H-K: This passage is best understood in light of Y. Kiddushin. There the opening pericope of Ketubot 7:8 is viewed as a challenge to Samuel's position. Samuel held that if party A presents damaged goods in a trade-off, he must prove that they were whole when he acquired his portion in the trade. In other cases, however, the law is that the party claiming damages must prove his claim before he will be paid.

Against this, at Ket. 7:8 we have a case where a husband demands a return of his kiddushin (marriage) payment because of an "acquisition in error" due to blemishes on his betrothed. In that case it is the bride's father who must prove that the woman was unblemished even though this is not a case of barter/trade-off.

The case of R. Huna, Phinehas, and Hezekiah before R. Yose is a separate, though conceptually related, incident. In that case the second section of Ket. 7:8 is adduced as proof for Samuel's view. Since the husband must bring proof for his own claim of an "acquisition in error" in order to withhold payment of the marriage contract, Samuel is correct in demanding that the owner of the damaged ass must prove that it was whole at the time of trade to retain his claim.

R. Yose responded that Ket. 7:8 provides no support for Samuel, even if we would consider kiddushin a form of barter. Samuel would agree that, had the ass been drawn into the cow-owner's possession, the cow-owner would have had to prove that the ass was damaged before he acquired it. So, too, Ket. 7:8, because the woman having been married, the ass's having been fully acquired by the cow-owner.

In sum, Ket. 7:8 provides no information about Samuel's case. Kiddushin (marriage) is not barter, and even if it were, Ket. 7:8 deals with a case of full acquisition while Samuel's case does not.

4:2, III.D: See Sh'are Torath Erez-Israel, p. 487, which supplies the following text based on Or Zaru'a: "If he retracts, he retracts. This is applicable to one who is rich, but not to a poor man [in which case the offer of a gift] becomes a vow.": In light of this version, III.D connects more easily to III.E.

4:3, I.A-B: Neusner's comments reflect PM. Alternatively, Rab and R. Yohanan may be arguing about whether one-sixth overcharge is the only measure of fraud or whether lesser amounts would also qualify, in some or all cases, as fraud. According to R. Yohanan, it is possible that any overcharge is fraudulent and a one-sixth overcharge is only an example, not a definition. Thus, the last statement of Rab would connect easily to that which precedes, as follows: "Rab says, 'This is an exact measure [of over-reaching].' R. Yohanan says, "This is not an exact measure [of overreaching].' Rab says, '[There is a case in which one-sixth is not a measure of fraudulent overreaching:] One who does business on condition that he shall not be overcharged [any amount], such a one has a claim of overcharging [for any amount].'"

See Yefeh 'Enaim, B.B.M. 49a.

4:3, II.A: R. Levi's teaching as reconstructed in the translation is again PM's understanding of the material, and, again, PM seems weak. Following in the line of comment above, Levi's view would be part of unit I, the purpose of which was to set the measure of criminal overreaching. Levi now states that overcharge of even a perutah, whether it represents a sixth or not, is retrievable because it is criminal overreaching.

Further, rather than considering the repetition of the phrase "and overreaching is a perutah" (Heb.: we-ha'ona'ah perutah) in the passage a question (so PM) which leads to a baraita, it seems reasonable to amend this phrase to "and an admission in a civil case is [measured] at a perutah" (Heb.: we'hahoda'ah perutah ("overreaching is a perutah") without repetition.

II.B. Rabbi's teaching should be regarded as a separate unit which deals with B.M. 4:3, O-Q.

4:3, III.B-I: Unit III, C-D represents a question about III.B, thus: "R. Jacob b. Idi, R. Abbahu in the name of R. Yohanan say, 'Just as the transaction is null for one party, it is null for the other [in the case at A].' [But how can that be since] it is taught elsewhere: 'There are four situations for those who sell: 1) If one has sold good wheat and it is found bad, the purchaser may retract [but not the seller]; 2) If one sold bad wheat and it is found good, the seller may retract [but not the purchaser]...' R. Yose b. Bun said, 'This case [at A] accords with that teaching which states, "He who does business with words, they do not subject him to the curse, 'He who punished, etc.'"....'" That is, since the transaction was incomplete, either party may withdraw. The cases at B.B. 5:6 are cases of completed sales.

4:4, I.E: Unit I.A-D discusses the weight requirements which render coin legal or illegal for circulation. So, a sela' may circulate as a sela' until it is equivalent in weight to a sheqel. At that point it must be removed from circulation lest it be used to fool people who might think it is a full sheqel when it is not. Note, even lessened weight caused by wear does not, of itself, invalidate the coin. Hence, its minted value is significant independent of its weight.

I.E may be understood in the context of I.A-D. Thus, concerns about fair weight and the mint value of coinage obtain here, too. Therefore, Y. says: "If the coin could be circulated in a sela' in unminted form [i.e., by weight], but only as a sheqel in terms of minted coinage [i.e., the coin looks like the minted sheqel], or if it could be circulated as a sheqel in unminted form [i.e., by weight], but it could also circulate as a sela' in terms of minted coinage [i.e., it looks like the minted sela'], [the one who possesses it] owns the [value according to] the form of the minted coin."

The minted form of the coin determines its value in the marketplace more than its actual weight, a position consonant with I.A-D and the Mishnah's teaching.

4:4, I.L: Y.'s text has "silver coins" in place of "copper coins." The rule at I.K obtains because the mint value of denars and selas determines their worth, but at I.L the coins are sold by weight.

5:1, VII.F-J: Y.'s text is: "... A received a field from B for 10 kor of wheat, and B said to him, 'Give me one sela'.' [A] said to him, 'I don't have anything but one kor of wheat. Take it.' He [B] returned and bought from him [A] for 24. This is not usury proper, but it is deception for the purpose of usury."

In Y.'s version, all parties are involved in a basically usurious arrangement which, however, circumvents the legalities surrounding usury. A is given a field by B for 10 kor of wheat. On the basis of this loan relationship, B requests a sela'. A, unable to provide cash, provides a kor of wheat, in effect paying an extra kor to B. In return, B buys 24 selas worth of produce. Though these "favors" are not formally usury because they are not actual repayment of a debt, they are forbidden because they are circumventions which, nevertheless, lead to usury.

5:2, I.E: Y.'s text is: "... that when you sell it, you sell it only to me... ."

5:2, I.H-J: Y.'s text is: "... all the time the seller [=debtor] uses the usufruct, it is permitted; all the time the buyer [=creditor] makes uses of the usufruct, it is prohibited."

5:2, I.N: Y.'s text is: "... Thus was the practice of Boethus b. Zonin on the instruction of the Sages." I.O-P Y. reads: They said to him, "From that [case] there is proof? He [Boethus b. Zonin] was a seller using usufruct!"

5:2, II.A: Y.'s text of the Mishnah is: "The year mentioned in the Torah regarding a walled city (Lev. 25:29), behold this is like usury, but it isn't usury."

5:3, II.T-V: In Y. the text is: "Y... when he sells he should not sell both together [produce purchased in partnership together with privately purchased produce], but he should sell this first and that last."

5:3, III.A: Y.'s text is: "One is bringing produce from a place where it is cheap to a place where it is expensive. He said to his fellow, 'Give them to me, and I shall give to you according to the way you give them at place X [i.e., at the more expensive market]. If the donor is responsible [in case of loss], [the arrangement] is prohibited, but [if] the purchaser [is responsible for loss], it is permitted.'" This version appears to be highly corrupted. See PM and Sh'are Torath Erez-Israel, p. 490.

5:3, III.R: This unit must be read in connection with Huna's statement at III.N even though discussion of III.N has intervened.

5:4, I.I-K: Y.'s text is: "More than that [amount of time] the portion of the householder and the assessment in his responsibility, all in accordance with local custom."

5:4, II.A-C: Y.'s text is: "In a place where they are accustomed to pay [the investment agent] for the carrying of the money [used for investment], they pay; [for the carrying of the] offspring of the beast, they pay; all in accordance with local custom."

III.B: T's text has: "18 months."

III. D: T's text has: "And if [the rancher] laid claim on him [for his share] during the stated [agreed upon] time, his fellow [the owner of the animals sent out for rearing] may demur."

III.E: Y.'s text is: "The care [given] for one year is not the same as [that given] for two years."

5:5, II.E-G: PM's comments on II.E-G are persuasive because they indicate a contradiction within the framework of M., which accords with the Y. formula "there ... here...." Yet, they are also problematic because they propose that the arrangement described at 5:5 A-B is permissible when the recipient of the flocks receives no portion of the profits. This violates the plain sense of 5:5 A-B which declares the arrangement prohibited and renders the phrase "paid bailee" incomprehensible, since the recipient of the flocks, according to PM, is not paid either a salary or a portion of the profits.

In view of these problems, it is unlikely that R. Jeremiah's comment at II.E refers to B.M. 5:5 A-B and is a transfer from some other locus (see Z. Frankel, Mabo Ha-yerushalmi, pp. 39 a-b). II.F refers to a Tannaitic source other than B.M. 5:5 in which a paid bailee is responsible for all accidental losses but is, nevertheless, permitted to enter into such an arrangement. The case of ass-drivers at 5:3 III is a possible point of reference; see RIDbZ' comments ad loc. In that case, R. Jeremiah holds that the ass-drivers are responsible for all losses.

Originally R. Jeremiah's question may have been a gemara on the baraita which discusses the case of ass-drivers at 5:3 II. It was transferred to 5:5 as part of a unit of questions by R. Jeremiah about the relationship of B.M. 5:5 to other tannaitic sources.

5:5, III: This unit appears to illustrate a contradiction between Mishnaic law at 5:5 and the biblical law at Lev. 25:35-36. The first part of Rabbi's question is not directed at B.M. 5:5, and his problems are not solved here. See, however, B.B.M. 71a.

5:5, V.D-G: R. Yose says, "[If] an Israelite borrowed from a gentile who subsequently converted, whether he settled them [the interests] on him [the Israelite] as a loan [i.e., along with the principal] or not prior to his conversion, he [the convert] may collect both principal and interest. If [he organized the loan so it would include the interest] after his conversion, he may collect the principal but not the interest."

By organizing the loan so that it includes both principal and interest, one circumvents the prohibition of usury. R. Yose indicates that whether or not this circumvention was used, if the Jew contracted it prior to the gentile lender's conversion, the convert may still collect the entire debt. If the debt was contracted after the gentile converted, then, as a Jew, he may collect only the principal from another Jew. Regarding or claiming the interest as part of the principal is not effective or permitted in allowing collection of the interest.

Y.'s test is: "[A] An Israelite who borrows from a gentile, or [B] a gentile who borrows from an Israelite and [the gentile] converts, whether one [of the lenders] included the interest in the principle before or after the conversion, he may collect the principal, but not the interest. [C] But if a gentile borrowed from an Israelite and [subsequently] converted, if prior to the conversion the interest was settled on him [as part of the principal], [the Israelite] may collect the principal and interest. Once [the gentile] has been converted, [the Israelite creditor] may collect the principal, but not the interest."

Bar Kappara's and R. Jacob b. Aha's comments relate to the case of an Israelite who borrows from a gentile, i.e., to case B in Y.'s text.

5:6, III.E: The full pericope indicates that a bargain may be struck for grain stacked on the threshing floor. This implies that such a deal may be made even though the grain lacked several stages of its processing.

5:6, IV.A: Alternatively, Abba b. Zamina gave a denar to the baker and bought bread throughout the year according to the season's cheapest price.

5:6, IV.G: PM's treatment of this baraita and its use in the passage at hand is highly problematic.

First, it is not common to quote directly material "placed in [a personal collection] of Mishnah." Second, the passage as it appears in Y. does not fit the case. PM would not only have us include the latter half of the baraita as found in T. but also revise its conclusion "permissible" to "prohibited."

More simply, this baraita appears to be a Tannaitic proof-text for Rab's position at IV.B, thus:

A. Abba b. Zamina gave a dinar to the baker [as a loan] and received bread throughout the year at the cheapest price.

B. Rab objected to this.

C. And so it is taught: [If] one owes money to another and [the creditor] came to claim his debt from him at the threshing floor, if the [debtor] said to him, "Consider the debt [payable in grain] according to the present market [price], and I will provide you [with grain at that price] throughout the year," this is prohibited....

Other material has intervened between Rab's opinion and its support baraita.

5:6, IV.C-G: The report should end, I believe, at "he went out and placed Rabbi's decision in his Mishnah." The passage should then continue with Rab's comments at H. G, as noted, refers to Rab at B.

5:6, V.C: Y.'s text is: "Bringing close profit and distancing loss, this is the way of the wicked. Bringing close loss and distancing profit, this is the way of the righteous. Near to this or that [i.e., profit or loss], or distant from this or that, this is [the way of] everybody."

6:1, IV.J: This is most likely a question because of the introduction 'ad kedun. Hence,

"I. R. Illa said: 'Only up to his wages.'

"J. Only up to his wage for the day or only up to his way for the hour?"

That is, if the work needed can be done in a few hours, can the employer take away up to a day's pay from the worker or only several hours' wages to pay the worker's replacement?

6:3, III.A-F: This appears to be an independent unit loosely attached to III.A-B, but not necessarily a comment on III.A-B. Thus, Abbahu quotes R. Yose b. Haninah to the effect that if the ass was seized in order to carry on a shortcut, then the one who rented out the ass need not supply another one. If, however, the ass was seized to carry on a normal route, i.e., for long-term service, then the one who rented it out must supply another one.

The common thread between R. Simeon b. Elazar and Abbahu-Yose b. Haninah is the degree of trouble the renter must endure in order to have a claim on a replacement. R. Simeon indicates that if the royal service takes the ass on the road it was going, the one who rents it out need not supply another. On the other hand, royal service which takes the ass out of the path chosen by the renter allows the renter to demand another ass from the supplier.

Units III.E-F represent the descriptive gemara which defines R. Simeon b. Elazar's position.

Though Jastrow (p. 980) emends Y.'s text at III.D to "in a basilica, forum," I believe that this is unwarranted since it does not effectively convey the opposite of compendaria, a shortcut. Silke is a long route, see 'Aruk Completum, ed. Kohut, s.v. silke, VI:64.

6:4, II-III: Y.'s text is: "How much must one add to its burden for him to be liable? Sumkhos says in the name of R. Meir. 'A seah for a camel and three qabs for an ass. A qab for a porter and three seahs for a wagon. And a ship -- according to what it is (i.e., according to its dimensions).'

"A caravan on which a band of robbers fell -- they reckon [for paying ransom] according to money [i.e., proportionate to the wealth of each person in the caravan]. [If] they sent a lookout before them, they reckon [the lookout's fee] according to souls [i.e., each one pays equally for this protection]. They may not deviate from the normal custom of caravans.

"A ship which was hit by a gale and they lightened its burden, they figure according to cargo or according to wealth, but not according to souls. [Thus, those with more property on board or wealth lose more. Someone without either has no demands made of him for his rescue.] But one who hires a wagon or ship from his fellow, they figure according to cargo and souls, but not according to wealth.

"A caravan on which robbers fell and one [of the party] arose and saved [the merchandise] from their hand -- he has saved it for the common fund. If they gave him permission, he has saved it for himself [and it belongs to him].

"Ass-drivers on whom robbers fell, and one arose and saved [their merchandise] from their hand -- he has saved it for the common fund. If he stipulated with them in court, he has saved it for himself.

"Partners who tax farmers released [from taxes] -- they have released to the common fund. But if they said, 'We have remitted for so-and-so's sake,' whatever they have remitted, they have remitted to him [alone].

"Collectors' and publicans' penance is hard [because they cannot return their ill-gotten gain to the original owners due to the great numbers of people they take from]. They should return [what they can] to those they recognized. As regards [the funds of] those they do not know, they should make of them [donations] to public needs."

Most of II and III has no relation to M. This may be a full quotation of Y.'s "Tosefta" which included Sumkhos's remarks. The entire passage -- arranged by association -- appears without editorial deletion of material unnecessary to the comprehension or extension of M. This is a common literary phenomenon in Talmuds.

7:5, I: Y.'s text is: "Anything the like of which has arrived [at the stage of] obligation to tithes or [if] another prohibition affects it, if [the employer] hired him [the worker] without specifying terms, he should redeem [the prohibition] and feed [the worker or] tithe and feed [the worker]. If he specified terms [of eating], behold, this one [the worker] eats. And anything the like of which has not arrived [at the stage of] obligation to tithes or prohibition [by virtue of] another prohibition, if one hired him [the worker] without specifying terms, [the worker] should not eat. If he specified [terms of eating], he may eat.

7:7, I.C: T. holds that food, clothing, and sexual rights are "monetary matters" and, as such, are subject to stipulation even against that which is written in the Torah. "Monetary matter" should be understood as a phrase for "that which is subject to waiver" by personal choice.

8:3, I.D: This section is translated in Neusner's text according to PM. Since it does not seem to be a specific case or ma^{c}aseh, the sudden introduction of "the old lady" is both jarring and unlikely. I would translate the phrase as an Aramic statement meaning "Take it beforehand." I.C-E would then read as follows:

C. "[If he said,] 'Lend me your cow for after ten days [during which ten-day period the cow owner loaned himself to the borrower],'

D. "[the lender] said to him, 'Take it beforehand.'

E. "[If] it died, it died under the indenture of the latter period. [Even though the cow was taken into the borrower's domain during the time its owner was 'on loan,' its indenture begins afterward. Therefore, the borrower must pay for the loss.]"

See Gilyon Ephraim, ad loc.

8:5, I.C: Traditional commentators have viewed R. Yohanan and R. Huna as disputants. This occurred because they read the phrase "between them" in R. Yosé b. Hanina's statement as a reference to those two sages'opinions which preceded R. Yosé's remarks.

It is clear, however, that R. Huna's statement does not answer R. Yohanan's question unless we add considerable editorialization. Moreover, R. Huna, a third- or fifth-generation amora, is not a contemporary of Yohanan (second generation). R. Yosé b. Hanina's comment can, without additions, serve as a response to R. Yohanan's question, and Yosé b. Hanina is Yohanan's contemporary. I would therefore render this passage as follows:

I.A. "R. Yohanan raised the question, 'If the trees thrived, what is their status [in law?]'

B. R. Huna said, 'If they were moved by the flood with their [original] earth clumps, R. Yosé b. Hanina says, "The orlah years [first three of fruit production] are shared between them."'"

Alternatively, I.B is a misplaced comment separating I.A from the response at I.C.

B. "R. Huna says, '[The Mishnah deals] with the flood having moved them with their clods. [Hence they share.]"

This comment is an explanation of the ruling at B.M. 8:55 and is independent of I.A and C. It is incorrectly interpolated between them. Then:

C. "R. Yosé b. Haninah [answering R. Yohanan's question] says, 'The years of orlah are [shared] between them.'"

See Rabin's formulation of Resh Laqish's statement at B.B.M. 101a which supports our first reading.

8:6, I.A: Y.'s text is: "About all these which they said...."

8:6, I.D-E: Y.'s text is" "As far as an olive-press is concerned [there may not be an eviction] throughout the season of olive pressing. As far as a wine-press is concerned [there may not be an eviction] throughout the time of wine-pressing."

8:9, I.A: Literally: "R. Simeon b. Laqish said, '[It is a case] in which he [the landlord] stood him [the renter] by it [and leased the house to him].'"

9:1, II: "One who rents a field from his fellow must harvest, make sheaves, thresh, winnow and sift. The digger, the measurer, the bailiff, city guards, and the town clerks collect from the common fund [i.e., each townsperson pays equally because these are public servants]. The well-digger, bathmaster, and the barber when they come because of the tenant-farmer, they collect [their fee] from the tenant-farmer. When they come because of the householder, they collect from the householder [because these are private businessmen]."

9:6, I.A-C: Y.'s text is: "'One who leases a field from an Israelite tithes [the produce] and gives him [the one who grants the lease produce which has been tithed],' the words of R. Meir. And sages say, 'Whether [he gives] of that [of grain which was stipulated] or from that field, he separates the heave-offering and gives him [produce still requiring separation of tithes]. But [if he gives] from another field [besides the leased one] or from another kind [of grain than the stipulated kind], he tithes and gives it to him [tithed].' R. Meir says, "Even from that field and from that kind one should separate the heave-offering and give him [untithed produce], but from another field or another kind, he need not tithe and give it to him.'"

9:8, I.C-D: Alternatively: "Flax exhausts the land for three years. And you may say: Thus explained R. Menahem, brother of R. Gurion before R. La, 'It is better to sow flax after flax than [to sow] barley after barley.'"

Flax after flax is less wearing for a field than continuous planting of grain. Therefore, if the owner leased the field for flax, he may not want it sown in wheat or barley because he intends to sow wheat or barley the year after, or did so the year before.

9:9: Y.'s Mishnah places E-G first followed by A-D. Also, zuz is replaced by dinar.

9:12, I.K-M: This passage is a typical halakic midrash. The Hebrew phrase "hbl thbl" (Ex. 22, 25), "if you shall surely take a pledge," is regarded as a repetitive phrase because of the use of the root hbl twice. The midrashist interprets each use of the root to derive another case in which one is required to fulfill the last clause of the verse, "thou shalt restore it to him...." The first use of hbl in the infinitive thus teaches that one who takes a pledge via the court's agent returns it daily. The second use of the root in the second person singular imperfect (thbl) teaches that even if one violated the law and personally exacted a pladge, he is not free of the law's latter clause requiring the pledge's daily return. So, essentially, PM; cf. B.B.M. 31b. which counters the tradition of Palestine. That baraita taught that one may take a pledge outside of court. According to this interpretation, hbl teaches the case of a pledge taken in court; thbl teaches that a pledge may be taken without the court's agency. Indeed, if the baraita at B.B.M. 31a based on Ex. 22:25 were lifted from its context, that is what it would most likely mean.

9:13, I.F: Y.'s text is: "... since he comes to her, he gives her a bad name."

10:1, IV.F-I: Y.'s text is: "[If] one's ruin was adjoining the wall of his fellow's courtyard, he [the courtyard owner] shall not say to him, 'I will rebuild with you [from] my courtyard wall and upward.' Rather he should rebuild from below [all the way] up. If [the courtyardp] was situated on ditches or on caves, [the courtyard owner] is not obligated [to share the cost of the wall]."

10:3, I.D-G: "If one's ruined building was adjacent to the ruined building of another, and the latter rose up and built it without his [the first ruin-owner's] permission, behold, this [the builder] tallies his expenses at the cost [at the time] he built, and [the ruin owner] gives him his expenses.

Gilyon Ephraim explains: "If one of the ruin owners (A) wants to rebuild and to do so he must utilize part of the adjoining ruin, he cannot force the other ruin-owner (B) to rebuild. If subsequently B decides to utilize the part of the ruin rebuilt by A, he must repay A for A's expenses on his part of the ruin. From this Y. deduces that B cannot be forced to rebuild in order to provide A with cover on the side where their ruins adjoin. A may take on this project alone and when B shall benefit from it, he will have to pay."

10:5, I: Y.'s text is: "One may unload his manure at the door of his courtyard in the public domain [if this is in order] to remove it immediately. But [if] to have it remain there, [this is] prohibited. [If] someone comes and is injured, lo, he is liable. R. Judah said, 'At the season of manure, one may unload his manure at the door of his courtyard in the public domain so that it will be pulverized by the feet of man and beast for thirty days. For it was on this condition that Joshua parceled out the land to Israel.'

"One may unload his dirt at the door of his courtyard in the public domain [in order] to keep it for immediate elevation onto a layer [of a wall]. [If] to leave it there [it is] prohibited. [If] another comes and is injured by it, he is liable.

"One should not mix mortar on this side [i.e., in a place other than the site of building], but rather at the place he is building.

"One may unload his stones at the door of his courtyard in the public domain [if he intends] to remove them immediately, [but if] to leave them, [it is] prohibited. [If] another comes and is injured by them, he is liable.

"If the quarry-man gaves [stones] to the camel-driver, the camel-driver is liable [for damages caused by the stone]. [If] the camel driver [gave it] to a porter, the porter is liable. [If] it was mounted on a pedestal [Y.: bimos], and someone shakes it and it fell, the architect is liable.

"[If] the stone cutter gave over [stones] to a porter, and someone was injured whether by chips or by a stone, the stone cutter is liable. [If] the stone cutter [gave stones] to a porter, and someone was injured by chips, the stone cutter is liable. [If] by a stone, the porter is liable.

"[If] the stone was raised and set firmly in a wall, and [sometime later] it fell, [all are] exempt."

Chapter 9

YERUSHALMI SANHEDRIN

David Goldenberg

Foreword

The following notes to Professor Neusner's translation of PT Sanhedrin-Makkot were written originally as supplementary material to that translation. They grew out of a proofreading of the translation and were meant to provide the reader with a commentary to the PT text. One of my major objectives in this commentary was to give a sense of the difficulty, which often exists in PT, of establishing a correct understanding of the text. Thus, I may quote several different interpretations of the same passage.

Since B. Ratner's Ahawath Zion We-Jerusholaim does not cover Sanhedrin-Makkot, I felt it worthwhile to list quoted passages of these tractates in later literature. For these quotations I have used editiones principes or modern editions based on manuscripts where available. References to parallel passages in the rabbinic corpus have been noted, as have variants of a substantive nature found in the parallels and citations.

This description of the following notes obtains only for Sanhedrin up to ch. 2, hal. 2 (ed. V, 17d-20a). At that point it became clear to me that to continue in the same manner would take me well over the time period allotted by the publishers for the task of proofreading the translation. Consequently, from that point to the end of the Makkot, I only commented periodically -- where I felt the translation unclear or wrong. This procedure was also followed in regard to Qiddushin.

Notes

1:1.A: Property cases -- or "monetary cases" (see below, 1:1.I.O) or "non-capital" (so Danby) or "civil" (so Schwab).

1:1.B: Damages for ḥblwt -- but M of PT in ed. V has ḥwbwt, debts, a reading tantamount to hwd'wt whlw'wt (cases of indebtedness) which BT 2b excludes from the laws of the M. PM, which Neusner is here following, says ḥwbwt and ḥblwt are identical, but this is based on the "correctness" of BT ḥblwt. See further M. Schachter, The Babylonian and Jerusalem Mishnah [Hebrew] (Jerusalem, 1959) pp. 258-59, 335.

Does the reading ḥwbwt -- if it is not an error of the ed. V printer -- reflect the gaonic decision that cases of damages may be judged only in Israel (see Taubes, p. 9)? The Palestinian reading was ḥblwt (cf. our M cited in PT, below, 1:1 II A), but did a Babylonian version of the M (ḥwbwt) somehow find its way into PT?

1:1:E: And sages -- or "And the sages" = waḥkhmym (so Yalon in Albeck's edition of the Mishna). Similarly 1:1.VII.B,D et passim. See below on 1:2.X.DD.

1:1.I.A-C: Neusner is following the first of two interpretations put forward by PM. However, the conclusion drawn in C (that Num. 35:29 proves careful cross-examination for both capital and property cases) is not at all clear. In BT (2b-3a) this conclusion is drawn far more understandably, from Lev. 24:22: "You shall have one law."

This problem has led to various interpretations and emendations of A-C, (see Sivitz ad loc. [p. 310]; PM's second interpretation; YE ad loc.; STEY ad loc. [p. 508], et al.) none of which are satisfactory.

It should be noted that C-G is basically found also in T. Sheb. 3.8, Sifra 'Emor, pereq 20, p. 105 a-b (cf. Yalqut Lev. 658), Midrash Leqaḥ Tob to Num. 35:24, Vol. 2, p. 284 (and see Sifra Num. 160, p. 219, and Yalqut Num. 788). By comparing the sources it appears that our text presents a corrupt sequential discussion which, reconstructed, would have: 1) assumed that capital and non-capital cases are alike; 2) drawn the conclusion that careful cross-examination is, then, required for non-capital cases as well; 3) drawn the tentative conclusion that non-capital cases do require a court of twenty-three, and 4) rejected the last conclusion by providing a separate exegesis for non-capital cases proving the need for courts of three only.

In the parallel sources the starting point for the comparison between capital and non-capital cases is Lev. 24:22. This verse, then, must have been original to PT as well. (Cf. ŠQ ad loc.) (Notice how the phrase hyyty 'wmr basically depends on the verse quoted before it.) PT. San., therefore, opens by asking "Whence does he produce evidence from Scripture [that non-capital cases require a court of three]?" and answers the question by quoting a tannaitic tradition extant in the parallel sources mentioned above.

Our tannaitic citation compares capital and non-capital cases and concludes that non-capital cases also require courts of twenty-three but never tells us how it is known that capital cases require twenty-three judges. A scribe, thinking that the opening words "Whence does he..." asked that very question, changed Lev. 24:22 to Num. 35:29. Num. 35 provides the Scriptural proof for the law of twenty-three judges in tannaitic literature (M. San. 1.6, T. San. 3.7, Sifre Num. 160, p. 220). The choice of verse 29 was natural due to the similarity of language between it and Lev. 24:22. Indeed, it may have been this similarity which caused the change to the verse in Numbers.

1:1.I.A: Whence shall we -- lit. "Whence does he."

1:1.I.A-Q: Quotation marks are highly interpretive of the text, and, therefore, preference should be given to having the authority's name followed by a colon (or some such), leaving the end of the ipsissima verba as ambiguous as in the original text. Two examples: 1:1 I B-G are, according to Neusner's punctuation, all the words of R. Josiah. But how do we know that they are J's words which begin in B? In fact, from BT parallel 3b one can say with certainty only that J's words begin in E. Or: 1:1 I M-N Neusner has being spoken by one person, Rabbi's interlocutor. Perhaps N is Rabbi's answer to M.

1:1.I.D-O: Paralleled in BT 3b-4a and (excluding O) in Mekhilta RI, mšptym, 15 (p. 302). On O cf. T. San. 1:1.

1:1.I.N: Rather: "When the Scripture says, '...whom the judges shall condemn (yršy^{c}n)', what is written is '...whom the judges shall condemn (yršy^{c}wn).' Since there...." (Although senseless, this is meant to give a literal non-interpretative translation of the text which is also senseless.)

STEY emends to: "When the Scripture says '...whom the judges shall condemn,' it is not written yršy^{c} but yršy^{c}n" (assuming omission by homoioteleuton). This emended reading follows Midrash Hakhamim. Friedmann (ed. Mekhilta, p. 92, n. 36) understands the exegesis thus without emendation. The PT text E-N as it stands, however, is parallel to Mekhilta to 22.7 (H-R, p. 302 with variants and see their note to line 6). In fact, I. H. Weiss (ed. Mekhilta, p. 98, n. 9) claims that Mekhilta was the source here for PT. Cf. ML 143.

1:1.I.O end: Three -- the text reads "...monetary cases should be decided by a court of five judges. In this way the decision will be reached by twenty-three judges." This, being obviously corrupt, can be variously understood following BT 3b: To emend "twenty-three" to "three" (thus, Neusner following PM, QH, and Sivitz); to emend "five" to "forty-five" (ŠQ ad loc. and I. Lewy, Ein Wort über die "Mechilta des R. Simon," Breslau, 1889, p. 24, n.2); by homoioteleuton: "R. Abahu raised the question, 'Now in accord with Rabbi, monetary cases should be decided by five so that the decision be reached [by three. If so the Great Sanhedrin needs 141 so that their decision be reached by seventy-one and the Lesser Sanhedrin needs forty-five so that their decisions be reached] by twenty-three.'" (kdy šygmr bšišh...kdy šygmr bšlšh w^{c}śyrm).

1:1.I.P-Q: Death penalty -- this is problematic, since we are dealing here with non-capital cases, see PM ad loc. It would seem, however, that the exegesis here is either based upon that found in Sifre Num. 160, p. 220 (and parallels) where this same exegesis is used to explain the "three" of the twenty-three needed to judge capital cases (YE to 3b), or the exegesis of Hezekiah is that found in Sifre, in which case "five" (Q) must be emended to "three" (Krochmal, ad loc., p. 103a). Neusner's translation ("majority of two"), however, makes it clear that while in Sifre the parallel may (see ibid. Horovitz's note to line 3) be between witnesses and judges, here in PT it is between witnesses and a majority of judges. The minimum number of judges needed to reach a majority of two is four.

1:1.I.P: Majority -- see above on 1:1 I P-Q.

1:1.I.Q: One more (='ḥd) -- Ms. L and ed. V: "another" ('ḥr).

1:1.I.Q: Five -- see above on 1:1 I P-Q.

1:1.II.A-C: Neusner's (so too QH) translation of A is literal but it is difficult to see how the answer given (B-C) which is based upon Ex. 21:1 answers the question posed in A as it is translated. Therefore PM and RYDBZ understand A based on BT 2b, to wit, "Are not theft and damages included in 'monetary cases'?"

The answer (B-C) is precisely that of BT (mh hn qtny) i.e. "theft and damages" are indeed included in the general statement of "monetary cases" and are stated as particulars of it just as the simple meaning of the verses (kpšwṭh dqryy'); or "the sequence of the verses" [from pšṭ, "to stretch out, unfold," see the dictionaries and the usage in nhr' nhr' wpšṭyh, Ḥul. 18b, 57a, and in nhr' kpšṭyh lyzyl, Giṭ. 60b]; see also MM ad loc. bpšwṭ' dqryyh hyynw bkl hmšk hpršh and M. Gertner, "Terms of Scriptural Interpretation: A Study in Hebrew Semantics," Bulletin of the School of Oriental and African Studies, University of London, 25.1 (1962), p. 19) show a general statement in Ex. 21:1 followed by its particulars. See also Lieberman's note in Mekhilta RaSHBI, ed., Epstein-Malamed, p. 253 (to p. 158, 1.4) and M. Kasher, Torah Shelemah, vol. 17, p. 225.

1:1.II.D-F: The bracketed words follow PM (see Hidushei Hagahot no. 6 on Tur, hm 12) but exactly how that which preceded -- whether it be "verse" or not (see YE to 3b) -- is in accord with the position of R. Yose is unclear (but see below). On this section see Alon, Mehqarim BeToledot Yisrael, vol. 2, pp. 30-31.

Dyn twrh here has the meaning "correct," "true" (cf. BT San. 6a and see Meiri to 5a [p. 11]: hdyn hgmwr r'l dyn twrh; BT BM 30b šh^c mydw dynyhm ^c l dyn twrh wl' ^c bdw lpnym mšwrt hdyn; QH to 2b s.v. kl mqwm šyš 'mt 'yn mšpt: d'mt hyynw dyn twrh). The litigants wanted to accept the decision only if it be a correct one. R. Yose replied that ultimate truth is known only to God who will punish the truly guilty party and that the litigants must abide by his decision whether or not it be ultimately a correct one. Thus the connection between EX. 21:1 and R. Yose's story may be that the verse is understood as giving asuthority to man to judge even without his knowledge of "Truth." (This verse is commonly understood as referring to the judicial system, see Mekhilta, ad loc., p. 246; BT San. 7b; PT Mak. 2.7, 31d; BT Git. 88b et al.)

^c Itur cites D-F on p. 53b and F ("R. Akiba said to them"!) on p. 52c. E-F (or Sefer Hefes citing E-F) is cited in SMG, II, No. 107 (p. 189d) (cf. Tur, hm, 12); Meiri to 6a, (p. 16); and Responsa of R. Joseph Colon No. 80. (On the value of PT citations in the SMG and other Rishonim see Lieberman, YK pp. xxiii-xxiv). On sec. F see M. Konitz, Ben Yohai (Vienna, 1815), 6:80, 40b, s.v. byn tbyn.

1:1.II.G: Cited by Meiri to 7a (p. 18).

1:1.III.A-IV.J: Quoted in ŚK, hm, 25:30.

1:1.III.A: Forty years -- see Mantel, p. 316.

In the PT parallel (San. 7.2, 24a) the reading, instead of Simeon b. Shatah, is R. Simeon b. Yohai. Such is also the reading of our passage in SMG, II, 107 (p. 189d; correct Metibot, p. 130 accordingly and see above on II.D-F). See also Tur, hm, 12; Kontiz, 40a; Mantel, pp. 307-308, n.6; and Alon, Toledot HaYehudim BeEreș Yisrael, vol. 2, pp. 58, 78.

1:1.III.A-B: Cited and discussed in Kontiz, p. 40a. (where the reading is mwryn instead of mydwn. Konitz (pp. 40b-41a) shows that a reading bdyn found cited in the Tur (hm 12, cf. ŚK, hm, 3:10) may be a misunderstanding and may not exist as a variant of PT. B is cited in SMG ibid. On the historical context of B see HZL, pp. 540-541, n. 46.

1:1.IV.A-B: Parallel in PT Ber. 7.1, 11a. See AZVY ad loc. and PT Ber. ed. Luncz where readings without the word "even" are cited. B is cited by Metibot, p. 97, ^c Itur, p. 52b, Tos. San 2b, s.v. dbry hkl. Tos. Git. 32b, s.v. wrb nhmn, and Tos. Yeb. 46b-47a, s.v. mšpt (see AY to our text). A alone is paralleled in BT 3a.

1:1.IV.C-L: Quoted (omitting D-G) by ^c Itur, p. 52b, bottom, and Metibot, p. 97. ^c Itur, in turn, is cited (including C-J) by NY, San. la, s.v. 'y qblwk ^c lyyhw (cf. ŚK, hm, 25:30).

NY San. 11b, s.v. dswgyyn b^c lm' cites C-L. Meiri 6a, (p. 16) cites 1:1.IV.H-L. Greater Mordekhai, as quoted in Responsa of BH No. 40 cites H-K.

1:1.IV.C-H: In an attempt to bring this section in line with its BT parallel (6a) some (QH; ŚK, hm, 25:30 and see YE to BT 6a) have reversed the prodoses of F and G. Others (MP ad loc.) do not see E-G as paralleling BT and translate thus: (E) "[The above mentioned interpretation of M. Bekh. must be so, for otherwise] how shall we explain this statement [of M. Bekh.]? (F) If it is... (G) If it is...."

Perhaps the best explanation, however, is that offered by RYDBZ (ad loc.) who reads F and G as declarative statements. Thus, the problem introduced by E is that either the court's decision is irreversible (if the decision was based on reasoning) or the judge must compensate the wronged party (if the decision was an error in Torah law), but not both. This explanation coincides with BT and leaves our text unmolested. At any rate, read as declarative sentences, our passage agrees with PT Ket. 9.2, 33a and with Sefer Ha-ma^{c}aśim (Tarbiz, I.3, p. 10 [Taubes, p. 43]).

1:1.IV.D: Two -- a variant, "three" is cited in Mar'eh Maqom WeHagahot, by Z. Braun et al. (printed in the margin of PT ed. Krotoschin).

1:1.IV.H-J: Cited in ŚK, ḥm, 3:10 and RḤ to San. 6a.

1:1.IV.K-R: On the concept of God's court see Urbach ḤZL p. 157 (correct n. 70).

1:1.IV.K: Standing -- PT (Ms. L and ed. V) has the participle in plural while in MT it is in the singular; cf. II Chs. 18:18.

1:1.IV.L: Book -- lit., "Writing," i.e. the seal of God.

1:1.IV.M-Q: M is paralleled in BT San. 38b. M-Q is cited in Metibot, p. 97, and P-Q (in reverse order) is cited in Mordekhai as quoted in Responsa of BḤ, no. 40, where "family" replaces "court" in P.

1:1.IV.Q-R: Concerning you -- text (Ms. L and ed. V too) has "concerning him" contra MT. But the parallel in PT Ber. 9.5, 14 (ed. V mistakenly 13)b has "you." So too the other parallels. PT in YM: 'lyk.

Neusner's explanation ("That is...mercy") is based on PM. But PM here is senseless and the meaning is as Margulies explains (ed. Lev. R., 24:2, p. 552): "And the Lord" of I Kings 22:23 teaches us that all "And the Lord"s connote the Lord and His court, since in I Kings 22:19-23 a court is implied (see Frankel, ed. PT Ber., ad loc.; and Luncz, ed. PT Ber., ad loc.) PM's interpretation seems to be based on a reading no longer extant -- a reading underlying his comment to PT Ber. 9.5: "Wherever it is written 'Elohim' it connotes justice; wherever 'Lord' it connotes mercy" -- and found partially in our text Ms. L and ed. V: "Wherever it is stated 'the Lord Elohim' it connotes Him and His court." This variant apparently arose from the reading kl mqwm šn'mr h' wh'... which is found in many Mss of the parallels, see Marqulies and Theodore ed. Gen. R. p. 533.

1:1.IV.S-W: See Gen. R. 81.2 (p. 971) and parallels cited there. U-V is paralleled in PT Ber. 1.8, 3C and W is cited in Metibot, p. 97.

1:1.IV.W: The text reads: "'I, the Lord, who am first,' for I did not accept dominion...colleague. 'And with the last am the same,' for the the end..." The biblical text before us is a combination of Isa. 41:4 and 44:6.

1:1.V.A: To cause trouble -- myṭrwp -- "to protest, complain" (Levy, Jastrow); "to throw oneself at" (Kohut, ed. Arukh, 4.93a, s.v., ṭrp 7). STEY emends to mytrws. Some understand myṭrwp absolutely and ^{c}l beginning a new sentence: "R. Ami entered and taught..." (KL,GE).

1:1.V.A: Sat down -- kpp = to force "the litigants to accept the sentence" (Levy) or, "the law requiring three judges." NY, la, s.v. 'y qblwk ^{c}lyyhw, citing PT has kph (cf. PM and Krochmal, ad loc.).

The last sentence of A is cited in RH to San. 6a and RN(2) to San. 5a, s.v. 'y qblwk.

1:1.V.B-C: Cited in Greater Mordekhai as quoted in BḤ on Tur, ḥm, 3:9 and in Responsa of BḤ no. 40; Mishnah Lamelekh to MT Sanhedrin 2.11; Meiri 5a (p. 11); ᶜItur 81 (p. 51b); ŚK, ḥm, 3:10 and (with the last sentence of A) in RḤ to San. 6a.

1:1.V.B: R. Abbahu...Caesarea is paralleled in PT Nazir 7.1, 56a.

Gate -- mdrt (mrdt') = the "Slope Synagogue," i.e. built on a slope, or the "Revolution Synagogue" (Kohut, Arukh, 4.264b, s.v. knš; Levy, 3.33, s.v. mdr'; Jastrow, p. 838, s.v. mrdt'; QH). The word is not found in the citations of our passage in ᶜItur, BH, and Meiri. See Midrash Samuel, 7.6, ed. Buber, p. 68, n. 32.

1:1.V.B: [People] -- i.e., reading 'ynwn (so PM, MP, and the sources cited above quoting our passage). Ms. L and ed. V. read 'twn which Levy, s.v. ytyb, translates as: "Since you see that I sit as a judge and people come to me..."

1:1.V.D: The Great -- or "The Elder," see the Talmudic dictionaries and below on 1:2.III.N.

1:1.V.F: We say -- or, subjunctively, "Let us say."

R. Eleazar and -- I should rather translate: "R. Eleazar [the associate and disciple] of R. Yohanan" in order to bring out the force of lrby Yohanan.

1:1.V.H-Ja, L: Cited in ᶜItur 82 (p. 53 c-d).

1:1.V.I: On the technical term kyny mtnyt' see MLH, 441-444; especially 442 where our passage is treated. On this quote from the Tosefta see TR, ad. loc. (vol. 2, p. 268).

1:1.V.J: To till around my palm tree -- this translation follows QH which must be based on a different reading. The reading in our text (dyswq tḥwty ldyql') can only mean "to climb the palm tree [to pluck the fruit] in my stead," as PM, Jastrow, and Levy s.v. tḥwt.

1:1.V.K: Cited in Meiri to 7b (p. 20).

1:1.V.L: For his time -- I should prefer: "for [the time of his] testimony." See TR ad loc. (vol. 2, pp. 268-269).

1:1.VI.A: See TR ibid.

1:1.VI.A-B: This section refers back to the above-cited M. Bekh. 4.6 which says the following: If one takes payment to judge, his judgments are invalid; to testify, his testimony is invalid. If, however, the judge or witness was a priest and the litigant caused him to become impure in regard to eating terumah, i.e., through his acting as judge or witness in the case he was forced to become impure, the litigant pays for the priest's ḥulin food. This is not considered making payment to a judge or witness. Thus the Mishnah paraphased. Now our section says that such a case came before R. Iaaac who dealt with matters in line with the Mishnah. The disciples added that from the amount paid for ḥulin (which is more expensive than terumah) the priest remits to the litigant the amount he, the priest, would have paid anyway for terumah. (Lieberman in Tarbiz 2, pp. 239-240 and p. 380.)

1:1.VI.B: [This...follows] -- see ŠQ ad loc.

1:1.C-EEE: This is, for the most part, found in Tos. San. 1:2-9, and BT San. 6b. Sections are found elsewhere -- see YE ad loc., to which add ARNA 12 (p. 48) for sec. H. See also Finkelstein's notes to his ed. of Sifrei pp. 28-29, and Urbach, ḤZL, p. 552.

1:1.VI.C: [After judgment...] -- this follows QH but is not in the text. R. Eleazar is of the opinion that justice should be done and not a compromise ("arbitration") while R. Joshua b. Qorha holds the opposite view (VI M).

1:1.VI.G: The bracketed words follow QH whose explanation is based on Tos. and BT 6b (but see the Mss). Our text, however, simply says "As did Moses." Cf. ŠQ who points out that the Bible never records Moses having said these words.

1:1.VI.H: See ARNA 12 (p. 48) and Lev. R. 3.6 (p. 71).

1:1.VI.J: Ground it into wheat, baked it into bread and How is such a person to say a blessing? It is no blessing but a curse. This follows Tos. and BT 6b (cf. BT BQ 94a). But our text reads: "And he brought it to a baker" and "This one blesses but, in fact, he's really cursing."

1:1.VI.L: So also Tos. BT has the referent as Judah and not "the brothers of Joseph." (Gen. 37:26, "And Judah said to his brothers: 'What profit....'") See QH, ŠQ, and STEY pp. 508-509 for various explanations.

1:1.VI.M-P: The opposition "judgment of truth" and "peace" follows the reading of Tos. Our text twice follows MT literally with the opposition truth/judgment of peace and once follows Tos. BT avoids any problem by posing the opposition judgment/peace. Incidentally Zech. in Tos. Ms. Erfurt reads "Truth and judgment and peace" ('mt wmšpt wšlwm).

1:1.VI.Q: (Rabbi says) -- found in Tos., BT, and PT San 2.3, 20a.

1:1.VI.R-T: An amalgam of Tos. and PT. Our text reads: "Scripture credits him as if he has done charity with the innocent and charity with the guilty. Charity with the innocent, for he returns to him his money; and with the guilty, for he removes the stolen goods from his possession." This reading need not be emended. Our text takes it for granted that justice was done to both parties when the guilty was declared guilty and the innocent, innocent. Beyond that, however -- says the text -- charity (ṣedaqah) was also done to both.

1:1.VI.U: The reference to Deut. 1:17 follows PM and YM. QH prefers (see ŠQ) Dt. 16:18-19. Of course, the text has neither. (Note that the root špṭ occurs twice in Zech. 8:16 itself.)

1:1.VI.V: The bracketed interpretation follows PM, MP, QH according to which VI W ff. is the answer. Alternatively VI W is part of the question (P, YM).

1:1.VI.FF-GG: PT in YM reads: htgl^c hryb...ntgl^c hryb.

1:1.VI.W-GG: This follows Tos. PT has some different wording, e.g., (DD) "you (the judge) are not permitted to arbitrate."

1:1.VI.HH: Cited in Meiri 5b (p. 15).

[The judge to] make up his mind -- better: "Majority opinion." See Jastrow p. 351, s.v. hkr^{c}h and A. Sofer's note to Meiri ibid. (But in support of Neusner's rendering see Levy, I, 469, s.v. hkr^{c}h.)

Tosafot (BT San. 6a s.v. tysgy): "It is explained in PT that the reason of R. Meir (requiring three people for arbitration) is that also arbitration requires hkr^c hd^{c}t." See MP, STEY, p. 509, and MM who, therefore, deduce a different reading of our PT text before the Tosafot.

1:1.VI.II-QQ: This follows Tos. Ms. Erf. Both Ms. Vienna and edd. have as PT in NN, "stronger." (So does Ms. Erf., in fact, but the scribe changed it into "weaker"; so Zuckermandel.) Similarly Ms. Vienna and edd. have as PT, "and the stronger one became his enemy" instead of "and the stronger one go after him." The passage also occurs in BT 6b.

Aside from those differences in PT bracketed by Neusner, note also that in PT neither LL nor OOb occurs. On whether the "him" of NN is the judge or the weaker litigant, the commentaries (on PT, BT and Tos.) disagree.

1:1.VI.RR: One was -- following Tos. Ms. Erf. But Ms. Vienna and edd.: "you were."

1:1.VI.TT: Lit. "do not gather in your words" -- which is a play on gwr/'gr (PM, QH, P and see Rashi on BT; cf. F. Brown, S.R. Driver and C.A. Briggs, A Hebrew and English Lexicon of the Old Testament, s.v. gwr II).

1:1.VI.UU-YY: An amalgam of Tos. (Ms. Erf.) and PT. In our text UUc as well as VV c-d are missing. In Tos. VVe ("It is He who...being") is missing.

1:1.VI.UU-AAA: Cited in Meiri 7a (p. 18).

1:1.VI.UU: For an explanation see Ḥasdei David ad loc.

1:1.VI.AAA: Whether or not justice is done will determine whether God must pay back Reuben the amount He declared for him. It is as if the judge, then, is judging God.

The bracketed interpretations follow PM. Alternatively "that man" may mean the other litigant (QH).

1:1.VI.BBB-EEE: Following Tos. Our Text (BBB): "R. Simeon b. Gamaliel says, 'Judgment is by three and arbitration by two.'" BBB-EEE is quoted (following PT) in Sefer Ma^{c}asim (B.M. Lewin in Tarbiz, I, 1, pp. 99-100).

1:1.VII.B-E: Cited by Meiri 8b (p. 24). B-C is cited by RḤ to San. 8a and D-E in part by RN(2) to 8a, s.v. psyln'.

Neusner is following PM who, in turn, is following Rashi in the latter's dispute with Rabbenu Tam (BT 8a). However, as Meiri (ibid) says, the wording of PT (n^{c}rh m'wrsh) argues against Rashi's interpretation (cf., however, Tos., 8b s.v. whby', end). For an alternative interpretation see, inter alia, the second explanation offered by QH, ad loc., s.v. 'bl bmwṣy' š"r.

1:1.VII.D: Lo..way -- various readings of this line: QH s.v., PM s.v., Meiri ibid., RYDBZ, ad loc. The last follows closely the reading of the parallel PT Ket. 4.4(5), 28c.

In view of the fact that PT Ket. reads 'yn, it is probably best not to translate our hn as "lo" (or as as relative adverb, "where") but as an interrogative adverb, "if" (cf. MAG p. 203 [12], HAS, Hebr. sec., p. 180). Further, since our line in San. contains two clauses, hn probably introduces a conditional sentence, as also in Biblical Aramaic (e.g. Dan. 2:6) and in the Genesis Apocryphon where hn and 'yn are each found twice serving this function. (E.Y. Kutscher, "The Language of the Genesis Apocryphon," Scripta Heirosolymitana IV, (1957), p. 4, cf. p. 19; HAS, p. 6, cf. p. 21). See Odeberg, §326 See also RH to San. 18a quoting PT San. 1.4, 19d: hn t^{c}byd...w'yn t^{c}bdynyh. In PT Ket. there is no condition.

Tnynth is a scribal error. Correct: tnyth (Ket.) or tnyt' (San. QH and RYDBZ; see D. Goldenberg, "HaTalmud BeFanim Hadashot," Bizaron, Nissan 5741, p. 78, n.4.) This word can be either a perfect 2 ps with objective suffix, t^{e}netāh, "You have taught it" (see MLH 884-885) or a participle, active or passive, in the determined state: tāneta', "the one (f.) teaching," or tanitā' (t^{e}nitā'), "the thing (f.) taught," respectively (Odeberg, §148). The perfect in the conditional is found elsewhere, see Kutscher, "New Aramaic Texts," JAOS 74 (1954), p. 234 [HAS, p. 38] and idem, "The Hermopolis Papyri," Israel Oriental Studies I (1971), p. 116 [HAS, p. 66]. Lieberman (Tarbiz 2, p. 112) points to this expression found elsewhere in PT.

The sense of the line is clearly that R. Mana has introduced a dispute (the betrothed maiden) between R. Meir and the Sages when the Mishnah has not, and vice versa. Therefore, the reading of PT San. is corrupt; the reading of QH is, "If the [tradition, law] taught [in the Mishnah] is disputed, do you make it undisputed?!"; and that of PT Ket. (and RYDBZ) is, "If the [tradition, law] not taught [in the Mishnah] is disputed..." (with apodosis understood).

1:1.VII.F: The parallel to the R. Mana -- R. Yose dispute is not in what follows (G) but in a R. Zeira -- Abbahu dispute found in PT Ket. R. Zeira was asked: If the husband brings witnesses to testify that his wife committed adultery and the wife's father brought witnesses to vitiate the testimony of the first witnesses (hzmh) and the father's witnesses are, in turn shown to be false (hzmh) -- are there two separate trials: a court of three for the father and one of twenty-three for his witnesses? R. Zeira answered in the affirmative. "R. Zeira is of the opinion that they are two separate cases; R. Jeremiah in the name of R. Abbahu: it is all one case [i.e. in a court of twenty-three]."

It would seem, however, that R. Mana's view (one trial for the accused -- the husband -- and his perjured witnesses) should rather accord with R. Abbahu. Therefore some would transpose the names of Abbahu and Zeira in F (QH) or would emend the opinion of R. Mana in C to be "husband tried by three; witnesses by twenty-three" (RYDBZ). PM leaves the text unmolested by dint of forced explanation.

1:1.VII,G-H: Parallel in PT San. 1.2, 19b.

1:2.B: Missing in many Mss. of the Mishna and also Ms. Leiden of PT. (In the latter a later hand has added it in the margin.) This line is not originally part of the Mishnah but is a baraitha added to the Mishnah (MLH, p. 963; J.N. Epstein, Tarbiz 6, p. 55, and see below to 1:2.I.A-B.

They said -- our text has, mistakenly, "(he) says."

1:2.W: PT text has: "lion, wolf," cf. Meiri to 15a, p. 47 and Sofer's note ad loc.

1:2.I.A-B: Follows PM which is not without difficulty; see MM. In fact, R. Abbahu's question does not relate to Mishnah 2 at all, the words, "Halakhah 2. [cases involving the penalty of] flogging are before three etc." (so in Ms. L and ed. V preceding I.A) being misplaced. Rather they relate to Mishnah 1, "And the sages say, 'He who brings forth an evil name is tried before twenty-three, for there may be a capital case'" (1:1.E-F). Based on this reasoning R. Abbahu asks that, according to the sages, flogging should also be before twenty-three, since there may be as capital case. This question of R. Abbahu is actually the second half of his query on Mishnah 1, the first part being according to R. Meir's view (1:1.VII.G) and the second, here, being according to the sages' view. (J.N. Epstein, Tarbiz 6, p. 55).

1:2.II.A-H: See the BT parallel (10b) and ML pp. 150-151, n. 19. Cited in RḤ to San. 10b.

1:2.II.B-D: The three verses contain three, five, and seven words respectively (QH following Rashi, BT San. 10b, s.v. kngd brkt khnym).

1:2.II.H: Ed. Zhitomir ff. has incorrectly rw'y. Ms. L and ed. V (and PT in YM) have as MT: mrw'y. Cf. BT San. 10b.

1:2.II.I-O: Cf. Num. R., 11.3.

1:2.II.I: "'From here we learn that the great Sanhedrin was composed of all Israel' -- and not only from the priests and levites as he concludes, 'And sixty men of the people of the land'" (QH and ŠQ).

1:2.II.N-S: Quoted in Tos. BT San 10b, s.v. šb^{c}h (q.v.).

1:2.II.N: Tnyy = tn'y. See the examples cited by Kohut, Arukh, 8, p. 250a (s.v. tn I). Bacher, Exegetische Terminologie 2, p. 241 (s.v. tn') cites Ber. 9c 'yt tn'y...w'yt tnyy which is an error. Ed. V (and Krotoschin), Ms. Leiden, SY, Ms. Vat 133 all read tny twice. PT Sirillo reads tn'y twice. On the double yod ending for the dipthong "ay" see Kutscher, SHY pp. 251-255; Zussman, Tarbiz, 43, p. 150; A.M. Rabinovitz, Ginze Midrash, p. 16 (and elsewhere; see index p. 318).

1:2.II.P-S: In the parallels (Shir. R 3.6, Num. R. 11:3, Gen. R. 70:8, pp. 807-808 with Theodor's notes) the "officer" spoken of is the mufla' of the court. Shir. R: "'And from the city he took an officer (srys)' -- this is the mufla' of the court. And why is he called srys? For he sryses the halakhah."

The mufla' either manages or handles the halakhah, i.e. the court case (Levy s.v. mwpl', Jastrow s.v. srs II) or he decides (i.e. cuts, as gzr, psq) the halakhah (commentaries; and see HJP, p. 66, n. 153).

1:2.III.A-B: A is explanatory of the Mishnah and does not, despite the BT parallel (Abbaye said, "learn (tny) 'sanctification of the month.'"), mean to emend the Mishnah. Samuel (B; cf. Meg. 4.4, 75b and BT San. 70b) disagrees with the Mishna's number of three for sanctification/intercalation of the month. He holds that (a minimum of) ten is necessary (MLH 371-372 and cf. QH). See Mantel, p. 184.

1:2.III.C: Apprentice-judges -- see STEY ad loc.

1:2.III.D: I came up with -- follows PM which is wrong. The root is ^{c}ll, i.e., "R. Samuel bar R. Isaac brought me in to the sanctification of the month [proceedings]." Similarly 1:2.III.H.

1:2.III.E-F: The bracketed additions follow PM. The text, however, simply says: (E) "It is self-evident that he did not count." (F) "Why?"

1:2.III.G: Note the switch from Aramaic to Hebrew.

1:2.III.K-L: Sofer's remark (ed. Meiri 11a, p. 33 n.5) that the Meiri was here dependent on PT may not be necessary, since BT's hškymw ly could provide the same deduction.

PT's yqrwny is an unusual form, since the pronominal suffix is not taken as the direct object of the verb, see Gesenius-Kautzsch-Cowley, Hebrew Grammar, §117x. The form occurs again in San.-Mak. at San. 1.7, 19c (bis), ktbtny, "you wrote for me" (cf. ktbwny and qb^{c}wny in BT Meg. 7a); San. 7.19, 25d ^{c}bdtyw (read thus for the nonsensical ^{c}bdtyn), "you have done to him;" San 10.2, 28c mhymnty, "he believes me." In Hebrew lh'mynw occurs at Mak. 1.5, 31a (bis), m^{c}ydh at San. 8.6, 26a (bis; = M. Ket. 9:7 and M. Shebu. 7:7), and h^{c}ydwhw at M. Mak. 1:3 (bis). Examples with the verbs h'myn (hymn) and h^{c}yd are not uncommon. Dr. Sol Cohen calls my attention to Targ. Onk., Gen. 49:24 (ed. Sperber) hwtyh.

1:2.III.N: The Small -- or "the Lesser." See PT Sot. 9. 13/14, 24b and above to 1:1.V.D.

In the BT parallel (11a) Samuel's answer is "I did not come to intercalate the year but to learn practical halakhah (hlkh lm^{c}śh)." Cf. QH.

1:2.III.O: The bracketed explanation follows PM. The text, however, is difficult. Whatever the correct text and explanation be, it seems certain that an analogy is being drawn between Samuel on the one hand and Eldad and Medad on the other. The latter were part of the seventy elders appointed by Moses but excluded themselves (Num. 11:25-26 according to BT San 17a and parallels). Samuel was also invited (BT San 11a) but denied it, excluding himself. (YM, MP).

1:2.III.P: They differed -- Jastrow (p. 34), Levy (I, 46) and Kohut (Arukh, I, 282a, s.v. 'wry(y)') read 'plgynwn (!) for the text's 'plgynh = "he diverted him!" YM: hplygwhw -- "they diverted him." Meiri (11a, p. 34) quoting PT has plgynyh = "he diverted him" (R. Gamaliel diverted Samuel?)

1:2.IV.A: Lit. "It is taught," tny (t^{e}ni) being a present passive particple (Bacher, Terminologie II, 238). But see J.N. Epstein, "Zur Babylonisch-Aramäischen Lexikographie" in the Adolph Schwartz Festschrift p. 321, n. 3, and p. 327.

1:2.IV.A-L: This section is paralleled in PT RH 3.1, 58d (top) (Goldman, HUCA 48 [1977] p. 230) and A-D is paralleled in PT Sot. 9.1, 23b (bot.). (On E-L see AZVY to RH 3.1, pp. 31-32 and add NY San. 13a end, s.v., 'bl blylh). It appears that the original place of A-D was Sot. (D: "Just as they differ here, so they differ in regard to testimony of the New Moon.") From Sot., A-D was brought into RH, including the pericope immediately preceding A which belongs to Sot. and has no place in RH. (This pericope has dropped out of Sot. [so ed. V, Ms. L. Ms. Vat. 133, ŚY pp. 217 and 343] by homoioteleuton, see QH, PM and ed. Zhitomir at Sot.) From RH, A-D and E-L (discussion on M. RH 1.3) were transferred to PT San.

Knowing the text history we can better understand the passage, thus: A-C is as tannaitic (tny, see also BT BQ 90b, RH 25b) statement dealing with the witnessing of a murder by the court (PT Sot. and RH read bet din; PT San, and BT parallels: sanhedrin). R. Judah bar Pazzi then comments that the same tannaitic dispute (BT names the disputants: R. Akiba and R. Tarfon) exists in regard to witnessing the new moon (D). On account of R. Judah's statement the entire section is transposed from PT Sot. to PT RH where Mishnah RH 3.1 says that if the court saw the new moon two of the court may serve as witnesses before the remainder, or if the court is only composed of three judges, two new judges are added to compensate for the two judges now turned witnesses. Immediately following PT RH is E which begins an entirely new discussion. E is a question asked on M. RH 3.1 as follows: "[What need is there to bring in two new judges; only one need be brought in to complete a minimum court of three, for] let one stand [and testify] while the other takes his seat [as a judge], and [vice-versa] the other will stand and the former will sit?"

The answer given is that such an arrangement would be legally different from the Mishnah's two-witness situation (shnyy' hy'), for once one has served as a witness to a case he can no longer serve as judge (F; cf. BT BQ 90b). (In the explanation to E-F I follow QH contra PM which Neusner follows.)

1:2.IV.G: PT RH reads: "As that case of R. Huna..."

1:2.IV.H: I.e., since it is beneath the dignity of R. Huna to testify in another court (PM, QH). See ŠQ, s.v. w^{c}bdyn kn.

1:2.IV.I: "What if he should, nevertheless, go and testify against you before another court?" (PM, QH).

1:2.V.A-VI.A: Parallel in PT RH 2.6, 58a-b (HUCA 47 [1976], pp. 207-212). For citations see also AZVY, ad loc., pp. 25-27.

1:2.V.A: Paralleled in BT San. 10b and RH 24a.

Taught -- lit., "teaches" tny (tāne) being a present active participle. See above on 1:2.IV.A.

1:2.V.D and F: See on 1:2.IV.A.

1:2.V.F: Follows PM and QH who, on the basis of PT RH, emend "month" to "year." But see AZVY, ad loc., and see below on H.

1:2.V.G: [The patriarchate] -- follows PM. QH: "Or the exilarchate." See also AZVY and Levy I, 228 s.v. byt'.

1:2.V.H: PT RH: "R. Hiyya bar Madeh, R. Jonah, R. Ba, R. Hiyyah in the name of R. Hiyyah in the name of R. Yohanan" by dittography. PT RH: "For the sanctification of the month...." So also in Meiri's citation of PT San. (to 13a, p. 41). But see the variants in Goldman, HUCA, 47, p. 208.

Alternatively H may be read as declarative, and not interrogative, explaining G (QH).

1:2.V.I-J: See AZVY, Goldman, ibid, and Meiri, ibid. The four statements ("say!" "he said," "had he said," "by saying") appear both here and in PT RH as: "in its intercalation" (b^{c}bwrh) all four times. But Ms. L and ed. V both here and RH have "in the intercalation" (b^{c}bwr) for the fourth instance. QHY, Nachmanides (AZVY), and Meiri have b^{c}bwrh - b^{c}bwr - b^{c}bwrh - b^{c}bwr. According to this reading (also Ms. L and ed. V) "its intercalation" refers to the eleven days by which the solar year is longer than the lunar year whereas "the intercalation" refers to the intercalation, i.e., the one which the sages added to the year which is the extra month of thirty days. (Perhaps the original reading in statement four was b^{c}bwr h^{c}bwr which became corrupted to b^{c}bwrh, cf. R. Hananel to San. 15a.)

Those who already had the same reading all four times had to add: "the sages added thirty days to it" to R. Yohanan's declaration (R. Hananel to RH, QH to RḤ, cf. ŠQ to San.; MM to San. and RH) or had to invent other fanciful interpretations (PM).

PT RH adds at the end of J; "And they intercalated it" (w^{c}brwh, cf. QHY, ibid., and QH to San.) which makes no sense here (although it does at the end of I). This may give us the clue to the correct reading of our text which, perhaps, was originally:

b^{c}bwrh - w^{c}bwrh - b^{c}bwrh - w^{c}bwrh (or b^{c}brwh - w^{c}brwh, etc). The interchange of b-w was not uncommon, see MLH, pp. 1225-1226; E.S. Rosenthal in Yuval Shay. A Jubilee Volume Dedicated to S.Y. Agnon, ed. B. Kurzweil (Ramat Gan, 1958), p. 308, n. 127; M.Z. Kaddari in Erkhe HaMilon HeḤadash LeSifrut Ḥazal, I (ed. Y. Kutscher), p. 163; Y. Zussman in Tarbiz 43, p. 149; and Z.M. Rabinovitz, Ginze Midrash, p. 205. "In it intercalation" implies its eleven extra days while "and its intercalation" implies the sages' intercalation of thirty days.

S. Gandz, "Studies in the Hebrew Calendar," PAAJR 17 (1948), pp. 9-13, reasoned a b-w change here and thought that our text read w^{c}bwrh - b^{c}bwrh and that "And..." implies the eleven extra days, while "in..." implies the extra month. The basis of this theory is the reading in M. Ned. 8:5, b^{c}bwrh, where the meaning is the intercalated month, as opposed to M. ^{c}Arak. 9:3 where the reading šnh w^{c}bwrh means the extra days of the solar year. This basis is, however, faulty. First, the reading of M. ^{c}Arak. 9:3 is not certain, BT ^{c}Arak. 31b quoting it as šnt ^{c}bwrh. More important is the fact that the reading of M. Ned 8:5, 'swr bh wb^{c}bwrh, shows that the b preposition is necessary for the particular syntactical construction of the Mishnah ("during the year and its intercalated month") which construction is not found in our passage of PT.

(On the terminology of "sanctification" applied to a year rather than, as is normally the case, to a month, see Gandz, ibid., pp. 13-17.)

The son of the blacksmith -- or "the inhabitant of Nafaḥ," see MLH p. 238, n.6.

1:2.V.K-N: For variants see Goldman, ibid., p. 209. Interestingly, "R. Yose" (N) in RH Ms. L is written just as our "R. Yasa," i.e. ys', but is vocalized as yose'.

The meaning of this section is unclear as the following differences of interpretation will show: In K "[to the court]" follows PM (see to RH). QH: "Appointed for intercalation." In L "[study in]" follows PM. QH: "For purposes of [sanctification of the month in] the meeting house." "Better able [to teach the law]" follows PM. The text has only hrgl (RH: hrgyl) which QH understands as those "more commonly found in the meeting house." See Mantel, p. 150, on this point and on M-N. On "to complete" in M see QH.

1:2.V.O-S: For variants see Goldman, ibid., 209-210, and AZVY to RH.

1:2.V.Q-R: Quoted in Bet Yoseph to Ṭur, 'oraḥ ḥayyim, 102, s.v. ktb.

1:2.V.Q: Va -- RH: "Ba." On the b-w interchange, see above on I-J.

But could not take his seat -- rather: "And took his seat;" see SQ to San. For our hsl and kywn dhsl, PT RH has each time mn dhsl "when he finished," on which form see MAG, pp. 31-35.

He did not want to pass in front of the other -- Midrash Samuel's dyfswq ("...to interrupt in front...") may be a corruption of dyfsw^{c} which would be equivalent to the PT account.

Behavior -- Mid. Sam. adds: "In Babylonia."

Master -- RH and Mid. Sam.: "Masters" or "superiors" (cf. YM to RH)

1:2.V.T: They removed him -- lit., "They brought him in."

Their gate -- i.e., dlhn. QHY reads dl^{c}l, abbreviation for dl^{c}lyt'? Cf. BT San 11a. Cf. also STEY. See S. Lieberman in Lev. R., ed. Margulies, pp. 869-70.

Possibly dlhn is from an original d'lhn, "of our God" and dl^{c}l in QHY is abbreviated from dl^{c}l'h, "of the Most High." The terms "Gate of our God" and "Gate of the Most High" are similar to the phrase tr' dmry swmy', "Gate of the Lord of the Heavens," part of a third-century synagogue inscription found at Umm el-^{c}Amed in the Galilee (N. Avigad, Bulletin of the Israel Exploration Society, Vol. 19, pp. 183-187 [1955; Hebrew]; an expanded English translation in Bulletin of the Louis Rabinowitz Fund 3 [1960], pp. 62-64).

I. Sonne (Tarbiz 27, pp. 557-559) thinks that "Gate of the Lord of the Heavens" is another expression for "synagogue" in general, and does not refer to the door of the synagogue in particular, a position which Avigad originally held but abandoned in his later English article.

F.G. Hüttenmeister (Israel Exploration Journal, vol. 28, pp. 109-112) has argued, partly on the basis that "there is no parallel to the... expression tr' dmry šwmy'," that tr' in the inscription is an error for 'tr' (see also M. Sokoloff in Bar Ilan 18-19 [1981], pp. 218-219). Our text may provide that parallel. At any rate, as Hüttenmeister admits, 'tr' dmry šwmy' is also unparalleled. See also J. Naveh, On Stone and Mosaic (Israel, 1970), p. 42, who argues for a reading tq' (= Gk. thḗkē, "ark").

1:2.V.U: Ms. L & ed. V: Qerispeda, RH: Qerispa

1:2.V.W-Y: Follows the parallel in BT San. 18b (cf. QHY p. 393). A literal translation of our text would be: "One said, 'The early and late [sowing] sprout in Adar,' and one said, 'In Adar the ox dies in his flock [or pen, reading with RH: b^{c}dryyh (but see Goldman, ibid.), cf. Jastrow p. 1046, s.v. ^{c}dr'] and sheds its skin [i.e., scratches itself, cf. Jastrow p. 1580 s.v. šlḥ following Rashi in BT] in the shade of the fig tree,' and one said, 'The East wind in Adar -- blow with your cheek [and] it will go out [Ms. L, ed. V, QHY: ypwq; RH: wpwq = "and go out"] against it [QHY: against you]'." See Jastrow p. 586, s.v. ypḥ; Levy 2.252, s.v. ypḥ.

On the ^{c}-ḥ interchange in lw^{c}' (PT San., QHY) and lwḥ' (PT RH), see MAG, pp. 43-49 and Zussman in Tarbiz 43, p. 149.

1:2.V.AA: May also be a declarative statement answering the question implied in U, see QH, RḤ to San. 15a and RH 25b, Goldman's punctuation (ibid, p. 211), and AZVY p. 26.

1:2.V.BB: PT Hor. 1.1, 45d.

1:2.V.CC: [Set of signs of intercalation] -- or "[herdsman]."

1:2.V.DD: Follows PM and QH, but there is no indication that the statement is interrogative.

1:2.V.EE: Ed. Zhitomir has mistakenly: ^{c}l ydy. Ms. L, and ed. V both here and in RH, as also QHY p. 394, have ydy ^{c}l. MT: ydy 'l (as RḤ to RH).

1:2.V.GG: [To a court] -- see below on 1:2.V.JJ.

1:2.V.KK: See AZVY, p. 27.

1:2.V.JJ: RḤ to San. 15a quoting our text has: "When they appointed him in the yšybh."

1:2.VI.A: PT RH (and see AZVY, p. 27): "The court below did not sanctify the month."

1:2.VI.B: Villages' [representatives] -- so Jastrow, p. 1419 s.v. qryh. Levy (4.379) understands "laymen" from qerāyāh originally "villager." So too Kohut (7.198). PM and

QH translate "wagons," cf. Kohut, ibid., s.v. qaryah; Levy, ibid., s.v. qaryah; and Alon, Toledot Hayehudim, vol. 2, pp. 97-98. See Mantel, pp. 182-185.

Domain -- lit., "house." Levy, ibid., "school." I. Halevy, Dorot Harishonim (Frankfurt a. M., 1901) Pt. 2, p. 70, n. 36 shows that byt rabbi is a term for the Patriarchate in general.

1:2.VI.C: Declaration [of the intercalation...] -- follows PM who understands symn' from swm, "to finish," i.e. the end of the intercalation process, or the declaration. But symn' never has this definition and means instead "mark, sign" and here "feature, distinction" (Jastrow, p. 981, Levy, 3.512). The "distinction" may refer to the intercalation itself, a distinctive feature of Judea. Cf. L. Ginzberg, Commentary on the Palestinian Talmud (New York, 1941), vol. 3, pp. 125-127. According to STEY, p. 509 and Halevy, ibid., p. 66 (cf. QH and Krochmal p. 104) symn' refers to sanctification of the month which was sometimes done by means of a "sign" or code.

1:2.VI.D-E: D may not be a unit unto itself, for Da may be a response to C and Db a new question to which the answer is E (Halevy, ibid., p. 68; Krochmal, p. 104; QH also understands E as an answer to D).

The commentators (whom Neusner is following) reverse the names Dan and Judah to conform to Josh. 15:29 and 19:44.

1:2.VI.F-G: Baalah -- Ms. L and ed. V: "Baalat" (as in D).

Some see F as a dittography of D (RYDBZ), i.e. G is an explanation of E (that Joshua puts one town in two different districts). Others understand F as a deliberate repetition of D in order to present an alternative answer, G (QH).

1:2.VI.H-K: In view of B above (that Lud is in Judah), H read as Neusner does ("Isn't Lud in Judea?") is difficult, for there is no problem causing the question in H to be posed (cf. Halevy, ibid., p. 69). Therefore, QH understands H as declarative, "But Lud is not in Judea!" (see Neh. 11:35, cf. I Chr. 8:1-12) and if so, why not intercalate there, since the decision in B was not to intercalate only in Judea (J)?

H-K is quoted in Meiri to 12a (p. 37) with the variant "Land of Israel" instead of "Judea" (H) and with the words "the year" added after "intercalate" (J) (on the latter cf. STEY, p. 510 and Halevy, ibid., p. 69).

1:2.VI.I-M: Cited in RḤ to San. 15b.

1:2.VI.M: Lit. "And so ['yṯh = Greek εἶτα] you've caused me to treat rabbis discourteously."

1:2.VII.A-J: Parallel in BT San. 11b. The translation follows the reading in Tosefta.

1:2.VII.A: [...spring] -- see QH (= Rashi to BT).

1:2.VII.E: "Also" is not in PT or BT. "On account of" implies that R. Simeon's statement refers to B, but BT is unsure if this is the case or if it refers to D; cf. QH (= Rashi to BT).

1:2.VII.L-N: Parallel in BT San. 11a. The translation is a combination of the readings in PT and in Tos. In L "lambs" follows Tos.; "sucking lamb" follows PT (according to PM; cf. TK 7 [to Ned.], 454). For "come" (L) BT has "fledged." Following Rashi in BT (= PM): "They do not intercalate the year because the kids and lambs [are still too thin to be brought as paschal sacrifices] or because the pigeons are unfledged [and are still too small]."

1:2.VII.O-P: Parallel in BT San. 11a. Translation follows Tos. although "[and in that of my colleagues]" is added from PT; see TR ad loc., vol. 2, p. 152, and Mantel, p. 3, n. 9.

According to BT, O-P is the text of a declaration used in a case described in sec. M.

1:2.VII.Q-V: Parallel in BT 11b, PT MŠ 5.6, 56c; see also Midrash Tannaim to 26:13 (pp. 175-176).

In session (Q) -- or simply "sitting."

The steps of the Temple (Q) -- lit., "steps on the Temple mount." PT MŠ has "the steps of the 'ulam [the court of the Temple] on the temple mount." See Mantel, pp. 26-27 and 28, n. 163.

1:2.VII.T-V: T precedes U in PT and follows it in the parallels. There is confusion among the parallels whether to read "we inform" or "I inform" in T, U, and V. In V the reading is either "I have added" (Tos., BT) or a nondescript infinitive (PT San. and MŠ).

Media -- PT San. and MŠ add: "and the residents of the Exile of Greece."

1:2.VII.W-BB: W-Y is paralleled in BT San. 13a; see also 12b-13a. The translation is a combination of Tos. and PT readings.

The translation of Z-AA follows PM whose reasoning is that since the omer must be brought in the "Nisan season," i.e. after the spring equinox, and since the day of the equinox is reckoned as belonging to the past season, therefore if it would happen that the sixteenth of Nisan (when the omer is brought) would fall on the equinox, we must intercalate the year to ensure that the omer-bringing falls after the spring equinox. R. Yose, however, feels that the festival of Passover, i.e., the fifteenth of Nisan, and not only the omer-bringing, i.e. the sixteenth, must be within the new season.

In BB R. Judah's statement refers to the autumnal equinox and not the spring equinox. Thus PM.

QH (following Rashi to BT 12b) understands "equinox" of W as the autumnal equinox and the dispute in X-Y as it is explained in BT 13a. Thus, the anonymous Tanna in X feels that the entire festival of Sukkot must be within the autumn season and therefore by the fifteenth of Tishrei (the beginning of Sukkot) the equinox must have taken place (the day of the equinox being reckoned as part of the new season). If not, we must intercalate a month.

R. Judah (Y), on the other hand, is of the opinion that only part of Sukkot need fall in the new season and therefore only if all seven days of the festival (until the twenty-first of Tishrei) would fall in the summer season is there need for intercalation.

According to QH, Z-AA refers back to Y and not to X, cf. Rashi BT 13a s.v. ššh ʿśr lpny hpsḥ, and BB refers to AA.

1:2.VII.CC: See BT San. 11a (bottom).

1:2.VII.DD: See Sifra, 'Emor, parashah 9:4 (p. 99d).

1:2.VII.EE-XID: Parallel in PT Ned. 6:13, 39d-40a.

1:2.VII.EE-GG: EE-FF is paralleled in BT San. 12a. EE and GG is paralleled in PT Sheq. 1:2, 46a; PT Pe'ah 5:1, 18d. (FF is also missing in the PT Ned. parallel.) On GG see also BT San. 12a, BT Ned. 53b, and PT Sheb. 6:4, 37a.

1:2.VII.HH: The bracketed addition is from Tos. but clearly belongs to our text as well, as can be seen from the parallel in PT Ned. The meaning of R. Meir's words are as follows: Since it was past the sixteenth of Nisan (for the people ate of the new harvest) and the crops -- save the species mentioned -- had not yet ripened, there was reason to intercalate the year.

1:2.VII.JJ: Follows Tos. in translation.

1:2.VII.KK-NN: Parallel in BT San. 12a-b; cf. T. Pes. 8:4-5. See B. DeVries, Studies in Talmudic Literature [Hebrew], (Jerusalem, 1968), pp. 66-69.

1:2.VII.KK: See Sifra 'Emor, parashah 9:6 (p. 100a).

1:2.VII.LL: The translation is a combination of Tos. (Ms. V and E) and PT San.

Issachar -- our text reads: "Israel."

1:2.VII.MM: Translation follows PT San. literally. However, this translation gives the impression that Simeon's statement deals with the law post factum (bdy^{c}bd). In fact PM ad loc., s.v. mpny š^{c}ybrw nysn, thus understands the statement. But PM is here basing himself not only on a literal translation, but also on the discussion in BT which injects the elements of ante factum (lktḥylh) and post factum. These elements are not found here in PT San. and the question before us, then, is whether Simeon meant to imply the element of post factum.

The reading in PT Ned. doesn't help for MM in Ms. L is omitted here due to homoioarktov (MLA 572) and its inclusion in ed. V may have been copied from our passage. Against the reading in PT San. stands that of Tos. and BT which read m^{c}bryn instead of m^{c}wbr, i.e., Hezekiah's intercalated Nisan is considered intercalated but he prayed for himself since we only itercalate Adar. The same variant occurs in RR between PT San. (m^{c}bryn) on the one hand and PT Ned. and Pes. (m^{c}wbr) on the other. So also 1:2.VIII.C (m^{c}wbr) and the parallels T. San. 2.7, BT San. 12a, BT RH 7a (m^{c}bryn). It seems likely, then, that "intercalated is only the month of Adar" = "we intercalate only the month of Adar."

1:2.VII.OO-CCC: Parallel in PT Pes. 9.1, 36c-d.

1:2.VII.SS: Parallel in PT Sot. 5.2, 20b (bis). Cited in Tos. San. 12a, s.v. š^{c}ybr and RḤ to San. 13b. The interpretation given follows PM which, however, is difficult, for a skull beneath the altar only shows that there was uncleanness in the Temple. But this fact does not speak to the question of whether the year is intercalated on account of the uncleanness. An alternative explanation is that the opinion that intercalation is prohibited accords with the view that a skull was found, i.e., corpse-impurity and not idol-impurity (idols placed in the Temple by Ahaz) was the cause of Hezekiah's intercalation, for were the people unclean by reason of the idols, Passover would have been prohibited and intercalation would have been a necessity (QH; see also YK, pp. 507-508, and ŠQ to Ned.).

1:2.VII.TT: This section begins a new topic.

And to do... judgments -- missing in PT Ned. and PT Pes.

1:2.VII.VV-WW: The exegeses turn on the meaning of the k in kṭhrt hqdš (II Chron. 30:19; note the reading in PT Pes. ^{c}śh kmh and not kmh ^{c}śh). According to PM and QH and following the reading in the parallels: One said, "Even though he did many things in order to purify the Sanctuary, he still did not fully carry out what is required for the purfication of the Sanctuary." And one said, "Even though he did many good deeds, he did not carry out what is required for the purification of the Sanctuary." Both interpretations understand the verse thus: Hezekiah did not do as is done for purification of the Sanctuary. The interpretations differ as to what Hezekiah did do.

1:2.VII.XX: Eight -- our text has "three," while PT Pes. has "eight" as MT. PT Ned. deletes this part of the verse.

1:2.VII.ZZ: See Ezek. 23:14.

1:2.VII.AAA-1:2.VIII.S: Cited in RḤ to San. 13b.

1:2.VII.AAA-CCC: Paralleled in BT Ber. 10b, BT Pes. 56a.

1:2.VII.BBB: He dragged... bier -- parallel in BT San. 47a, BT Mak. 24a. See S. Lieberman, "Some Aspects of After Life in Early Rabbinic Literature," Harry A. Wolfson Jubilee Volume (Jerusalem, 1965), vol. 2, pp. 506-508.

He pulverized... serpent -- 2 Kings 18:4.

1:2.VII.CCC: He closed... Gihon -- 2 Chron. 32:30; See YK p. 508.

He cut... Temple -- 2 Kings 18:16.

He intercalated... itself -- cf. 2 Chron. 30:2.

1:2.VIII.A-C: Paralleled in BT San. 12a, BT RH 7a.

The court may sit to discuss intercalation after the New Year, but not before it. Whenever they sit, however, only one month may be intercalated: Adar. (Cf., however, the reading in Tos. Ms. V and edd. where C reads "henceforth" instead of "nonetheless.") See also above, to 1:2.VII.MM.

1:2.VIII.D-IX.G: Paralleled in PT RH 3.1, 58c (Goldman, HUCA, 48 [1977], pp. 225-228) and PT Shebi. 10.2, 39 b-c. 1:2.VIII.E-K is missing in PT Ned. by homoioteleuton.

1:2.VIII.D: The parenthetical definition here of an intercalated Nisan (and in K for an intercalated Tishre) is necessarily accepted by the commentaries due to the following discussions (E-I and L). However, the usual definition of an intercalated month is that it lasts thirty days (instead of the regular twenty-nine) and has nothing to do with the month before it. See Sirillo's commentary to Shebi. and RḤ to BT San. 13b. In line with the definition here is the statement 1:2.IX.A: qydšwhw qwdm zmnw 'w l'ḥr ᶜybwrw.

1:2.VIII.F-I: The text reads only: "If the ḥdš comes on time." These words could be part of T. RH 1:4 (= T. Sheq. 2:7) as Neusner has it, but they could also be part of M. Sheq. 4:5. Epstein, MLH, pp. 888-891, thinks that tnynn usually cites a Mishnah.

The reading in H, "new [sheqels]" as well as the interpretation after I follows PM who understands ḥdš (H) to refer to the new sheqel offerings. Alternatively ḥdš may mean "month," i.e. Nisan (QH; ŠQ to RH; Melekhet Shelomo to M. Sheq. 4:5; Commentary of Sirillo to Shebi.; Aryeh Loeb ben Asher, Ṭure 'Eben to RH 7a, s.v. w'm). Note that in M. Sheq. Ms. Kaufmann, in PT Shebi., and PT Sheq. Ms. (ed. A. Sofer; N.Y., 1954) p. 39, the reading is ḥwdš. On the answer, "If it came, but it never did," and below, "If it was, but it never was," see Lieberman in Tarbiz 5, pp. 102-103.

1:2.VIII.K-S: Cited in RḤ to San. 13b.

1:2.VIII.K: See above 1:2.VIII.D.

1:2.VIII.N-Q: Paralleled in Sifra, 'Emor, parashah 11.5 (p. 101d); PT RH 4.6, 59c; BT RH 32a.

1:2.VIII.R: When the new month begins on the thirtieth of the previous month, Rosh Ḥodesh (the new-moon festival) is observed only one day. When it begins on the thirty-first, the festival is observed two days, the thirty-first of the previous month and the first of the new month. (This question, R, is asked also in BT RH 32a.)

1:2.VIII.S-U: The interpretation of T as an independent question follows our text in San. and Ms. Sirillo Shebi., mhw... wmhw.... However, Ned. reads mh byn hr' šwn lšyny (Shebi. ed. V, Ms. L and Ms. Vat.: mh byn hr' šwn wmh byn hšyny) which may be taken as the conclusion of S thus: "That year things were miscalculated somewhat between the first and second days." U, in either case, provides an alternative answer to R. (PM to Ned. and RH).

Against this interpretation, see BT RH 32a m'y šny lywm šny lšnh hb'h, which would seem to parallel T-U. Sirillo in his commentary to Shebi. preserves a different reading for T ("And has it not been taught 'On the first and on the second'?") which is meant to vitiate the answer given in S. Elijah Gaon, in his commentary to Shebi. (see also RYDBZ to San. and cf. STEY, p. 78) has the following order: U-V-S, omitting T.

1:2.IX.A-Ca: Paralleled in Sifra, 'Emor, pereq 10.4 (p. 100a). Cited in RḤ to RH 26a. See Tos. RH 2(3):1-2.

1:2.IX.A: [If the court] -- cf. TK vol. 5, p. 1037 (to T. RH 2(3):1).

1:2.IX.C: The exegetical basis is the word 'wtm ("which") and the exegesis is as Neusner has it. The exegete deliberately incorporates biblical phraseology into his exegesis ('lh hm mw^{c}dy), which has led Goldman (HUCA 48, p. 228) into error thinking that the exegesis turns also on the word hm.

Prior to its... the month is probably not part of the argument, but an unconnected statement of definition: "'Prior to its time' means the twenty-ninth day; 'after its intercalation' means the thirty-second day." (TK, vol. 5, p. 1037, to T. RH 2(3):1).

1:2.IX.D-F: Parallel in Sifra, 'Emor, parashah 9.1 (p. 99d). On D, see BT San. 11a and T. San. 2:12.

1:2.IX.D: The parenthetical "home" here in D and below in G follows I.H. Weiss' commentary to Sifra, ibid. PM and QH understand the movement of those in exile to be in the opposite direction: from their homes to Jerusalem. (See also R. Meir Simḥa's commentary to our text in San.) The reading in PT Ned., hgy^{c}w lmqwmn, supports Weiss, while that of Ms. Sirillo Shebi., šyṣ' w mmqwmn (cf. BT San. 11a), supports the opposing view. Similarly -- as Weiss notes -- the reading s^{c}lw (PT RH; QHY, p. 394; Sifra, Ms. Vat. 66; Krochmal, p. 104) would indicate direction to Jerusalem (unless we translate as a pluperfect: "Those in exile who had come up [to Jerusalem and were now returning] but have not yet reached [their homes]").

Weiss is of course right that ascent implies direction to Jerusalem. Thus we may, incidentally, correct a translation of Josephus, Antiquities 17.214 where it is said that on Passover (4 B.C.E.) the people káteisi, "came down" (so Marcus in the Loeb ed.) to Jerusalem from the country (chṓra) and from abroad (hyperoría).

How could Josephus have used such terminology in this context? (a) Josephus was influenced by hyperoría, lit. "beyond the border" the prepositional prefix of which may mean "above" as well as beyond." Or (b) Josephus was influenced by hyperoría, "abroad," to use kateisi in the sense, "'to return home,' the reference being generally to the return from an exile..." (V. Tcherikover, Hellenistic Civilization and the Jews, [New York, 1975; trans. S. Applebaum], p. 483, n.25). Tcherikover says this of katérchomai but the same applies to káteimi, see Liddell and Scott, Lexicon, on both words. Neither (a) nor (b) is a suitable answer since the parallel to Antiquities in the War 2.10 reads káteisi mèn ek tēs chṓras, omitting hyperoría. The meaning "to return home" gives no sense in the War, since Jerusalem was not specifically home to the Jews over aginst Judaea as Judaea would have been in contrast to hyperoría.

Thackeray's theory of Josephan assistants is also an unlikely answer, since they would have known from the rest of the War (and, later, Antiquities too) that one went "up" to Jerusalem. Besides, such a blatant error would have been caught by Josephus in proofreading.

The answer seems to be simply that káteimi and katérchomai may also mean "to return" (Liddell and Scott, s.v.), i.e. to return to Jerusalem each year or so for Passover. (Note also that the examples given in the Lexicon for this meaning, under both entries, refer to returning from the country [agrothen] to the city or town [eis ásty or pólinde].) Alternatively, Liddell and Scott (s.v. katérchomai) notes the usage simply, "to come to a place," cf. Whiston's and Schalit's translations. At any rate, the Marcus translation is definitely wrong.

1:2.X.A-C: Translation is a combination of the Tos. (edd. and Ms. V) text and our text. Parallel in BT San. 11b and cited in She'iltot, Exodus, 49 (ed. Mirsky 3.80) where Mss. read in B "it is deemed not to have been intercalated," see below on F and TR, vol. 2, pp. 152-153.

1:2.X.D-F: Abroad -- i.e., outside of Israel. D is cited in RḤ to San. 13b. The point in E is that once the prohibition of intercalation in Galilee is said, the prohibition of intercalation abroad becomes redundant. So PM.

In F Ms. L reads "In Galilee they do not intercalate the year. And if they did so, it is not intercalated. Abroad..." The word "not" has deletion marks above it and is also erased by a later hand (MLA, 595).

1:2.X.G-N: Cited in RḤ to San. 13b.

1:2.X.H: Cited in Tos., BT San. 11b, s.v. 'yn.

1:2.X.I: See Tos., ibid.

1:2.X.J-M,O: The story, with variants, is found in BT Ber. 63a-b. Parts are cited also by Meiri to 13a (p. 40).

1:2.X.J: Rabbi -- see STEY, 404; W. Bacher, Aggadot HaTannaim, vol. 2, pp. 110-111, n. 3; Mantel, p. 194, n. 131 and p. 240, n. 487; MLT, p. 570, n. 181.

With -- or "to," (i.e. "via"), STEY ibid. Cf. Bacher and MLT, ibid.

1:2.X.M: Thorny wilderness -- or "the wilderness of Atad" (Levy, 1.59, s.v.; Jastrow, 42, s.v.; Kohut, Arukh, 1.60, s.v.).

The intention of the statement in M is that if Hananiah would not accept Palestinian authority he may as well set up an altar, or temple, in Babylonia and renounce Judaism altogether (Levy, ibid. and 1.55, s.v. 'ḥyh).

Nehunyon is Onias, the founder of the Jewish temple at Leontopolis (Levy, 3.371 s.v.; QH; On Onias -- BT Men. 109b, Josephus, War 7.423 ff.) or a variant for the BT 'hyh, a leader of Babylonian Jewry (Rashi in BT; Bacher, ibid. p. 111, n. 2; cf. PM). See Krochmal, p. 104.

1:2.X.N: Did obeisance -- lit., "he honored them."

1:2.X.P-R: PT Ned 6:13, 40a reads in P: "And read: It is written in the Torah..." and in Q: "They said to him" (cf. T below). The reply of R. Isaac to the people (R) is, "[Indeed, the reading 'festivals of the Lord' is the reading] with us [but you Babylonians who follow Hananiah make it the 'festivals of Hananiah.']" So PM, YM and QH. (Ms. L and ed. V have here in P: "The festivals of the Lord. Hananiah...")

The force of R. Isaac's lesson turns on the genitive construct, "festivals of the Lord," and therefore the verse cited must be Lev. 23:4 (and not 23:2). We should, accordingly, delete hm.

1:2.X.S: Lit. "R. Nathan arose and completed: "For from Babylonia..." "Completed" may refer to the homily (QH cf. Levy 4.563, s.v.), or the verse (Jastrow, 1586, s.v.).

1:2.X.U: Or, "[Indeed, the reading 'For from Zion will Torah go forth, and the word of the Lord from Jerusalem' is the reading] with us [but you Babylonians who follow Hananiah make it 'For from Babylonia will Torah go forth, and the word of the Lord from Nehar Peqod.']" So QH. See above, on P-R.

1:2.X.V: After them... after them -- i.e., after the authorities in Israel (PM, YM) or, after the calendrical calculations established in Israel (QH). See S. Abramson, Sinai 74, p. 2, n. 2.

1:2.X.W-X: What tells -- PT Ned: "Who tells" (lit. "informs"); so also Meiri, p. 40, and RḤ to San. 13b. See Mantel, p. 182, n. 44. According to YM, PM and QH, R. Judah's answer comprises Wc-X thus: "Since [he, Hananiah, says that if] they are not so well informed as he in calculating the calendar, they should listen to him, now that they are, in fact, masters of calculation as much as he, he must listen to them." This interpretation is clear in the PT Ned. parallel where "he says" is explicitly in the text.

1:2.X.Z: Places which... the ones -- lit., "where... where."

1:2.X.AA-BB: Cited in RḤ to San. 13b. The connection between this exegesis and the prior discussion is that it argues against the stand taken in W (ŠQ).

1:2.X.CC: The craftsmen... sages -- see BT San. 38a and parallels.

1:2.X.DD-HH: See Gen. R. 41 (42).3 (p. 404) with variants and Theodore's notes for parallels. GG-HH is cited in RḤ to San. 13b. where instead of "apprentices" the reading is "sages." This entire unit (QH) or just GG-HH (PM ad loc. and to Ned.) may be seen as an answer to CC thus: AA-BB follows the opinion of the rabbis who do not interpret II Kings 24:16 as referring to disciples of sages. (QH ad loc. is corrupt; see to Ned.)

And rabbis -- or "And the rabbis" = warbnn. Similarly passim. See above on 1:1.E.

Councillors -- bwlbwṭyn, Ned: Bwlwwṭyn = Gk. bouleytēs (Krauss, p. 140, s.v.). For an interesting variant (glywṭym = Lat. galeotae) for bwlbwṭyn and a consequently different exegesis, see D. Sperber, "Greek and Latin Words in Rabbinic Literature," Bar-Ilan 16-17 (1979), pp. 16-19. On this word and on the entire passage, see also Sperber in Researches in Talmudic Literature: A Study Conference in Honour of... Shaul Lieberman (Jerusalem, 1983), pp. 195-199.

1:2.XI.A: "R. Hoshaiah, when he would receive witnesses [concerning the new moon] at ᶜEn Tob, would say to them, "Know that you are really providing many testimonies and that many sums of money for rental of houses depend on your evidence." On ᶜEn Tob see Mantel, p. 183, n. 46.

Many testimonies -- those who profane the various holidays whose inception is based on the witnesses' testimony (PM). Based on the witnesses' testimony the court-appointed messengers travel the land and testify before the local courts as to the inception of the new month (QH, see ŠQ).

Sums of money... -- false testimony can cause a loss of a day's rent to the lessor (PM, QH).

1:2.XI.D: Paralleled in PT Ket. 1.2, 25b. Ms. L and ed. V: "If the court decides to intercalate, the signs of virginity do not return, and if not, the signs of virginity do return." But PT Ket. (cited in Shulḥan Arukh, Moses Isserles, 20:1) and PT Ned. read as our translation.

1:2.XII.A-R: Parallel in PT Sot. 9.1, 23c; B-G is paralleled in BT San. 13b and Sifra wyqr', ḥwb', pereq 6.1 (p. 19b); A, D-G in BT San. 3b, and A alone in Tos. San. 1.1 and BT Ket. 101b. I-L and R are paralleled in BT San. 14a and BT Sot. 44b.

1:2.XII.C: PT Sot. ŚY reads, "And the elders shall lay on hands...." See PM and QH.

1:2.XII.H-L: Our text has R. Simeon's exegesis of five judges followed by R. Judah's of three which is obviously corrupt. Neusner, therefore, follows the emendations of PM. However the correct text is in PT Sot. ŚY: R. Simeon's exegesis of three followed by R. Judah's of five; cf. the structure of B-G and see AH pp. 78-79, n. 111.

1:2.XII.M-N: If we substitute "and that" for Neusner's "then," (N) we have the second explanation of N offered by QH; and see also ŠQ.

No interpretation of N (see also Sivitz, p. 312) appears felicitous to me. Furthermore, M is difficult, since the reason Rabbi prefers R. Judah's exegesis is equally applicable to R. Simeon's.

A part of M (as in PT Sot.) is quoted by Meiri to 13a, p. 42.

1:2.XIII.A-XIV.D: Cited in part by RḤ to 14a and RN(2) on San. 5a s.v. w'm, and in its entirety by Meiri to 14b (p. 44) and (excepting C) by Barzilai, Sefer HaSeṭarot (ed. S.J. Halberstam; Berlin, 1898), pp. 133-134. Metibot (p. 97) cites XII.R-XIII.D. On ordination see Alon, Toledot HaYehudim, II, 140 ff, 150; idem, Meḥqarim, I, 272; II, 33 ff.

1:2.XIII.A: Cf. Tos. San. 1.1 = BT San. 13b.

1:2.XIII.A-B: Metibot, ibid., understands smykwt as the plural of smykh rather than as a singular abstract noun (l' hy' sm[ykh] hn smykwt).

1:2.XIII.C: See Mantel, pp. 206-207, n. 225 and H. Albeck, Studies in the Baraitha and Tosefta and Their Relationship to the Talmud [Hebrew], (Jerusalem, 1969), p. 87. Metibot, ibid., vocalizes thus: taman q̄ārayyin lmanwyyā'.

1:2.XIII.E: See Mantel, p. 212, n. 260 and MLT, p. 148.

1:2.XIV.A-C: B-C explains A. On A see L. Ginzburg, "Some Abbreviations Unrecognized or Misunderstood in the Text of the Jerusalem Talmud" in Students' Annual of the Jewish Theological Seminary of America (New York, 1914), pp. 145-146.

1:2.XV.A: Paralleled (with variants) in T. Yeb. 12:15.

She came... brother -- paralleled in PT MQ 3.3, 82a (see AZWY ad loc., pp. 107-108); PT Yeb. 12.7, 13a; BT Yeb. 39b. "On the ground" is cited in Tos. Yeb. 106b s.v. ᶜd. "At first they would write a deed of ḥaliṣah" and "At first they would write a document of the exercise of the right of refusal" (B) refer to the period before the Hadrianic persecutions (TK vol. 6 [to Yeb.], p. 147).

Removed -- Ed. V šḥt, corrected in ed. Cracow etc. to šrt as in Ms. L and the Palestinian parallels.

Before him -- following the emendation of QH which is based on BT Yeb. 39b (cf. the quote from Pesiqta Zuṭarti Ms. in TK, ibid., p. 148: qdm ybm). However, the Tosefta and PT texts read: "before us." On the question of whether bpnyw of Deut. 25:8 meant "before him" or "in his face" see TK, ibid., pp. 147-150 and Albeck, Mishnah, Moᶜed, p. 10.

1:2.XV.B: Paralleled (with variants) in T. Yeb. 13:1 and BT Yeb. 107b-108a.

I do not want... to him -- paralleled in PT MQ 3.3, 82a.

At first... -- see above on A.

In our presence -- this is the end of the preceding sentence and does not begin the following one as can be seen from A and from BT Yeb. 108a.

Stay with him -- following PM. Others, based on the reading in MQ -- šwyn' -- understand "I am not equal to (or, in agreement with) him" -- so Levy IV, 518; Kohut in Arukh VIII, 39; Jastrow, p. 1532 (all s.v. šwy/').

Actually, however, šwyn' is only špyn' with a w-p interchange which is the reading of T. Yeb. 13:1 (špy') i.e., "I am not comfortable with him" (TK, VI [on Yeb.], 152). (Although I could find no other instance of a w-p interchange, the interchanges of w-b and b-p are well known; on w-b see above to 1:2.V.I-J; on b-p see Sokoloff, pp. 6-7; MLH, 1220-1222.

1:2.XVI.A-L: Parallel in PT MŠ 4.3, 54d-55a (AZWY ad loc., p. 186). A and H are quoted in Responsa of Bezalel Ashkenazi (Venice, 1595), end of Responsum 2 (printed incorrectly as 1), p. 16d.

The translation follows the text in San. However, the commentaries (PM, QH, RYDBZ) emend the text to follow the parallel in MŠ which interchange C with J and, consequently, E with L. That this emendation is correct may be seen from F which may properly be asked only on the J/L statement and not on C/E.

Thus the interpretation of our section would be as follows: The answer to B is that since it is common for one to be generous about things consecrated, therefore if one has redeemed the consecrated for more than its true value, we assume it was done so deliberately.

The answer to I is that since the Temple treasurers would demand the fifth for consecrated objects but not for second tithe, the law was declared that redeemed second tithe without its fifth is invalid in order to assure that the owner would pay the fifth. Such a law would be unnecessary for consecrated objects (BT BM 54a).

In regard to D and K a variant reading (see AZWY; so also emended by QH) preserves the statement with clauses reversed, thus: "This reason is valid from the viewpoint of one who said that it [i.e. second tithe] is in the status of one's own property. [Then there is a distinction between it and consecrated objects to God.] But in accord with the one who said that it is not in the status of one's own property [and is, rather, considered the property of God] what is the difference between a consecrated object and a second tithe?"

1:2.XVI.C: There is a demand -- (so also in E) -- lit., "there are those who demand," (i.e. the Temple treasurers; see BT BM 54a).

1:2.XVI.D: It -- i.e., produce in the status of second tithe.

1:2.XVII.B-XVIII.K: Paralleled in PT Meg. 4.4, 75b. (AZWY, Meg., pp. 91-92).

1:2.XVII.B-C: The text chosen by PM is that of PT Meg. Our text reads: "That which you've said applies in the case of one who consecrates his field itself. But if he says 'Behold a maneh is incumbent upon me for consecration' [what is the law]?"

1:2.XVII.D-F: D-F is difficult whether we accept the interpretation of PM, QH, or Neusner. Perhaps the text should be understood thus: (D) The Mishnah states that valuation vows for moveables are evaluated by three judges. (E) But is there such a thing as valuation vows for non-moveables which would seem to be implied in the Mishnah's terminology? (Alternatively: But is there such a thing as valuation vows for moveables: [Understanding š'yn = šhn; see MLH p. 547. This reading would make E equal to the question in BT San. 14b]). Of course not, since valuation vows (^{c}rkym) is a term applied only to human beings (Lev. 27:1-8). (F) Therefore, the word "moveables" in the mishnaic term "valuation vows for moveables" (^{c}rkym hmṭlṭlyn -- sic!) refers to the method of payment rather than the object of the vow which is, of course, a human being. (See BT San. 14b-15a.)

1:2.XVII.D: Perhaps delete the parenthetical remarks here since the very meaning of the Mishnah's ^{c}rkyn hmṭlṭlyn are under discussion, see my remarks on D-F and PM. Epstein (MLH p. 548) thinks that D is not a citation from our Mishnah but from T. San. 1:2.

1:2.XVII.G: This section is the answer to the question posed in C, thus: "[Is not the law governing] him who says, 'My valuation is incumbent upon me' the same as [the law governing] him who says, 'The valuation of my field is incumbent upon me'?"

1:2.XVII.I: Lit. "If he should become wealthier, he is judged according to the law of 'as much as he can pay.' (hsg yd)." This law says that if one cannot pay the full value of the pledge when the time comes for payment, one only pays what one can. (See BT ^{c}Ar. 20a.) Our text, then, claims that if one pledged a maneh but could not pay it, he pays only what he can and does not have to pay the remainder should he later come into money. (This statement of PT clearly contradicts BT ibid. and, therefore, the commentators either re-interpret the term hśg yd [QH, PM, MP] or manipulate the text [STEY p. 314].)

1:2.XVIII.A-C: See BT Ket. 100b.

1:2.XVIII.B-K: Paralleled in PT Ket. 11.6, 34c.

1:2.XVIII.B: The parallel in PT Meg. 4.4, 75b and PT Ket. ibid., have: "What is a deed of inspection? R. Judah...."

1:2.XVIII.D: The less people making the assessment the better so that word not be spread and allow the slaves to hear that they are to be sold. (PM; QH similarly; see the citations in AZWY, Meg., p. 92).

1:2.XVIII.H-K: See BT Ket. 100a.

1:2.XVIII.I: Forefathers -- PT Ket. "forefather." See AZWY ibid. (AZWY cites ^{C}Itur as reading zqynk in quoting PT Ket. However, ed. pr. of ^{C}Itur (p. 73c) reads zqynyk.

But if they...inspection. -- this reading is difficult, for it was the rabbis, and not R. Simeon b. Gamaliel, who said that the sale is valid only if a deed of inspection was issued (M. Ket. 11:5). Based on BT Ket. 100a, QH would emend our text, accordingly, to read instead: "Otherwise what power does the court have?"

1:2.XVIII.K: [Simeon b.] -- so PT Ket. and PT Meg. See AZWY ibid.

1:2.XIX.B-C: Paralleled in PT San. 1.1, 18b.

See above, 1:1 VII with notes.

1:2.XIX.D: What has the ox done... -- "What has the owner done? (PM).

1:2.XIX.E: Brigand -- Ms. L and ed. V read lystys.

1:2.XIX.G-H: See BT San. 15a; Mekh. RI, Mšptym, 10 (p. 285); Mekh. RaSHBI to 21:29 (p. 181); T. San. 3.2 and TR ad loc. (2.153). In other words, the words "also its master will die" in Ex. 21:19 are not to be taken literally but are to be interpreted as the exegetical fulcrum whereby the trial of the ox is likened to the trial of the master. On the question posed in ŠQ s.v. 'p mytt, see L. Ginzburg, "Some Abbreviations..." (above, on 1:2.XIV.A-C), p. 146-147.

1:3.I.A: One...following -- lit., "Come and see."

[Namely...priest] -- so PM. Alternatively, the two refer to the law that two people may not stand trial (in a capital case) in one day (M. San. 6.4 and parallels; QH and Sivitz, p. 123.

1:3.I.B: Patriarch - nśy'. Paralleled in BT San. 15b-16a.

1:3.I.C: See BT San. 16a and RḤ ad loc.

1:3.II.A-B: In BT San. 16a the exegesis is: "Just as the case of the rebellious elder (Deut. 17:12) requires a court of seventy-one so too does the case of the false prophet."

1:3.II.C-D: See above on II.A-B. The "speaking" in the case of the rebellious elder may refer to Deut. 17:9, "And they shall declare unto thee the sentence (dbr) of judgment" (QH) or to Deut. 17:10 "And thou shalt do according to the sentence (dbr) (PM) or Deut. 17:11 "Thou shalt not turn aside from the sentence (dbr). On dybr (=dbwr) see Sokoloff, p. 274 [38], Kutscher in Erkhe HaMilon HeḤadash LeSifrut Ḥazal, I (ed. Y. Kutscher), p. 72; and N. Bergrin in HaṢofeh, 18 Nissan 5703 [= Koveṣ Ma^{C}amarim BeLashon Ḥazal, ed. M. Bar-Asher, (Jerusalem, 1972), p. 254].

1:3.III.B-H: Paralleled in PT Shebu. 2.3, 33d (partly cited in RḤ to BT Shebu. 15a).

1:3.III.B: At the outset -- see STEY ad loc., pp. 510-511.

1:3.III.C: In Jerusalem -- so MT. Our text: "The God of Israel."

1:3.III.D-G: The section is problematic, since, first, the exegetical bases in D, E, and F are unclear and, secondly, G, seemingly belonging to the structural pattern of B-G (verse followed by exegesis), yet has no exegesis. The commentaries, therefore, understand Deut. 32:7 as proof for D, since this verse connects "father" and "elders" (=Sanhedrin) (PM, QH). "The song" then introduces its proof (rather than following it) which is Neh. 12:32 (continuing until 12:36 -- so QH; or the proof may be from a reading in the verse šry yhwdh rather than śry yhwdh -- so Krochmal, p. 105). Similarly, "thank offerings" introduces its proof, Neh. 12:31.

1:3.III.G: Upon the wall -- MT: m^{c}l lḥwmh. Our text: m^{c}l hḥwmh.

1:3.III.H: Neusner's translation tries to make sense of a difficult passage, which is, literally: "Why is it written 'walked in processing' (mhlkwt), not 'moved in procession' (thlwkwt)?" The passage is difficult, since Neh. 12:31 does read thlwkwt. Note, however, that LXX reads dielthon in the active voice and MT in 12:38 has the active hwlkt. See YE to Shebu. 15a.

1:3.III.I: And of all its furniture -- MT: "And concerning the pattern of all its furniture."

1:3.III.I-N: Cited in RH to San. 16b.

1:3.III.N-P: See above on 1:3.III.D-G, according to which Deut. 32:7 is unnecessary in our section (N). It is accordingly deleted by QH.

1:3.III.P: Dung -- MT: h'špt. Our text: h'šph.

1:3.III.Q: See above on 1:3.III.H.

1:3.III.S-BB: See BT Shebu. 15b.

1:3.III.W-X: Toward -- lit., "Opposite" which means here "side-by-side," cf. BT Shebu. 15b.

QH interchanges the clauses of W and X, since it is only if the two parties are walking one after the other that a single offering -- the one of the first party -- sanctifies ("atones for") each step ("every place") of the new additions to the city. If the parties are side-by-side, the new ground being gradually covered in the procession is sanctified by both offerings simultaneously.

1:3.III.Y: [T. San. 3:4.E] -- also M. Shebu. 2:2 (above, III.A). The "inner one," i.e. the second in the procession (see BT Shebu. 15b) has come into an area already sanctified by the "outer" party and may, therefore, be eaten.

1:3.III.Z: Toward -- see above on W-X.

1:3.III.BB: QH understands this section as an answer to Z while PM (cf. STEY, p. 511), following BT Shebu. 15b, sees it answering also the view of "one offering after the other," since M. Shebu. 2:2 requires two offerings for sanctification and, therefore, the second party never entered a sanctified area.

1:3.III.CC-DD: See YE to Shebu. 16a.

1:3.III.CC: On tānayyi (tmn) see MLH, p. 891 and MAG, p. 26 ff.

1:3.IV.D: The translation follows PM and the meaning is that once the area is consecrated, work on the walls becomes similar to a sinful "trespass" in the order of the sacrifices (Lev. 5:15-16; M. Tractate Me^{c}ilah). Alternatively (and seemingly correct): "They do not regard the walls as if they were standing." Once the walls are destroyed we do not view the area as consecrated and therefore building may take place. (QH; YE to Shebu. 16a [= Ruaḥ Zekenim, ad loc.]; see also RYDBZ ad loc.).

1:3.V.A: Courtyards -- lit., Temple (hykl).

1:3.V.B-C: Following BT Shebu. 15a-b the answer given in B refers to the two loaves of leavened bread brought on Shebuot (Lev. 23:17). The question in C resolves, according to BT, into the following: Consecration must occur at the time of the building and building may not take place on a festival (see MP).

1:3.V.E: Building may not take place on the Sabbath (BT Yeb. 6a) and see above on C.

1:3.V.G: Building may not take place at night (BT Shebu. 15b) and see above on C.

1:3.V.H: See BT Shebu. 15a and QH.

1:3.V.I-J: The assumption is that the Temple area in Ezra's days, although lacking a rebuilt Temple, was yet considered consecrated. Therefore sacrifices could be brought and the meal offering with them. (The meal offering without a prior sacrifice is not considered sanctified; see BT Shebu. 15b with Rashi.) However, at the building of the first Temple the Temple area had not yet been consecrated with a prior Temple and therefore no sacrifice could be brought, (PM, QH, RYDBZ).

1:3.V.K: Nob and Gibeon -- where sacrifices were brought before the first Temple was established.

1:3.VI.A-E: Paralleled (with variants) in BT Shebu 16a. See TR 2:153.

The translation follows the text of T. Ms. V and ed. T. Ms. E and BT Shebu. (cf. also the PT text), however, read in B-C thus: (B) "The lower one was sanctified with all these procedures, but the upper one was not sanctified until the exiled came up -- without a king, without Urim, and without Thummim. (C) In the lower one..."

In D PT reads, "while the associates would eat Lesser Holy Things and second tithe.

On the form hyt (as opposed to hyth) in E (Ms. L and ed. V) see MLH pp. 1208, 1252-3 and Sokoloff, p. 27.

1:3.VI.A: Valleys -- see Kohut, Arukh 2:155 (s.v. bṣ^{c}3) and vol. 9 ("Additions"), p. 101.

1:3.VII.A-B: The scriptural proof may be only to show that each tribe's sanhedrin must judge its own tribe (QH and see T. San. 3.10 = BT San. 16b) or that each tribe must have its own sanhedrin (PM, STEY, p. 511).

1:3.VIII.A-F: See T. San. 14.1; T. Neg. 1.13; BT San. 16b.

1:3.VIII.E: Gentiles -- so Ms. L and ed. V. Ed. Zhitomer and following have the censor's substitution: "idolators."

1:4.E: In addition to -- or "over."

1:4.L: I derive the inference -- PT text is here corrupt reading š'mr hyh which is most probably from an original š'hyh becoming separated to š' hyh and š' being understood as an abbreviation for š'mr.

1:4.L-O: The exegesis is as follows: From "You shall not follow the majority opinion to do evil" (i.e., to condemn) I derive the inference that a majority to acquit is followed. There is no reason then for the last part of the verse, "Follow the majority," for if it refers to condemning it contradicts the first part of the verse, and if to acquittal the law is already derived by inference.

In answer, the verse is explained by reference to two different types of majority thus: "You shall not follow the majority (of one vote) to do evil (i.e. to condemn)," from which I derive the inference that a majority of one vote to acquit is followed. The last part of the verse, "Follow the majority," refers to a majority of two votes and to a verdict of guilt.

1:4.I.A-F: Parallel in PT Ber. 7.3, 11c (AZWY, p. 174, to which see PT Ber. ed. Luncz, ad loc., note to line 4); PT Meg. 4.4, 75a; and Gen. R. 91.3 (p. 1110). A is found below, PT San. 4.10, 22b. and C-D (with variants) in BT Ber. 21b, BT Meg. 23b, and BT San. 74b.

1:4.I.A: (Num. 35:24, 25): Here Neusner is following PM's statement that the "congregation" spoken of is that in Num. 35. This would be so if A-F were original to PT San. as PM to Meg. believes is the case. However, from R. Simon's statement (C-D) and R. Yasa's statement (F), which have nothing to do with the subject in San., it would appear that A-F is original to either PT Meg. (so QH to San.) or to PT Ber. (See Albeck's note to Gen. R. ed. T-A, and Sivitz, pp. 312-313).

The laws under discussion in PT Meg. and PT Ber. as well as BT Meg., BT Ber., and BT San. (note also tny Samuel...qydws in PT Meg.) all deal with matters of sanctification. R. Simon's statement and R. Yasa's statement are therefore fitting and R. Yohanan's "congregation" is thought to refer to either Lev. 19:2, "Speak unto all the congregation of the children of Israel, and say unto them: Ye shall be holy (qdwsym, 'sanctified')" (so Frankel ed. PT Ber., ad loc., and QH to San. and Meg.) or to Psalms 82:1, "God standeth in the congregation of God" (so Gen. R. according to some Mss. and Luncz, ed. PT Ber.). (The verse cited in the name of Azikri, the author of Sefer Ḥaredim, to PT Ber., ad loc. [printed in ed. Zhitomer and following] does not exist.)

1:4.I.E: The translation follows PM (to San., Ber., and Meg.), which is, however, based on BT (see MP to Ber. and San.). R. Yasa's objection is, rather, as follows: "If from the usage of 'within' (of Gen. 42:5) you wish to derive the matter, then they are many," i.e. the preposition "within" is syntactically connected to "the others" which follows it. "The others" who came to Egypt were many more than ten. (So QH; Frankel, ed. PT Ber.; Luncz, ed. PT Ber.; and Albeck in Gen. R.).

1:4.II.B-X: Paralleled in T. Ḥag. 2.9 and BT San. 88b (with variants). Partly quoted (excluding G-S) in RH to San. 18a.

The text underlying the translation is T. San. Ms. E excepting F and R which is taken from the PT text. For a discussion of this section see Goldenberg, pp. 22-35.

1:4.II.B: Ms. V and edd. of T. San. and T. Ḥag., BT and PT: "Said R. Yose, 'At first there were no dissensions in Israel, for the court (PT: Sanhedrin) of seventy-one was in the hewn-stone chamber.'" So too in RH.

1:4.II.C: Other courts of three -- Ms. V and edd. of T. San., T. Ḥag., PT (and see also BT) and RH: "Two courts of three."

Rampart -- ḥyl.

1:4.II.F: Distinguished member -- mwpl', which may be the title of an officer of the court.

1:4.II.K: Court -- PT: "Sanhedrin."

1:4.II.L: See BT Soṭ. 45a and BT San. 37a.

1:4.II.T: Law -- halakhah. PT and RH: "Torah."

1:4.II.U: Paralleled in BT Soṭ. 47b and PT Ḥag. 2.2, 77d. After "Israel" Tos., Ms.V and edd., parallels and RH read: "And there became two Torahs" (BT Soṭ.: "sects").

1:4.I.V: Prudent -- špwy, Jastrow (p. 1614, s.v. špy I): "humble." Levy (4.594, s.v. špy): "prudent, tranquil." Kohut, Arukh (8.126, s.v. šp II): "tranquil, serene." Ms.V and edd.: w^c nyw wšpwy (edd.: wšpl), "humble and contrite" (Jastrow, ibid.).

Good repute -- cf. BT Ta^c an. 16b. Lit., "a good age." PT and RḤ have: "Wise, deeply humble (^c nyw špwy; cf. Levy, ibid.), benevolent, content (npš šplh), a lowly spirit, a good heart, a good nature, a good lot." On the meaning of prq/ḥlq ṭwb see GJP, pp. 72-75

1:4.II.W: Wanting in PT as is the first clause of X. RḤ has the text as in Neusner's translation.

1:4.II.X: See above, W, and T. Sheq. 3.27.

Ms. V, edd., PT and RḤ add: "They promote him and seat him on the court of the Temple mount" before the promotion to the Rampart's court.

1:4.III.A-C: Quoted in RḤ to San. 18a.

1:4.III.A: The text behind the translation is the Mishna. PT reads: "The sanhedrin was arranged like the half of a round threshing floor and the chief officer (nasi) sat in the center so that they could see him and hear his voice." Apparently A together with B-C is a citation of T. San. 8:1.

1:4.III.B: Elders -- i.e., judges.

1:4.III.C: The parenthetical remark is not in the PT text.

1:4.IV.A-F: Parallel in BT San. 18a and PT San. 10.2, 28d. See Sifrei Deut. 14 (p. 23) with Finkelstein's note.

1:4.IV.H: [One out of ten male residents] -- or "[One for every ten...]"

Those who are on trial...: The text reads: "And those who are on trial..." (without a preceding colon). The passage is difficult and the attempts made to harmonize it with BT San. 17b (PM, QU, MM, YE) are not convincing.

Chief of the court -- ḥzn, "attendant;" see Kohut, Arukh, 3.359a, s.v.

1:4.V.A: In addition to -- see above on 1:4.E.

1:4.V.B: Of the people -- MT: lbny. Our text: bbny.

1:4.V.B-H: Paralleled in BT San. 17a, Num. R. 4.10, Sifre Num. 95 (p. 96), and quoted in Arukh, s.v. ptq (6.466-467). B-E is cited in RḤ to San. 18a.

1:4.V.D: Slips -- pyṭqyn (= Greek: pittákion).

1:4.V.E: Urn -- qlpy (= Greek: kálpē).

1:4.V.I-N: Paralleled in Num. R. 4.10.

1:4.V.I: His fellows -- see below on 1:4.V.CC.

1:4.V.O-P: Quoted in Arukh, s.v. ptq (6.467) and RH to San. 18a.

1:4.V.O: The ed. Zhitomer (and following) reading, tnyyn', "the second [Tanna]" is a corruption of Ms. L and ed. V tnyy', "a Tanna." See below, 1:4.V.HH.

His fellows -- see below on 1:4.V.CC.

1:4.V.R: [Abbahu] -- see below, 1:4.V.JJ-KK.

1:4.V.S-T: Paralleled in Num. R. 4.9 and BT Bekh. 5a. Cited in RḤ to San. 18a.

On the various names preserved for the Hegemon (and on the variant "Rabban Gamaliel") see Kohut, Arukh, 7.135, s.v. qwnṭrqws.

1:4.V.T: Priesthood -- i.e., Levites.

1:4.V.U-GG: Paralleled in BT San. 17a, Num. R. 15.19, and Sifre Num. 95 (pp. 95-96).

1:4.V.CC: His colleagues -- ḥbryy'. ŚY, however, here and in HH reads: ḥbryh which may indeed be vocalized ḥabrayāh, "colleagues," but may also be vocalized ḥabreh, "his colleague." The latter would seem more apt in the context, especially considering the expression hg^c ^cṣmk in the singular (O and HH). Cf. KL.

1:4.VI.A-G: Paralleled in BT Bekh. 5a-b. Cited in RH to San. 18a. The first part of A (Antoninus...accounts) is in Num. R. 4.19. The following charts will be found useful for this unit.

I.

1 mina/litra = 25 sheqels

II.

	talent/ centenarius		minas/litras		sheqels		half-sheqels
	1	=	60	=	1500	=	3000
or	1	=	100	=	2500	=	5000
sanctuary weight	1	=	120	=	3000	=	6000

III.

	603,550 half-sheqels
at 1:60	= 201.1 talents
at 1:100	= 120.7 talents
at 1:120	= 100.5 talents

IV.

		70 talents/centenarii	+	96 minas/litras (or 2400 sheqels)
at 1:60	=	71 talents/centenarii	+	36 minas/litras (or 900 sheqels)
at 1:100	=	70 talents/centenarii	+	96 minas/litras (or 2400 sheqels)
at 1:120	=	70 talents/centenarii	+	96 minas/litras (or 2400 sheqels)

V.

		1775 sheqels		
at 1:60	=	71 minas/litras	=	1.1 talents/centenarii
at 1:100	=	71 minas/litras	=	.71 talents/centenarii
at 1:120	=	71 minas/litras	=	.59 talents/centenarii

1:4.VI.A: Centenarius -- Targum Ps.-Jon. translates kkr ("talent") of Ex. 38:25 as qnṭynryn, "centenarius."

Libras -- libra is the Latin for the Greek lítra which is what our text has. What is termed a litra in PT San. 8.2, 26a is termed a maneh in BT San. 70a.

1:4.VI.B: Our teacher -- rbn. Not only when we compare rbn with rbkm above, 1:4.VI.A, but also when we compare rbn with the reading in ŚY, rbynw, Kutscher's statement that rbn = "our teacher" ("The Aramaic of the Samaritans" [Hebrew], Tarbiz, 37, pp. 403-404; [HAS, pp. 262-263 in the Hebrew section]) is substantiated.

He continued -- this translation follows the commentaries and the BT parallel, however, 'mr lyh, "he said to him," usually connotes a change in speaker. "He said to him, 'Is it not written...'" is the formulaic expression used to introduce each of R. Yohanan's three answers (B,D, and F).

And the copper from the wave offering was seventy... -- so the Biblical text and ŚY. Ms. L and edd. are corrupt.

1:4.VI.B: [One libra...convenient] -- this is unclear and incorrect I think. Rather: [One libra being twenty-five sheqels. Now, ninety-six libras = one talent and thirty-six libras (or 900 sheqels) (at the rate of a talent = sixty libras) which is what Scripture should have said.] Yet Scripture gives the amount in the smaller weight (2400 sheqels). See Šiṭah Mequbbeṣet to BT Bekh.

1:4.VI.C: Into libras -- rather: "Into talents." See above, on B.

The centenarii do not amount to a talent -- the rate is one talent = 100 libras and not 1:60 so that ninety-six libras do not equal even one talent.

[I maintain...sheqels.] -- the entire argument is not in the text and is supplied from BT Bekh. via the commentaries.

1:4.VI.D: [Yet Scripture...libras] -- rather: "Yet Scripture gives the amount in the smaller weight (1775 sheqels)." See above, on B.

1:4.VI.E: The centenarii did not amount to a talent -- the rate is one talent = 100 libras (or 2500 sheqels) and not 1:60 so that seventy-one libras (= 1775 sheqels) do not equal even one talent.

ŚY adds: "But if you insist that they do, [I maintain that Scripture was interested only in a large round number of talents but not in listing one talent.]" See above, on p. 80 C, Rashi to BT Bekh., and PM.

1:4.VI.F: See BT BB 90a-b and BT Men. 77a.

And fifteen sheqels -- so ŚY and ed. Z ff. Ms. L and ed. V have wrongly "And twenty-five sheqels."

2:1.I.A-E: Quoted in RḤ to San. 18a.

2:1.I.A: See Ṭur, ḥm, 124 and J. Falk, Derišah, ad loc.

2:1.I.C-E: Quoted in Arukh s.v. 'nṭlr (1.146); Ṭur; ibid; Naḥmanides, Novellae on Shebu. 30a, s.v. wky tym'; Mordekhai to BM 39a, s.v. 'pwṭrwpws; SMG II, 97 (p. 186c); Responsa of R. Isaac b. Sheshet, #392, s.v. w^{c}th, Yom Tob ben Abraham Ishbili, Novellae on Shebu. 30a, s.v. šm; RN(1) to Shebu. 30a, s.v. mn'; Asher ben Yehiel, Novellae to Shebu. 30a, s.v. wky.

2:1.I.C: Mandatary -- 'nṭlr = the Greek entoleýs.

2:1.I.I: Paralleled in BT San. 18b.

Tos. (Ms. Erfurt) and BT have: "Intercalation of the year."

2:1.I.J-L: In ŚY J-L is followed by the opinion of "the other" (wḥrnh ') which would seem (the text is not entirely preserved and a defninite statement cannot be made) to be identical to the first opinion except in L where the first opinion ends with, "...station of the king," and the second opinion continues to the end of L.

ŚY in J has, "The King of Israel." See BT 19a and ŠQ.

2:1.II.A-III.P: Paralleled in PT Hor. 3.2, 47a which is quoted in Yalqut Šimeoni ed. Salonica, ŚY, p. 336 (but incorrectly identified by Ginzberg as the San. text). 2:1.II.A-2:1.III.A (beginning) and part of P are quoted in Barzilai, Sefer HaŠetarot (ed. S.J. Halberstam), pp. 131-2. On 2:1.III.A-P see Midrash Samuel 7.5. 2:1.II.A-2:1.III.C is cited by Kesef Mishnah and David ben Zimra to MT, Sanhedrin 17.8.

2:1.II.C-D: Found in ŚY on our San. text (p. 257; see also p. 336) as well as in the PT Hor. parallel. (Also in PT Hor. printed in BT edd. after BT Hor. However, the value of these readings for our section is nil, for the following reason. In BT ed. pr. [1521] and the early edd. of BT our section is missing, since it was missing in the PT Ms. before the printer of ed. pr. [The scribe had deleted the section, since it already occurred in PT San.] In the later edd. this lacuna was filled in from the printed edd. of PT. So Lieberman, "Yerushalmi Horayot," Sefer HaYovel LeRebbi Ḥanockh Albeck [Jerusalem, 1963], pp. 295-297.)

2:1.II.F: R. Haninah Ketobah -- see PT Pes. 1.8, 28b; PT Meg. 1.11, 71c; Sivitz, to San., p. 313; Epstein in Tarbiz, vol. 6, pt. 1, p. 40.

Anointed priest -- so in PT Hor., ŚY on San., and Sefer HaŠetarot. Our text, however, and ŚY, p. 336 (Yalqut) have: "High priest." "Anointed priest" is an alternative term for "high priest."

[By the judgment... judges] -- although missing in our text, the line is found in every source mentioned in the previous note.

2:1.III.A: Ruler -- or Patriarch, nśy'.

2:1.III.D: Judah the Patriarch -- this is Judah II, otherwise known as Judan, grandson of Rabbi.

Goths -- ŚY and PT Hor. read gwtyyn.

[R. Simeon b. Laqish] fled -- so in PT Hor. (including the BT ed. and Yalqut in ŚY p. 336). PT San., however, has: "[R. Simeon b. Laqish] struck them [ŚY: and] fled."

To the Tower -- or, more probably, to Magdala, the town. San. Ms. L has ld' Magdala and lhd' Kefar Hittayya while ŚY San. and Hor. (including in ed. BT and Yalqut) read bd' or bhdh. The interchange of the prepositions l- and b- has been shown; see Sokoloff, p. 139; Kutscher, "The Language of the Genesis Apocryphon," Scripta Hierosoloymitana 4 (1957), pp. 29-30 [HAS, pp. 31-32]; MLH, pp. 1110-1129 and especially 1119-1129; Margulies ed. Lev. R., p. 165; Lieberman in Ginzei Kedem vol. 5, pp. 180-183. See also Gen. R. ed. Theodor-Albeck, p. 771; Mekhilta, pisḥa 3 (p. 11) lbyt 'b; and BT Hag. 14b 'rb^{c}h nknsw lprds or bprds depending on the variants.

All the sources (excepting San. Ms. L), both here and below in J (except Yalqut) prefix the relative d to Magdala and Kefar Hittayya, which led Jastrow (p. 726, s.v. mgdl) to translate, "He fled to the synagogue (and schoolhouse) of Magdala," basing himself on Koh. R. to 10:8 knyšt' deMagdala. However, one may more readily translate, "The field of Magadala" (certainly a better place for R. Simeon b. Laqish to hide from the authorities), basing oneself on PT Ma as. 3.1, 50c, bzw šebeMagdala, where there is an antecedent ḥṣr.

Of course this interpretation is somewhat difficult here as there is no antecedent to the pronoun. Perhaps the correct reading is preserved in Yalqut (ŚY, p. 336) br' deKefar Hittayya and (at J) l'br' deMagdala, i.e. the forest, or woods, of Magdala and Kefer Hittaya. See Targ. Ps.-Jon. to Deut. 20:19 for br' = field. 'br' with this meaning (assuming prosthetic aleph) is unattested but cf. 'br'y in Levy, vol. 1, p. 16 (Jastrow, p. 9). (The l' may be metathesis for '''l ["He said to him"] missing only in this source.) Br' in Syriac commonly means "field" (Payne Smith, Thesaurus Syriacus, s.v., Col. 576). In Mandaic: "Country outside towns" (E.S. Drower and R. Macuch, A Mandaic Dictionary [Oxford, 1963], p. 50 s.vv. bar and barai; see also p. 69, s.v. braia with variant ᶜbraia). The Mandaic Dictionary (ibid., s.v. barai) records the reading labarai in Aspar Malwasia 72:18. In the published Ms. (D.C. 31) of this work, however, the reading does not have the first "a" (E.S. Drower, The Book of the Zodiac [London: 1949]).

2:1.III.F-G: Cited in part in Tos., MQ 27b, s.v. ṭpwḥ,"He clapped with one hand and no sound was produced. He clapped with both hands and a sound came out" (Midrash Samuel 7.5) -- i.e., R. Yohanan's word of Torah without first bouncing off R. Simeon would not have much of a sound. See Goldenberg, p. 181, n. 3.

2:1.III.H: Nor is Ben Laqish here -- ŚY, Hor., and Yalqut read instead of wl', w'yn lww ('yn l', w'y l'w) so that literally H would read: "No, and without Ben Laqish -- no!"

Between H and I ŚY, Hor. (but not in ed. BT), and Yalqut add: '''l l', "He said to him, 'No.'" This reading is very difficult, since it would mean that I was said by R. Yohanan and J by R. Judah. It would, therefore, appear that '''l l' is some dittographic error from the preceding l' and succeeding '''l ('l' [this word itself may be a dittography as it is missing in all the parallels]).

2:1.III.I: Where is he hidden -- followng PM and so also Lieberman, YK, p. 22 (see Kohut, Arukh, vol. 9 ["Additions"], p. 347, s.v. ptḥ). Lieberman is basing himself on the euphemistic phrase found elsewhere in PT gbr' mpth' where the latter word as an attributive adjective can take the definite article. Although here, as a predicate adjective, we should not expect the article, exceptions occur. In Syriac, see T. Nöldeke, Compendius Syriac Grammer (London, 1904), Sec. 204B and C. Brockelmann, Syrische Grammatik (Leipzig, 1960q) Sec. 191g; in Mandaic, T. Nöldeke, Mandaische Grammatik (Halle, 1875), Sec. 217, R. Macuch, Handbook of Classical and Modern Mandaic (Berlin, 1965), Sec. 242, and W.S. McCullough, Jewish and Mandean Incantation Bowls in the Royal Ontario Museum (Toronto, 1967), p. 17 s.v. "Bound." in Babylonian Talmudic Aramaic, M. Schlesinger, Satzlehre der Armäischen Sprache des Babylonischen Talmuds (Leipzig, 1928) Sec. 17. Odeberg (Sec. 337) says, "The participle in adjectival force usually stands in... the absolute state... when a predicative." But he cites no "unusual" cases. Nöldeke, Syriac Grammar, ibid.: "Pure participles are always in the abs. st."

Despite this support for Lieberman I do not think a euphemistic idiomatic expression can provide proof for regular usage of the term. It would be tantamount to saying that sgy means "little, lacking" in regular speech since the euphemism sgy nhwr means "blind."

2:1.III.M: [Judah] -- all the sources read "you (pl.) set... your (pl.) Creator."

And not only so, but -- following the reading of ŚY and Hor.

Retinue -- or "Troop." From the Greek droýggos or drakōn. See Kohut, Arukh, 3.142, s.v. and 9 ["Additions"]. 150, s.v. and the literature there cited.

2:1.III.N: Found in Hor. (also in BT ed.) and in Yalqut, ŚY, p. 336. The ŚY San. fragment does not cover this section, having ended at M.

2:1.III.P: Because I was afraid -- mh dḥyl. Hor.: my dḥyl; Yalqut: mdḥyl.

"The people of the Lord spreading about (m^{c}byrym)" is interpreted to mean "The people of the Lord remove (m byrym) [him]."

2:1.IV.A-VII.O: Paralleled in PT Hor. 3.6, 47d-48a. (PT Hor. in BT early edd. is missing this section as above, 2:1.II.A-III.P. See note to 2:1.II.C-D.) A-K is paralleled in PT MQ 3.8, 83d in a different sequence (H-I, D, C, A-B, E-F, J-K). On A-K see BT Hor. 12b. VII.B-O is paralleled in PT Pes. 8:8, 36a-b.

2:1.IV.E: [Who does... deceased] -- and who requires a tear "above the binding" for all upon whom mourning is obligatory.

2:1.IV.G: This -- following the reading d' in PT Hor. rather than dl' in our text.

2:1.IV.H-K: After I, we have shown that the Mishna is in accord with R. Eleazar's interpretation and follows the view of R. Meir. Therefore, the ordinary priest tears his garment above as stated in the Mishna. But a problem remains in regard to the high priest who does not tear above (J). The answer given (K) is that the high priest is exceptional and still our Mishna follows R. Meir and R. Eleazar.

This interpretation rests on the reading in K š'ynw found in PT MQ. The reading in PT San. and PT Hor., however, is šyh', in which case K is merely read as interrogative, thus: "Should the more strict ruling of the high priest demand undoing the binding [as an ordinary priest?! Of course not. The high priest is exceptional and does not require tearing above]. This entire unit IV follows PM.

2:1.VI.A-C: Paralleled in Sifra, 'Emor, parashah 2.5 (p. 94d).

2:2.B: Rather: "And the appointed [prefect of the priests] places him [= the high priest] between himself and the people."

2:2.I.B: PM translates A-B thus: (A) "The statement... overturning the bed. (B) [it being understood that] the high priest is subject to that requirement of overturning the bed. QH translates B thus: [And] the high priest is subject to that requirement of overturning the bed, [for otherwise why have him sit on a stool? Let him sit on his bed].

2:2.II.C: On the phrase 'yt bh ^{c}nh see Lieberman in Tarbiz 5, pp. 106-7.

2:2.II.G: Will begin to answer 'Amen' -- i.e. the point at which the congregation answers 'Amen' to the Messenger's prayer; see QH.

2:2.II.K: Ordinary day -- see the parallel in PT Ber. 3.2, 6b.

2:3.V.K: And thus... -- rather: "And thus shall you salute the living one -- ['the living one' means] for life -- Peace be to you...." (MT is being followed here, for PT's exegesis depends upon it. See Lieberman, GJP, p. 65.

2:3.V.L: This is a play on the word wynwḥw (PM).

2:3.V.V: Translation follows MT for the text's exegesis.

2:3.V.OO: Cause of grief goes forth -- rather: "Doubts goes forth (typwq pqpwqtk).

2:4.III.F: To relieve himself -- lit., "To cover his feet," (lhsk 't rglyw).

2:5.III.P: The "he" of "he defended it" refers to the owner of the field (PM).

2:5.III.Q: The "he" of "he defended it" refers to the owner of the field (PM).

2:5.IV.H: The quote from the Mishnah is the concluding remark to the previous discussion, i.e., the teaching spoken about in G is that "[the king] may exercise..." (PM).

2:6.I.A: I would add to you as much more -- lit., "I would add to like them and like them (again)."

2:6.II.W: Wept -- so in Koh. R. to verse 2.2.

3:4.II.A: Neusner has the last part of T. San. 5:1 being quoted with the PT addition: "He can retract." It would seem, however, that if the Tosefta is being quoted at all, it is the earlier part (ed. Zuckermandel, lines 27-28) and T has left out a self-understood "he accepted it."

3:4.III.B: PM has the reverse, i.e. Yose's remark refers to the defendant's statement.

3:5.I.G-H: Trains -- lit., "Races, incites."

3:5.II.WW: I -- following MT for purposes of the exegesis.

3:9.III.D-E: Rather (following PM): (D) Before a court... single witness [without a corroborating witness whose testimony before a court is not valid].

(E) In a case in which they said to him, "Lo, you are ... witnesses." Is it... liable [to a sacrifice if he did not give testimony? see Lev. 5:1-10]?

3:9.VI.E: [Josiah's] -- a neutral, "his," would preserve the ambiguity; see PM and QH.

3:12.I.F-G: Rather (following PM; see also MM): (F) ...One said, "[The litigant may introduce evidence] until he declares invalid any evidence he may have."

(G) The other said, "[The litigant may introduce evidence] until he denies that he has any more evidence."

4:5.I.D: Rather (following PM): "Rather the question in A is: 'What is the source of the rule that if he erred and judged -- even the beginning of the judgement -- by night, that the sentence is valid?'"

4:7.II.E: Now if one says... obvious. PM's explanation of "reasonableness" is too farfetched. QH sees Memucan as representative of their trials and Judah of ours. Since they both spoke first, our trials are like theirs.

4:8.I.B-II.C: Lieberman, GJP, 146 reads this section entirely differently (see also STEY p. 518).

5:1.III.A: Idolator -- the uncensored texts (Ms. L, ed. V and Assis' fragment) have: "Gentile."

5:3.D-H: I.e., "At the second hour after sunrise [i.e. 8:00 A.M.]" and so for all the hours in this sec.

5:3.II.N: Neither Assis nor QH could find anywhere that R. Meir held that "But" is to limit.

5:5.II.B: [The one who declares he has no opinion is treated as if he is not present] -- according to PM just the opposite is the case.

6:8.I.C and D: Rather (following PM): He who said glyny understands the word as meaning "light" [i.e. it is not light, but weighty]. He who said ql 'ny understands the word to mean "I am burdened."

6:11.I.B: His ancestors would free him from the rigors of judgment -- So indeed the PT text here. But PM and QH based on BT interpret: "His ancestors have been freed from the rigors of judgement." PT MQ 1:5 [80d top].

7:1.III.H: The last clause of T. San. seems to be a conflation of readings in Tos. and PT.

7:2.Summary: I don't think the language of II D does not necessarily show [80d top] an amalgam of two different theories, since km( )n may mean kmh (see Sokoloff, pp. 25-26). Our passage may then be translated: "As that (kmh) which he (the Tanna) said."

7:5.IV.F: PM treats the two statements as question and answer.

7:8.V.K: PM reads this unit as interrogative and as the second part of the J-K answer.

7:8.VI.D-F: Following the translation a distinction exists between a Gentile and an idolater, a distinction which does not exist, however, in Ms. L and ed. V which reads goy for idolater. (So also in G the reading is goy.)

7:9.F: He who carries out a vow -- PM and others understand mqyym = to take an oath.

7:10.III.O-P: Following PM: If one passes himself through [he is exempt,] for isn't he passing through by foot [cf. F]. For passing oneself through [is, therefore, not considered "passing"]. But if he drew [his son] through and passed him through [he is liable].

7:11.IV.A-D: "Minor" -- less than twelve years and a day. "Maiden" -- twelve years and a day until twelve and one-half years and a day. "Pubescent girl" -- twelve and one-half years and a day and older.

8:1.C: Full -- i.e., until the outline of the entire bears is visible (lnqp = to surround). So also 8:6.A-B.

8:9.I.G: This line of T makes no sense. I'd therefore accept the reading of PT (mmḫyn) and T ed. (mwḫyn; unrecorded in ed. Zuckermandel) over T Mss. (mnyḫyn) and translate accordingly: "For if they would attempt to stop him the incident may come to murder."

10:1.VII.C: Scribe -- or, "Book," referring to the Torah.

10:2.III.F: The walls went and trembled -- a doubtful translation. Rather as translated below, 10:8.I. Q: "Their funds declined." (Y. Abramsky: "His children between Abiram and Segub gradually died" -- also doubtful.)

10:5.I.A: The world to come ... the world to come -- in the text a distinction is made, the first term being l^{c}wlm hb', the second l^{c}tyd lb' (cf., however, T. San. 13:12).

11.4.II.R: Equivalent to two ephahs - add: "Each ephah is three seahs."

Mak. 1:3.I.B: Fifteenth... fifteenth -- Fifth... fifth (PM). PT text: Fifth... tenth.

Mak. 1:4.I.A: The first part of M. BQ, which is crucial to the following discussion, is omitted.

Mak. 2:3.II.A-B: PM: "And does he have the right...," i.e., he should be guilty of homicide. The answer (B) is that since the wall was about to fall, passers-by should have been careful. See Albeck's notes to the Mishnah.

Mak. 2:6.IV.A-L: Our text of PT on this section is corrupt and is missing the following:

> They asked the Torah, "As to a sinner, what is his punishment?" She said to them, "Let him bring a sacrifice and he will be forgiven."
> They asked David, "As to a sinner, what is his punishment?" He said to them, "'Let sinners be consumed from the earth' (Ps. 104:35)."

See Lieberman, Shkiin, p. 76, and Midrash Debarim Rabbah (Jerusalem, 1974^3) who cites the sources for this omission.

Mak. 2:6.VI.B-D: Lit., "And is it not written 'And God spoke...' etc." The scribe here with the word "etc." (grsh) calls attention to -- but does not complete -- the rest of this rabbinic midrash. The continuation, however, is found in a Ms. fragment to our text (published in Tarbiz, 17, pp. 133-134; see also Lieberman in Tarbiz, 5, p. 109), from which we translate (following Wieder's annotations, ibid.) as follows: And is it not written "And God spoke to Noah (and to his sons) saying" (Gen. 8:15)? What new point is being made here?! The new point is the prohibition of eating a limb torn from a living animal (Gen. 9:4). And is it not written, "And Abram fell on his face, and God spoke with him saying" (Gen. 17:3)? What new point is introduced here? The new point is the law of circumcision (Gen. 17:10). And is it not written, "The Lord has sent a word against Jacob" (Isa. 9:7)? What is new here? The prohibition of eating the sciatic nerve (Gen. 32:33). But is it not written, "And God spoke to Moses and said to him, I am the Lord" (Ex. 6:2)? What new point is connoted here? Sanctification of the Name. But, again, is it not written, "And God spoke to Joshua saying" (Josh. 20:1)? What new point is being made here? If you answer, "The institution of six cities of refuge" -- but this point was already made to Moses at Sinai. In the case of Joshua, however, the "speaking" introduces a new factor not found in the verses dealing with Moses (Num. 35:6-28; Deut. 4:41-43). "He shall flee to one of these cities and shall stand at the entrance of the gate of the city, and explain his case to the elders of that city; then they shall take him into the city, and give him a place, and he shall remain with them." What is the meaning of "And they give him a place"? The Rabbis of Caesarea say...." (E).

On the scribal use of grš see B. Bokser, "An Annotated Bibliographical Guide to the Study of the Palestinian Talmud," Aufstieg und Niedergang der römischen Welt, II. 19.2, p. 180.

Mak. 2:6.VII.C-D: D, and not C, may be the Tosefta quote. See the variants listed by Zuckermandel where both Ms. V and edd. read "R. Nehorai" instead of "Abba Saul" and also read (so too Ms. E) "Lo, fifteen."

Mak. 3:13.C: Following is PT to Mak., Chapter 3, missing in our texts but found in a Ms. fragment (Wieder in Tarbiz, 17, p. 135; see also Lieberman, Hilkhoth Ha-Yerushalmi of Rabbi Moses Ben Maimon, pp. 67-68 and E.S. Rosenthal, "HaMoreh," PAAJR, 1963, pp. 32-33): R. Hananiah ben Akashiah said, "God (lit., 'the place'), blessed be he, wanted...." [M. Mak. 3.13]. Why do we call God, "[Place?" For He is the place of the world and the world is not his place.

R. Hunah in the name of R. Imi: "It is written, 'The eternal God is your dwelling place' (Deut. 33:27) to teach that He is the dwelling place of the world and the world is not his dwelling place."

R. Yose ben Halfta said, "It is written, 'And the Lord said, Behold there is a place by me' (Ex. 33:21) to teach that He is the place of the world and not that the world is his place."

R. Isaac said, "It is written, 'The Lord came from Sinai into the holy place' (Ps. 68:18 RSV conjecture; lit. Heb., 'The Lord among them Sinai in the holy [place]'). The logical order, 'The Holy [One] at Sinai,' is reversed to teach that He is the place of the world and not that the world is his place."

R. Judan said, "It is comparable to a warrior riding a horse and his weapons are hanging on either side. It is not the horse which governs (lit., 'bears') the warrior but the warrior who governs the horse."

R. Aha said, "It is written 'The Lord was pleased for his righteousness' sake.' (Isa. 42:21). For your righteousness' sake. For your benefit I said it to you."

(In addition to the above, Lieberman, ibid., gives also the reconstructed text to PT Mak., Chap. 3, hal. 1, 2, 3, 5, 7, 11, 12, 17, based on parallel sugyot found elsewhere in PT.)

ABBREVIATIONS AND BIBLIOGRAPHY

(Dates refer to editions used)

AH	S. Lieberman, ᶜAl HaYerushalmi (Jerusalem, 1929)
ARN	Solomon Schechter ed., 'Avot deRabbi Nathan (Vienna, 1877; New York, 1967[2])
AY	Israel Eisenstein, ᶜAmudei Yerushalmi, Lvuv, 1880; second rev. ed. printed in text of PT, ed. Vilna
AZWY	B. Ratner, Ahawath Zion We-Jerusholaim, 12 vols. (Vilna, 1901-1917; repr. Jerusalem, 1967)
BḤ	Joel Sirkes, Bayit Ḥadash (printed with, and commentary on, Ṭur) __________, Responsa: Bayit Ḥadash
GE	Efrayim Dov Kahohen Lof, Gilyone 'Efrayim (printed in text of PT, ed. Vilna)
GJP	Saul Lieberman, Greek in Jewish Palestine (New York, 1961, 1964[2])
Goldenberg	David Goldenberg, "Halakhah in Josephus and in Tannaitic Literature: A Comparative Study" (Ph.D. dissertation, Dropsie University, 1978)
HAS	E. Y. Kutscher: Hebrew and Aramaic Studies, ed. A Ben-Hayyim et al. (Jerusalem, 1977)
HJP	Saul Lieberman, Hellenism in Jewish Palestine (New York, 1950, 1962[2])
ḥm	ḥosen mishpat

H-R, Mekh.	H. S. Horovitz and I. A. Rabin, ed., Mekhilta deRabbi Ishmael (Breslau, 1930; Jerusalem, 1970)
ḤZL	E. E. Urbach, Ḥazal: Pirqei 'Emunot WeDe^{c}ot (Jerusalem, 1970; in English translation as The Sages: Their Concepts and Beliefs, 1975)
^{c}Itur	Isaac ben Abba Maari, Sefer Ha^{c}Ittur (Venice, 1608)
KL	Hayyim Azulai, Kikar Le'Eden (printed in text of PT, ed. Vilna)
Krauss	S. Krauss, Griechische und Lateinische Lehnwörter in Talmud, Midrasch und Targum II (Berlin, 1899)
Krochmal	A. Krochmal, Yerushalayim HaBenuyah (Lemberg, 1867)
Levy	Jacob Levy, Neuhebräisches und Chaldäisches Wörterbuch uber die Talmudim und Midraschim, nebst beiträgen von H. L. Fleischer (Leipzig, 1876)
Luncz	A. M. Luncz, Talmud Heirosolymitanum Ad Exemplarin Editiones Principis, I - V (Jerusalem, 1907-1919)
MAG	Y. Kutscher, "Meḥqarim Be'Aramit Gelilit," Tarbiz 21, pp. 192-205; 22, pp. 53-63, 185-192; 23, pp. 36-60
Mantel	Hugo Mantel, Studies in the History of the Sanhedrin [Harvard Semitic Series XVII] (Harvard Univ. Press, 1965)
Meiri	Menaḥem HaMe'iri, Beit HaBeḥirah to Sanhedrin (ed. with notes by A. Sofer, 2nd impr. ed., Jerusalem, 1945)
Metibot	B.M. Lewin ed., Methiboth... to which is Appended Sepher Hefez (Jerusalem, 1933)
ML	Ḥanokh Albeck, Mavo LaTalmudim (Tel Aviv, 1969)
MLA	J. N. Epstein, Mevo'ot LaSifrut Ha'Amor'aim (Jerusalem, 1963)
MLH	J. N. Epstein, Mavo LaNusaḥ HaMishnah (Jerusalem, 1964^{2})
MLT	J. N. Epstein, Mevo'ot LaSifrut HaTanna'im (Jerusalem, 1957)
MM	Yeḥiel Michal Epstein, Mikhal HaMayim, in Hashlamah LiYerushalmi (= Supplement Volume to Vilna-Romm edition, 1928, and reprints)
MP	Moses Margalioth, Mareh HaPannim
MT	Moses Maimonides, Mishneh Torah
NY	Joseph Ḥabiba, Nimmuqei Yoseph (printed with, and commentary on, Alfasi)
Odeberg	Hugo Odeberg, Short Grammar of Galilaean Aramaic (Lund, 1939) [Lunds Universitets Arsskrift, N. F. Avd. 1. Bd. 36. Nr 4]
P	Perush ("Anonymous" Commentary of David Darshan. First printed in margin of PT, ed. Cracow and then ed. Krotoschin)
PM	Moses Margalioth, Pene Moshe
QH	David Frankel, Qorban Ha^{c}Edah

QHY	"Qiṣur Hagadot HaYerushalmi" in Louis Ginzberg, *Genizah Studies* (= *Ginze Schechter*) (New York, 1928), I, pp. 387-429
RḤ	R. Ḥananel, Commentary on BT (printed in Vilna-Romm ed. and following)
RN(1)	Nissim ben Reuben Gerondi, Commentary on, and printed with, Alfasi
RN(2)	___________, *Novellae to Sanhedrin* (in *Sefer Ḥamishah Shiṭot*, Salzbach, 1762)
RYDBZ	Jacob David of Slotz, *Perush HaRidbaz* (in Vilna-Romm ed. of PT)
Shkiin	S. Lieberman, *Shkiin* (Jerusalem, 1970^{2})
SḤY	*Sefer Ḥanokh Yalon*, ed. S. Lieberman, S. Abramson, S. Esh (Jerusalem, 1963)
Sivitz	M. S. Sivitz, *Sefer Mashbiaḫ* (Jerusalem, 1929^{3})
ŚK	Shabbetai ben Meir HaKohen, *Śiftei Kohen* (printed with, and commentary upon, Shulkhan Arukh)
SMG	Moses of Coucy, *Sefer Miṣvot Gadol* (Venice, 1547)
Sokoloff	M. Sokoloff, "Ha^{c}Ivrit Shel Bereshit Rabbah Vat. Ms. 30," *Leshonenu* 33, pp. 25-42, 135-142, 270-279
ŠQ	David Frankel, *Shire Qorban*
STEY	Z.W. Rabinovitz, *Sha^{c}are Torat Eretz Yisrael*
ŚY	Louis Ginzberg, *Śeridei Yerushalmi* (*Yerushalmi Fragments from the Genizah*; New York, 1909)
Taubes	Hayyim Taubes ed., *'Osar HaGeonim to Sanhedrin* (Jerusalem, 1966)
Terminologie	W. Bacher, *Die exegetische Terminologie der jüdischen Traditionsliteratur* (Leipzig, 1905)
TK	Saul Lieberman, *Tosefta Ki-fshuṭah*. I ff. (New York, 1955 -)
TR	Saul Lieberman, *Tosefet Rishonim*. 4 vols. (Jerusalem, 1937-1939)
YE	Aryeh Leib Yellin, *Yefeh ^{c}Enayim* (in Vilna-Romm ed. of BT)
YK	S. Lieberman, *HaYerushalmi Kiphshuto* (Jerusalem, 1934).
YM	Samuel Yafeh Ashkenazi, *Yefeh Mareh* (Venice, 1590)

Chapter 10
YERUSHALMI SHEBUOT
Baruch M. Bokser

1:1.I.B: Lieberman (YK, p. 3 and n. 1) suggests that the phrase "and four to exempt from punishment" is an addition generated by the structural parallel in the preceding phrase. If so, the question would be whether or not M. Shebu. should be interpreted like M. Shab. 1:1. Specifically, does the Mishnah's reference in C to two sets, which yield four subdivisions, mean two that yield four instances of both liability and exemptions or does it mean an absolute number of four cases of liability?

1:1.I.D: The difference in sequence between Y. Shab. and Shebu. is either intentional and reflects Y. Shebu.'s use of traditions that originated in Y. Shab. or else is the result of a corruption. See Lieberman, YK, p. 3.

1:1.I.I: If we follow Lieberman and delete the clause "and four to exempt from liability," I concludes the discussion.

1:1.I.M: QE suggests that M is an alternative answer to K. It would be inappropriate to teach "twelve for exemption," since the present use of the term exemption (PTWR) means "exempt and permitted." The cases and usage in the latter part of M. Shab. 1:1, however, are of "exempt but not permitted."

1:1.III.E: Yerushalmi fragments (GYF, pp. 264ff.) preserve most of the missing material.

1:1.III.K: "Do" is the rendering of S'YNN, which is equivalent to SHYNN. See Epstein, ITM, pp. 201, n. 4, 202, n. 3.

1:1.III.L: "This passage...sages" makes up a pattern that avers that the forthcoming opinion and not the previous ones is normative. See Bokser, Samuel's Commentary, p. 196 and J.N. Epstein, Tarbiz 6 (1924):49-50.

1:2.I.E: Cf. the reading and interpretation in Ramban, cols. 14-15 and n. 96.

1:2.I.O: Pene Moshe and QE reverse "outset" and "end" and provide a different argument to the same effect: by the above logic, since it is not necessary for the verse to indicate knowledge at the "end," apply the requirement of knowledge to the "outset." But the latter requirement would run counter to accepted principles. Line P responds to this problem with an explanation that the verse's specification of knowledge at the "end" is needed for certain "end" situations. See also SQ. This rendering makes the question somewhat smoother.

1:4.V.B: "Of the New Year," which falls on the Sabbath -- thus Lieberman, TK 1:41, n. 37.

1:4.V.E: "The two goats of the New Year" -- one is offered on account of the beginning of the new month; thus Pene Moshe and QE. Rabinovitz (p. 538) emends the text to fit this rendering. He also changes the attribution from "R. Yose" to "R. Ba bar

Mamel." This is to make F's reference to the latter understandable. The reading of the former name would have been generated by the name in D. Cf. QE, who for the same logic, in F, replaces "R. Ba bar Mamel: with "R. Yose."

1:4.V.L: See Lieberman, TK 5:1062, n. 68.

1:4.VI.E: "Through designation." On the basis of the parallel phrases in Y. Yoma 5:1, 42b, and Y. Sheq. 4:5, 48b, Rabinovitz (p. 538) emends the text and replaces BQBW^{C}H, "designation [at the outset]" with BSHYTH or BQRYBH, "slaughtering." QE assumes this rendering.

1:5.I.A: On the attribution cf. Rabinovitz, p. 538, with Epstein, ITM, pp. 398-99. The latter discusses the dynamics of the Amora's response to the Mishnah's text.

1:5.II.A: Neusner follows the version of the baraita in T. Shebu. 1:2 (p. 445, ll. 26-31) to supply the required number of items.

1:6.I.B: The phrase "positive and a" is lacking in Y. Shebu. but found in the Y. Yoma 8:5, 45b parallel. See Epstein, ITM, pp. 336-37.

1:6.V.D: The phrases "Rabbi admits that" and "thus" are added on the basis of the Y. Yoma 8:6, 45b parallel. See Lieberman, TK 4:826, esp. n. 49.

1:6.VI.K: PT Yoma 8:6, 45b also has "Yohanan."

1:6.VI.L: GYF, p. 266, and the Y. Yoma 8:6, 45b parallel have DBRY HKMYM, "the words of the sages," instead of HKMYM 'WMRYM, "the sages say." See n. 7 and especially the reference to Epstein.

1:6.VI.T-Y: See Lieberman, TK 4:834, n. 75; Ramban, col. 47; and Pene Moshe to the Y. Yoma 8:6, 45c parallel.

1:6 end: See, e.g., Lieberman, TK 4:826.

M.1:7.A: Epstein (ITM, p. 957) suggests the Mishnah originally lacked this and certain other phrases. This helps him explain the Talmud pericope I.A-E. See n. to 1:7.I.C

1:7.I.B: Epstein emends this to "indeed is," switching the phrase with one in clause C. See n. to 1:7.I.C

1:7.I.C: Epstein emends this to "there is no." See n. to 1:7.I.B. According to Epstein, D refers to B of the Mishnah, which -- he claims -- originally lacked the phrase "annointed priest." See n. to M.1:7A.

1:7.II.Q: "By the confession and the casting of lots." The Leiden MS and editio princeps have "by the confession" alone and commentators, on the basis of logic and the Y. Yoma 6:2, 43c parallel, emend the text to read "the casting of lots" (BHGRLH). See Pene Moshe; QE; and Duenner, p. 221.

2:2 end: See Lieberman, OY, p. 23.

2:3.I.E: Lieberman (TK 4:744) suggests we add a prefix and read [K]LPNY LPNYM, "and went forward..." The person must prostrate himself with his face -- and not his back -- toward the holy precints. See n. to 2:3.I.G.

2:3.I.G: Lieberman (TK 4:744-45) corrects S'SH' to SSH', "has bowed." He explains that the Talmud asks rehtorically, "Is not the individual liable if he merely bows?" Hence why does it state "Until he remains for an interval sufficient for prostrating himself"? Therefore we learn even if he went forward inside, he is not liable until he prostrates himself or has remained for an interval sufficient for him to prostrate himself.

2:4: See Lieberman, "Yerushalmi Horayot," p. 289.

3:1.II.C: Pene Moshe and in a different way Rabinovitz (p. 541) preserve some of the section while deleting the rest. On the other hand, QE and Duenner (p. 225) preserve the basic structure through emendations. They have a basically identical rendering for the initial portion: "Rather we interpret the issue to be a case of." They differ in the formulation of the next section. Pene Moshe: whether or not [eating] any amount [even a small amount] constitutes eating." [See Lieberman, TK 4:834, n. 74.] QE and Duenner: "An oath [or a 'general oath'] inclusive of any amount. Is any amount considered eating?" Pene Moshe without the latter question, connects the next clause to the former: "for R. Aqiba believes eating any amount is also included." QE and Duenner: "It is explainable in accord with R. Aqiba [QE: 'R. Simeon'] who holds that [eating] any amount is considered eating."

3:2.I.B: Instead of "derived the two of them" read "heard it," i.e. the proposition that drinking is subsumed under eating. The latter is the reading in the parallels in Y. Yoma 8:2, 45a, and Y. M.S. 2:1, 53b. See Duenner, p. 225.

3:2.I.C: Neusner follows Pene Moshe and the other commentaries who adopt the reading in the parallels. See n. to 3:2.I.B.

3:2.I.D: If we follow the Talmud parallels, we should delete lines 8-10. If the lines are secondary, they may have been generated by a pericope in Y. 3:1. See above n. to 3:1.II.C and text thereto.

3:2.I.G: The Talmud parallels read, "R. Jonah heard it [the proposition] from as follows," See n. to 3:2.I.B.

3:2.I.R-S: The parallels differ in the wording of clauses R and S and their place within the sugya. Epstein (ITM, p. 72) suggests the clauses belong between clauses O and P. Cf. Duenner, p. 226.

3:5.IV.T: The passage has been transferred from above, Y. 3:1, 34b. Lieberman (OY, p. 17) suggests that the scribe mistakenly transcribed the phrase "one cannot say so, for," words that do not fit the new context and that naturally posed problems to the commentators.

M.3:6.G: Clause G is an explanatory gloss to the Mishnah.

3:6.I.A: This explanation of Mani's comment is based upon an interpretation of Rashi. Epstein (ITM, pp. 401-3) offers a different rendering of pericope I along with II. Mani explains the import of C of the Mishnah: C is not a rhetorical statement that leads into D-F, according to which Mani would agree with the anonymous authorities in F. Rather, C represents an autonomous statement asserting that the individual is liable. D serves to provide a reason for the opinion in C.

3:6.II.A: "Eat [carrion]" = Epstein, ITM, p. 402. At the end, commentators and Epstein (see p. 402, n. 3) supply an additional clause: "and a yes [is not treated] as no different from a no" [such that one who takes an oath that "I shall eat carrion" is exempt, and that one who takes an oath that "I shall not eat" is liable]?

3:7.I.A: Follow Epstein (IAL, p. 276) and add the negative: "and he did not eat it."

3:7.I.G: The "and" (W-) is probably an instance of the disjunctive usage meaning "or" see Meiri, p. 7, and QE.

3:8.I.A-B: On A-B see Weiss Halivni, ST 1:292-94.

3:8.V.L: The text reads, literally, "even an egg [BY^{C}H] and a pearl." The word for "egg" is preserved in the Y. Ned. 3:3, 35a parallel but corrupted in Y. Shebu., in the editio princeps to BYTH, which was further corrupted to BYT'.

3:8.VI.D-F: Certain medieval citations vary in the reading of D-F. See Ramban, col. 127; Rashba, p. 67; and Lieberman, TK 7:418, who discusses the readings and the whole pericope.

3:8.VII.A: Lieberman (GJP, p. 34, n. 32) cogently suggests that the correct reading is TYNYN, "figs," and not TRYN, "two [things]," and that, therefore, the individual swears that "figs are figs."

3:8.VII.B: See Lieberman, GJP, pp. 33-37, and "More on the Leiden MS to Yerushalmi," Tarbiz 20 (1950):116-17. Since rain is already falling, this prayer for rain is useless and therefore takes God's name in vain, which constitutes an instance of a vain oath.

3:9.I.D: Alternatively: "It was said not in reference to this [baraita] but in reference to this baraita." See the Y. Ned. 3:3, 38a parallel.

3:9.III.E: Epstein (ITM, p. 552 and n. 2), supported by two medieval citations, suggests instead of "a rash oath" we read "a vain oath and a rash oath." This accords with the interpretation of the Mishnah that clause D refers to a rash oath in addition to the vain oath.

4:1.I.L: While the version of the sugya in Y. Sanh. 3:9 (10), 21c has this chain of tradition, the versions in Y. Yoma 6:1, 43b and Y. Shebu. 4:1, 35b add the name of "R. Huna" after R. Yose b. R. Bun." Huna may well have been an intermediary in the tradition's citation. See Bacher, Tradition, pp. 435, 498.

4:1.I.O: The Y. Shebu. 4:1 and Y. Yoma 6:1 versions add the additional injunction that the judge "not be forbearing toward one and brazen toward the other." See the version of the baraita in T. Sanh. 6:2, p. 423, 1.33 to p. 424, 1.6.

4:1.I.P: The Y. Shebu. 4:1 and Y. Yoma 6:1 parallels include a second portion in Judah's comment. It explains how the equal justice presecribed in O may still be maintained: "['What is' = Y. Yoma] the prohibition? That one should not stand and the other sit." The clause is probably not secondary to the text, since it is attested in the baraita's versions in the T. Sanh. 6:1 and Sifra, Qedoshim, 4:4 (Weiss ed. p. 89a). Since the latter two sources likewise have the introductory question, "what is," found in Y. Yoma, it too is probably original.

4:1.II.F: The reading of F as a conclusion of the preceding material and G as a question follows Y. Shebu. and not Y. Sanh., in which both are presented as questions. See Pene Moshe to Y. Sanh. and QE to Y. Shebu. Lines Q-R provide an analogue to this pattern of a deduction and then a question.

4:1.II.H: To explain logically why the witnesses should not be related to one another or to the judges, the texts of the Talmud present two reasons but associate each with the wrong clause. Commentators, including GE and QE to Y. Shebu., Pene Moshe to Y. Sanh., and Duenner (p. 180) already observed that logic required the switch, which is further supported by the Talmud's citations of Rif to b. Sanh. chapter three (p. 8b [= p. 16]) and RN to b. Ket., chapter two (p. 12b [= p. 24]).

4:1.II.T: See n. to 4:1.II.H, above.

4:1.III.B: In Y. Shebu. the verse is introduced by the question, "how do we know this?"

4:1.III.J: We read "two," following Y. Shebu. and not Y. Sanh., which mistakenly has "one." See Pene Moshe to Y. Sanh.

4:1.IV.A: On the introductory terminology and the origin of the whole sugya, cf. Moshe Assis, Parallel Sugyot in the Jerusalem Talmud (Ph.D. diss., Hebrew University, 1976), pp. 115-17, and the additional literature cited there.

4:1.IV.C: The Y. Sot. 1:1, 16c, Y. Ket. 2:4, 26c, and Y. Shebu. 4:1, 35c parallels to the Y. Sanh. 3:10, 21c version contain the name of an additional tradent: "R. Jeremiah, R. Samuel b. R. Isaac [+ "in the name of R. Isaac" = Y. Shebu.] in the name of Rav."

4:1.IV.N: The Y. Shebu. version alone precedes this clause with an actual tradition attributed to R. Yudan, that "the matter is subject to dispute." This may have been generated by the present clause.

4:3.II.A: Epstein (ITM, p. 480) suggests that II.A constitutes a citation of the Mishnah and not an explanation and hence does not add anything to the Mishnah. The clause serves as an introduction before Yose's explanation in B.

4:3.II.B: The opening of the tradition reads MTNYT' WHW' SYHZWR... Epstein (ITM, p. 480 and n. 1) cogently suggests that MTNYT' is unnecessary and represents a scribal addition generated by the phrasing in line H. This interpretation is supported by the usage of the next phrase, WHW' S-. The latter makes up a form that directly glosses the text it explains, here the Mishnah, and is used to set out the circumstances of that text. See Bokser, Samuel's Commentary, pp. 190-91.

4:5.II.B: Rabinovitz (p. 545) observed that, first, the reference to "the status of the generality of plants" does not make the best sense here, and second, that the analogue in T. Sanh. 6:1 has a more appropriate reading, viz., "the [nature of the] claim." Zalmon Dimitrovsky (oral communication, March, 1971) suggests, however, that the reading "they follow the generality of the claim" fits the context better and requires more modest emendation. On the issue of clause A see Lieberman, Caesarea, p. 38, n. 37.

4:5.II.C: Here too perhaps we should read, "They follow the generality of the claim." See n. to 4:5.II.B.

M.4:7.I: This clause is lacking in most MSS of the Mishnah, including K, P, L, and N and the Leiden MS to PT. The authorities in the Talmud (those in unit II, and R. Mana in unit I on the next Mishnah), who discuss the meaning of the Mishnah did not have this clause in their text. Cf. Epstein, ITM, p. 730.

4:7.I.B: A more literal rendering of the clause would be: "And this yes is not [an instance of] a 'yes of righteousness' and [the Torah requires] a 'yes of righteousness.'" While Y. Shebu. 4:7 is somewhat abbreviated, the several parallels to the pericope present a more complete form of the statement. See Y. Shevi. 10:9, 39d; Y. M.S. 4:7, 55d; Y. Git. 6:1, 47d; and Y. Shebu. 10:9, 39d.

4:7.II.E-G: On E-G cf. the renderings and emendations of QE and Duenner, p. 233.

4:10.II.A: "Thus does the Mishnah teach...," renders KYNY MTNYT', the reading in the printed texts. But the Leiden MS and the editio princeps have KMTNYT', i.e., "like the Mishnah." Thus R. Yannai follows the anonymous Mishnah and its formulation of the matter. But R. Yohanan, as represented in the next clause, avers that the matter is disputed by R. Meir and R. Judah. Epstein (ITM, pp. 275-76) suggests that the reference in the Mishnah is to line I and not E. If so, the issue would then be whether or not the case in I is under dispute.

4:10.III.F: See Ramban, cols, 154-55. While he lacks the negative, L', his explanation and reading supports the text of the Talmud and the rendering adopted here. Cf. QE.

5:1.I.A: GYF (pp. 268-69) provides further evidence for the Talmud text and with several exceptions it supports the readings of the Leiden MS. See n. to 5:1.II.A.

5:1.II.A: Several medieval authorities, esp. Ramban (cols. 172-76) and Meiri (pp. 126-27), in their analysis of b. Shebu. 37b cite and discuss Y.II.A-J. They include several variant readings and explanations, two of which are presented in the following nn. They apparently contain a clause between H and I that responds to the objection in H. It is similar to the answer in J. In all, the citations support the present structure of the sugya, and thus argue against several rearrangements suggested by some commentators.

5:1.II.D: That is, they do not rely on this ruling but rather specify that "they are responsible and pledges for one another." See Ramban, col. 173; Meiri, pp. 122-23; and Pene Moshe.

5:1.II.F: The translation of E-F follows the simple reading of the Leiden MS, supported by GYF (p. 268), which open F with WY^{c}SH KKWPR. The initial W- should be taken as an explanatory W-. See the references in Bokser, Samuel's Commentary, p. 27, n. 56, and Post Mishnaic, pp. 93 and 162, n. 349. The medieval citations, on the other hand, lack the W- and take the clause as the continuation of E. MSS and citations end E with the phrase 'YN SWM^{c}YN LW. But the citations, instead of reading it as an apodosis, "they pay no" take it as a conditional, "if they," with the 'YN as equivalent to 'M, a usage known elsewhere. See ITM, p. 890, n. 4, and Lieberman, TK 7:423. These readings, though, support the present understanding of the question and answer.

5:1.II.I: On this rendering see Meiri, p. 127. According to an alternative rendering, also found in Meiri, it is the same individual who takes the oath several times.

5:1.III.A: Since the Leiden MS and GYF (p. 2678) both have TRYHWN, "both of them," perhaps we should take the subject of the verb as R. Yohanan and R. Simeon b. Laqish. We would then delete the W- that presently precedes R. Yohanan's name. Thus R. La is the tradent of the joint tradition. Elsewhere he transmits the teachings of Yohanan and Simeon b. Laqish. See Bacher, Tradition, pp. 400, 470-71, 563.

5:1.IV.B: The translation follows Pene Moshe who makes the text conform to his reading of Sifra, Vayiqra 22:6, (Weiss ed. p. 28a). But in both the Talmud and Sifra, variants exist for the first two cases. The Leiden MS has "one knows about a lost object and about the one...; one knows about the lost object but not about the one...." GYF (p. 269) is identical for the first case, but for the second has what Pene Moshe suggests: "one knows about the one...but not about the lost object itself." Sifra first edition and Vatican MS, Codex 31 (published in facsimile as Torath Cohanim [Sifra] [Jerusalem: Makor, 1972]) supports Pene Moshe's reading, but the other Vatican MS (Sifra or Torat Kohanim

According to Codes Assemani LXVI, intro. Louis Finkelstein [New York, 1956], p. 124) does not. For the first case it is identical with the Leiden MS to the Talmud but for the second it agrees with the printed Sifra editions. Hence the reading overall agrees with GYF. On the rendering of the sugya, cf. Aryeh Loeb Yellin, "Yefeh Enayim," to b. B.Q. 105a (printed in the back of the Vilna BT editions).

5:2.V.B: The translation follows the Talmud text of the parallel, above on M. Shebu. 4:2 (Leiden MS and editio princeps = 4:3) section V.B-C. The Talmud text here is made up of one line: "As to an oath taken at others' initiative, what is the law as to one's being liable for a guilt-offering worth two shekels?" The subject apparently remains the same as that in the previous line, V.A, i.e., "in the case of real estate." Cf. Pene Moshe.

M.5:3.D: Literally, "not you, and not you, and not you." See Epstein, ITM, pp. 552-54, and below, unit IV of PT on M.5:4.

5:3.II.A: The Leiden MS reads "R. Eleazar." As pointed out, MSS and citations of the Mishnah and Gemara have diverse spellings of the name. Epstein (ITM, pp. 552, n. 3, and 1180) believes that Eleazar is the correct reading.

5:3.II.B: The rendering of B as a continuation of R. Yohanan's delineation of the positions of R. Eliezer/Eleazar and the rabbis is supported by the reading of Rashba, p. 112.

5:3.II.C: Duenner (p. 235) cogently suggests that we supply a protasis before C. It is appropriate in the pericope since it analyzes the significance of the difference between Eliezer/Eleazar and the rabbis. Duenner proposes we read, "If he made mention of it at the end and did not make mention of it at the outset," a clause identical to the one at the end of B. The apparent repetition caused someone to delete the instance of the wording that belongs with C.

5:4.I.H: On the pericope see Lieberman, TK 7:530.

5:4.IV.A: Weiss Halivni (ST 1:608-10, esp. n. 4) throws light on IV. A-F. He suggests that the Mishnah originally lacked the clause "Mr. So-and-so divorces Mrs. Such-and-such." that R. Yohanan and R. Simeon b. Laqish originally differed concerning what are the circumstances of the Mishnah, and accordingly that the comment in F would not have been inconsistent with the Mishnah.

5:4.IV.L-K: On the text and variants of L-Q and their parallel in Y. Git. 9:7, 50b-c see Epstein, ITM, p. 550-51.

5:4.IV.P: See Epstein, ITM, p. 555, n. 8, and Bokser, Post Mishnaic, p. 171, n. 436.

5:5.I.G: On the pericope see Yellin, Yefeh Enayim, to b. Shebu. 38b [published along with his notes to b. A.Z.].

5:5.II.E: See Pene Moshe and Ridbaz and, on the plain meaning of the positions of Simeon and the sages, Lieberman, HY, pp. 51-52, nn. 60-400, 1, and Weiss Halivni, ST 1:182-84. Cf. the renderings of Duenner, p. 238, and Rabinovitz, p. 548.

5:5 end: More specifically, 5:5 explains what monetary claims are involved in the different cases. Unit I treats rape and seduction, and unit II defamation of a woman. See Pene Moshe.

5:6.I.M: See Pene Moshe, who follows the reading in the Y. Ket. 3:9, 28a parallel, and QE in Y. Ket.

6:1.III.G: In accord with the citations of Ramban (col. 191) and Rashba (p. 126), delete the title "R." and read "Samuel." The name with the title refers to a master different from the one designated by the appellation without the title (see Bokser, Samuel's Commentary, pp. 98-99, n. 275). Our context requires the reference to the latter.

6:2.III.D: The word WHWRH, "who ruled," which is supplied by commentators, is found in the citations of Tosafot (to b. 42a, s.v. KL MYLT'); Ramban (cols. 209-10, cf. 211), and OZ (4:2d, Sanhedrin #12). Undoubtedly the original reading of RBY WHWRH became corrupted to RBY YHWDH. See Lieberman, OY, p. 8.

6:2.III.E: See GE and Rabinovitz (p. 248), who likewise, contra Pene Moshe, follow the text of the Talmud, which is supported by the citation of Ramban (col. 210). We must distinguish between the R. Jeremiah's in D and E. See Lieberman, YK, p. 25, and Caesarea, p. 102; and Albeck, Introduction, pp. 203, 295, 340.

6:2.IV.A: Rabinovitz (p. 549) suggests that the geneology of the masters requires us to read "R. Hama, father of R. Hoshaiah, and Bar Qappara." See Lieberman, Caesarea, p. 93, and Albeck, Introduction, p. 160.

6:3.end: Cf. Lieberman, TK 2:779-80, who likewise points to the difficulties in the text. He observes (n. 9) that PT cites the baraita to indicate that the laws of second tithes differ from those of M. Shebu. 6:3.

M.6:4.Q: The sequence of the clauses to refer to "utensils" and then "real estate" is the preferred reading. See Epstein, ITM, p. 481. Epstein also points out that some readings of the Mishnah lack line P and the word "conceded," in line O, and that the resulting sequence of phrases enabled the interpretation in the Talmud, line X. I.e., Q is a continuation of O and refers to additional instances of denial.

6:4.I.O: Weiss Halivni (ST 1:258), following the reading of the Y. Ket. 13:4, 36a parallel, adds here: "and he conceded one of them." O then makes the point: Why then did the sages say that the confession is not of the same kind as that which is subject to the claim?

6:4.I.P: Weiss Halivni, likewise here, prefers the Y. Ket. reading: "If he laid claim for oil, and the bailee conceded [only] that he had jars, all parties will concur that what is conceded is not of the same kind as that which is subject to the claim." Hence, why does Admon maintain that within the confession is an element of what is claimed? See n. E to 6:4. I.O.

6:4.I.X: This reading is one of several possible emendations of X so as to make the line comprehensible. Cf. Pene Moshe. Epstein (ITM, p. 481) prefers a different reading and rendering: "Thus does the Mishnah state [= is to be interpreted]" If he denied the claim for part of the utensils he is liable; for part of the real estate he is exempt." This interpretation is to be correlated with one of the readings of the Mishnah. See n. to M.6:4.Q, above.

6:5.I.E: Cf. Duenner (pp. 240-41) and Rabinovitz (pp. 549-50) who replace the unusual usage of PSYT' "teaching," with PLYG', "dispute."

6:5.III.M: M makes up a popular idiom. See Lieberman, GJP, p. 124, n. 74. On unit IIIi and its legal issues see Lev. R. 6:3, Margulies ed. 1:132-36, and nn.; and esp. Weiss Halivni, ST 1:536-47.

6:6.I.E: Cf. the renderings of GE and Rabinovitz, p. 550.

6:6.end.(re IV): Rabinovitz (p. 464) also explains Huna's saying in this way, though he emends some of its language.

6:8.III.C: Albeck (Introduction, p. 330) following Ramban (col. 241), reads "Dromiya" instead of "Diyoma."

6:8.III.D: See Ramban (cols. 280-82), whose citation of the Talmud basically follows that of the present text [= Leiden MS], contra the various emendations suggested by commentaries, and whose explanation accords with that adopted here.

M.7:1: This clause is an explanatory gloss and is not found in the Mishnah MSS.

7:4.I.D: Alternatively: "until he breaks up his scenery."

7:6.II.B-C: Rabinovitz (p. 552) and Joseph Engel (Giljonei Haschass [Vienna, 1925. Reprint in 2 vols., n.p., n.d.] 2:135a) suggest we delete the word DMR, "which said/reported," and read B-C thus: "This is in line with the following: R. Judah bar Shalom made arrangements..."

7:6.II.C: Jastrow (p. 602): "paid porters with orders drawn on the retailers."

M.7:7.G: Mishnah MSS (K.P. Lowe, Naples) and the Leiden MS read "testified." See Epstein, ITM, p. 1137.

M.7:7.H: Most of the MSS that read "testified," in clause G, have "Rabban Simeon b. Gamaliel says," in clause H. See Epstein.

7:7.I.A: Alternatively: "In all of these cases, an oath like that of the one deriving from the Torlah applies." This could be rendered in one of two ways. First, "the oath [imposed by the rabbis] is like -- but not exactly the same as -- the one deriving from the Torah." This accords with the interpretation presented in the text. Second, "the oath [imposed by the rabbis] is of the exact same status as the one deriving from the Torah." This, in turn, could be a question or a statement. Clause(s) B- would then be a continuation or response to clause A. See Pene Moshe and QE to Y. Ket. 9:7, 33a, and Duenner, p. 246.

7:7.II.C: The pericope is also abbreviated and found in a fuller form in Y. Ket. 3:7, 33b and Y. San. 8:6, 26b. See Lieberman, TK 6:338-39, and cf. Duenner, p. 246.

7:7.III.Q: See Pene Moshe; Duenner, pp. 245-46; Lieberman, OY, p. 21; and esp. Weiss Halivni, ST 1:228-29.

7:7.VI.A: The interpretation in the text follows the explanation of most commentaries. Weiss Halivni (ST 1:228-29) and Lieberman (TK 6:334-35), however, suggest an alternative rendering which more closely fits Talmud usage. Simeon refers to a case in which the husband dies and the wife receives maintenance from his estate. The heirs may impose an oath upon her (that she has not taken anything not her due) only when she claims her marriage settlement. For the same reason, Hanan believes that in a case in which the husband goes overseas and the wife receives maintenance from his estate, they may impose an oath upon her only when she collects her marriage settlement.

7:7.VII.A-E: Since our texts of Y. B.M. may represent a recension of Gemara different from the one from which unit VIII was transferred, we note several variants in the Y. Shebu. version: clause A is attributed to "R. Hiyyah bar Ashi in the name of Rab" and clause C to "R. Avinah in the name of Samuel." A uses the Hebrew word "document"

(STR) and not the technical Greek loan-word "codicil" (SYMPWN). Clauses D-E are missing or deleted. See Lieberman, Caesarea, p. 45, esp. n. 63.

7:7.III.C: The sytle of this clause is problematic. Hence Yellin (Yefeh Enayim to b. Qid. 28a), NY, and Rabinovitz (p. 593) suggest we read it as a question and answer. The questioner assumed that the reference, in B, to a "slave" is to a gentile slave and therefore asked: "Take note of the possibility that the defendant was a priest [and, if so, could not be a gentile slave]?" The next two words supply the answer: "It is a case of a Jewish slave." This rendering requires us either to emend W^{c}BD BRY to B^{c}BD BRY or to understand the opening vav, W-, either as an explicative or as a shortened form of the word WHW'. Lieberman has pointed to other instances of the W[HW'] used as a prefix. See Bokser, Samuel's Commentary, p. 27, n. 56, and Post Mishnaic, p. 162, n. 349.

Clause IV.A is also difficult and Rabinovitz emends it and sees it as a continuation of III.C. Cf. Duenner, p. 246; and Lieberman, TK 2:588, and the reference there, in n. 23.

8:1.II.C-D: Lieberman, on the basis of the Mekhilta D'Rabbi Sim^{c}on B. Jochai to Ex. 22:6 (ed. J.N. Epstein and E.Z. Melamed [Jerusalem, 1955], p. 200) offers a different explanation of C: "If the item is stolen from the person's home and the thief is not caught, the person is liable for an oath. But if it is stolen from the top of the person's roof, whether or not the thief is caught, he is liable to pay -- for he has not properly guarded the item." According to this rendering, Eleazar's comment, in D, constitutes an appropriate gloss to C. See Lieberman, TK 3:448, n.22.

8:1.III.EE: The printed editions of the Talmud read SYS, "[that] is," which is the corrected reading in the Leiden MS. Commentators emend this to S'YN, "[that] is not," which accords with the reading of the text of the Leiden MS before the "correction."

8:1.IV.G: The text of G reads: "R. Hanina in the name of R. Yudan, 'The following statement of the baraita supports the position of R. Zira.'" See Duenner (pp. 247-48), who likewise emends G and sees the baraita in H as a support for Hanina. Duenner, in addition, takes E as a support for Zira and emends D accordingly.

8:1.IV.K: This follows the emendation of Pene Moshe, Ridbaz, and others, who delete the negative L', "not," from "does not make restitution."

8:1.V-VI: Lieberman (OY, p. 17) suggests units V-VI, which are not directly relevant here, were mistakenly cited along with IV.T-V from the gemara to M. B.M. 3:13. See also Caesarea, pp. 50-51.

8:1.V.A: Epstein (ITM, pp. 310, 1034) renders the clause "what is the meaning...took [wine]" thus: "How was our Mishnah said: 'To take [wine]' or 'took [wine]'?" See n. to 8:1.V.B.

8:1.V.B: Instead of "because the man has spoiled it?" Epstein (ITM, p. 1034), following the Y. B.M. 4:1, 9c parallel, reads TYLTWLH, "[because the man has] moved it?" The question is based upon a part of the baraita not cited in our texts, though found in full in T. B.Q. 10:34, which reads: "If he lifted and took from it a quarter [-log of wine] and it broke..." The point is, since the text says "if he lifted [it]," he is liable even if he did not take it. Epstein argues that the discussion originally concerned whether or not "raising" was sufficient to make one liable. Later the controversy of whether a person's "intent" is sufficient or whether "actual action" is required to make one liable was superimposed upon the earlier interpretations.

8:3.I.F: Alternatively: "committed the transgression *and [hence]* took the oath in error..."

8:3.I.G: Alternatively: "*and* took the false oath..."

8:3.I.H: The sense is clear, though the text of the second half of line H poses difficulties. Cf. the commentaries for other emandations.

8:3.II.A: Epstein (*ITM*, p. 896) adds a negative, "[he] does not [pay]." This accords with a different rendering of the pericope. B provides an alternative presentation of the law, i.e., that he *does* pay. C then provides support for Yohanan's position. See n. to 8:3.II.D.

8:3.II.D: Epstein emends this to: "It was stolen." See n. to 8:3.II.A.

8:3.VII.A: Alternatively, emend the last phrase, from "selling the meat" to "stealing" (*GNYBH*). See GE; Duenner, p. 251; and cf. Pene Moshe. But note: The Leiden MS to C contains a reference to "selling" that has been crossed out. It reads: "witnesses to the act of selling theft did not come along." If the word "selling" is original, it might support the reading of "selling" in A.

8:4.GG-HH: On the addition of GG-HH see Epstein, *ITM*, p. 1043.

ABBREVIATIONS

Albeck, *Introduction*	Chanoch Albeck. *Introduction to the Talmud, Babli and Yerushalmi*. Jerusalem, 1969.
Bacher, *Tradition*	Wilhelm Bacher. *Tradition und Tradenten in den Schulen Palästinas und Babyloniens*. Leipzig, 1914. Reprint, Berlin, 1966.
Bokser, *Post Mishnaic*	Baruch M. Bokser. *Post Mishaic Judaism in Transition: Samuel on Berakhot and the Beginnings of Gemara*. Chico, 1980.
Bokser, *Samuel's Commentary*	Baruch M. Bokser. *Samuel's Commentary on the Mishnah: Its Nature, Forms, and Content*. Leiden, 1975.
Duenner	Joseph Zevi Duenner. *Haggahot*. Vol. 3: *Tractates Sanhedrin, Makkot, Shebuot, and Horayot. Bavli and Yerushalmi*. Frankfurt, 1902.
Epstein, *IAL*	J.N. Epstein. *Introductions to Amoraitic Literature*. Jerusalem, 1962. [Hebrew]
Epstein, *ITL*	J.N. Epstein. *Introductions to Tannaitic Literature*. Jerusalem, 1957. [Hebrew]
Epstein, *ITM*	J.N. Epstein. *Introduction to the Text of the Mishnah*. 2nd ed. 2 vols. Jerusalem, 1964. [Hebrew]
GE	Ephraim Dov HaKohen Lapp. "Gilyon Ephraim." In *Talmud Yerushalmi*. 7 vols. New York, 1959. [= Reprint of Vilna, 1922, edition with additional commentaries].
GYF	Louis Ginzberg. *Yerushalmi Fragments from the Geniza*. New York, 1909. Reprint, Jerusalem, 1969.
Lieberman, *Caesarea*	Saul Lieberman. *The Talmud of Caesarea*. Jerusalem, 1931.

Lieberman, GJP — Saul Lieberman, Greek in Jewish Palestine. New York, 1965.

Lieberman, HJP — Saul Lieberman. Hellenism in Jewish Palestine. New York, 1950.

Lieberman, HY — Saul Lieberman. Hilkhot HaYerushalmi. The Laws of the Palestinian Talmud of Rabbi Moses Ben Maimon. New York, 1947.

Lieberman, OY — Saul Lieberman. On the Yerushalmi. Jerusalem, 1929.

Lieberman, TK — Saul Lieberman. Tosefta Ki-Fshutah. 1-. New York, 1955-.

Lieberman, "Yerushalmi Horayot" — Saul Lieberman. "Yerushalmi Horayot." In Sefer HaYovel leRabbi Hanoch Albeck. Pp. 283-305. Jerusalem, 1963.

Lieberman, YK — Saul Lieberman. HaYerushalmi Kiphsuto. Jerusalem, 1934.

Meiri — Menahem HaMeiri of Perpignan. Bet HaBehirah ᶜal Masekhet Shebuot. Ed. Abraham Liss. Jerusalem, 1968.

NY — Yehoshua Isaac of Slonim. Noam Yerushalmi. 2 vols. Vilna, 1863-69. Reprint, Jerusalem, 1968.

Pene Moshe — Moses Margaliot. "Pene Moshe." In Talmud Yerushalmi. Reprint of Vilna, 1922 edition.

QE — David Frankel of Berlin. "Qorban HaEdah." In Talmud Yerushalmi. Reprint of Vilna, 1922 edition.

Rabinovitz — Z.W. Rabinovitz. Shaᶜare Torath Eretz Israel. Jerusalem, 1940.

Ramban — Nahmanides. Hiddushe HaRamban HaShalem. Shebuot. Ed. Elijah Lichtenstein. Jerusalem, 1976.

Ridbaz — Jacob David of Slotz. "Perush HaRidbaz." In Talmud Yerushalmi. Reprint of Vilna, 1922 edition.

Rashba — Solomon ben Adret. Hidushe Ha-Rashba on the Treatise Shebuoth. Ed. Abraham Screiber. Jerusalem, 1964.

RN — Nissim b. Reuben Gerondi. Commentary on Alfasi. In Talmud Bavli. Reprint of Vilna, 1895 edition.

SQ — David Frankel of Berlin. "Shire Qorban." In Talmud Yerushalmi. Reprint of Vilna, 1922 edition.

Weiss Halivni, ST — David Weiss Halivni, Sources and Traditions. 1-. Tel Aviv and Jerusalem, 1968-.

INDEX